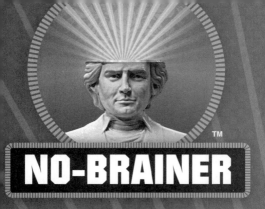

NO-BRAINER™

PLA
UKULELE

WE MAKE PLAYING UKULELE A NO-BRAINER!

Alfred
SINCE 1922

Alfred Music • P.O. Box 10003 • Van Nuys, CA 91410-0003

alfred.com

ISBN-10: 0-7390-9535-8 (Book & DVD)
ISBN-13: 978-0-7390-9535-5 (Book & DVD)

Ukulele photos (left to right): Firebrand™ (photograph by Jennifer Harnsberger)
Tiny Tenor ʻukulele designed by Pepe Romero & Daniel Ho (www.RomeroCreations.com) • Beethoven bust photo courtesy of www.Statues.com

 Alfred Cares. Contents printed on environmentally responsible paper.

CONTENTS

About the DVD

The DVD contains valuable demonstrations of all the instructional material in Part 1. You will get the best results by following along with your book as you watch these video segments. Musical examples that are not performed with video are included as audio tracks on the DVD for listening and playing along. The audio tracks are all accesible through the chapter selection on your DVD player and also as downloadable mp3 files on your computer.

ABOUT THE AUTHORS

The Meeting of Great Minds

In order to enlighten you, we have gathered together a stellar group of authors who specialize in different facets of teaching ukulele. Every one of them has contributed knowledge to make playing ukulele a no-brainer. Here is a little information on each of them.

Shana Aisenberg

Multi-instrumentalist *Shana Aisenberg* plays ukulele, acoustic guitar, lap steel guitar, mandolin, fiddle, banjo, fretted dulcimer, and more. In addition to being a respected author, Shana has recorded, produced, and played on over 50 albums. She has also composed music for films. In 1981, Shana was a triple winner at the prestigious Walnut Valley National Flatpicking Championships, held in Winfield, Kansas, where she placed in the categories of fingerstyle guitar, mandolin, and fretted dulcimer. Shana performs regularly with duo partner Beverly Woods and teaches private lessons and group classes in New Hampshire and online. You can visit Shana on the Web at: www.shanasongs.com

L. C. Harnsberger

L. C. Harnsberger studied music composition at the University of Southern California. Since finishing school, he has been composing and performing as well as writing best-selling instructional books. His *Kid's Guitar Course* (co-written with Ron Manus) has received numerous awards and continues to grow in popularity. Other publications include guitar methods, ukulele methods, reference books, and performance music for band and orchestra. He is currently the editor-in-chief of the Musical Instruments division at Alfred Music.

Daniel Ho

Daniel Ho's simple philosophy of presenting music with sincerity and artistry encompasses six consecutive GRAMMY Awards, #1 albums on national airplay charts, and Top 10 albums on the Billboard charts. In 2010, his solo 'ukulele CD, Polani (Pure), was the first 'ukulele album in music history to receive a GRAMMY nomination. Daniel brings the same integrity to his instructional video 'Ukulele: A Beginning Method as well as his other instructional methods and song collections.

Greg Horne

Greg Horne is a multi-instrumentalist, songwriter, author, and teacher in Knoxville, Tennessee. He is the author of several books and DVDs published by Alfred Music, including the *Complete Acoustic Guitar Method*, *Teach Yourself Songwriting*, two volumes of the *Complete Mandolin Method*, and the *Couch Potato Guitarist/Bassist* books. Greg holds a bachelor of arts in music from the College of Wooster, and pursued graduate studies at the University of Mississippi. To contact Greg, hear his music, or see his videos, visit: www.greghornemusic.com

Paul Lidel

By the time Paul signed his first major-label recording contract at age 23, he had already been playing professionally since age 14. Paul has over 2,000 shows under his belt, having toured abroad and performing in 45 states in the U.S. Paul's latest project had him recording and performing with the band Dangerous Toys. In addition to performing, Paul also enjoys teaching guitar at the University of Texas and has been on the faculty of the National Guitar Workshop.

Ron Manus

Ron is co-owner of Alfred Music and its sister company, Daisy Rock Guitars. He is one of Alfred Music's most prolific and top-selling authors, with over 100 published titles to his credit. Ron has written instructional books for guitar, bass, banjo, harmonica, and ukulele. In addition to holding prominent positions with Alfred and Daisy Rock, Ron also plays guitar and sings in the rock-solid, no-nonsense, punkrock band sASSafrASS.

HOW TO USE THIS BOOK AND DVD

No Brainer™: Play Ukulele provides all the information you need to get started playing soprano, concert, or tenor ukulele. The DVD contains video explanations of basic techniques and musical concepts, as well as audio demonstrations of the pieces and exercises to help you reach your maximum potential on the keyboard.

Video demonstrations of all the instructional material in Part 1 are included on the DVD. You will get the best results by following along with your book as you watch the video. Musical examples that are not performed on the video are included as audio tracks on the DVD Rom for listening and playing along. The audio tracks are all accessible through the chapter selection on your DVD player and also as downloadable mp3 files on your computer.

You may find it best to have your DVD player's control or remote positioned near you so that you can use the book as you watch and play along with the video. Sometimes you might prefer to first work with the book before using the video, carefully reading the instructions and playing the music. Other times, you may want to start by watching the demonstration. You decide what works best for you. There is no wrong way to use this book and DVD!

If you are just getting started and do not own a ukulele, there are tips on choosing an instrument on page 7.

Here are some important things anyone learning to play music should keep in mind:

- **It is better to practice a little a lot than to practice a lot a little**. In other words, never miss a day of practice, even if you spend just a few minutes that day. Skipping a few days of practice and then practicing once for a long time will not be nearly as helpful as regular daily practice.

- **The quickest way to play fast is to take the slowest route**. You will learn to play fast music by practicing slowly. Playing too fast too soon can lead to confusion, difficulty, and bad habits that will slow your progress. Taking your time is well worth it.

- **Practice with a metronome**. A metronome is an adjustable device that beats time for you. Electronic metronomes are inexpensive and very accurate. Get one that makes a click loud enough for you to hear. Practicing with a metronome will teach you to play with accurate rhythm.

Although this book is perfect to teach yourself, **there is no substitute for a good teacher**. A teacher can watch and listen to you play, and give you guidance and encouragement to do your best. If you find yourself having trouble understanding the concepts, consider finding a local teacher.

PART 1: THE BASICS

SELECTING YOUR UKULELE

Ukuleles come in different types and sizes. There are four basic sizes: soprano, concert, tenor, and baritone. The smallest is the soprano, and they get gradually larger, with the baritone being the largest.

| Soprano | Concert | Tenor | Baritone |

Soprano, concert, and tenor ukuleles are all tuned to the same notes, but the baritone is tuned differently. Each ukulele has a different sound. The soprano has a light, soft sound, which is what you expect when you hear a ukulele. The larger the instrument, the deeper the sound is. Some tenor ukuleles have six or even eight strings.

The soprano ukulele is the most common, but you can use soprano, concert, and four-string tenor ukuleles with this book. Because the baritone ukulele is tuned to the same notes as the top four strings of the guitar, you can use *Learn to Play Baritone Uke* (Alfred item 380) to start learning.

THE PARTS OF YOUR UKULELE

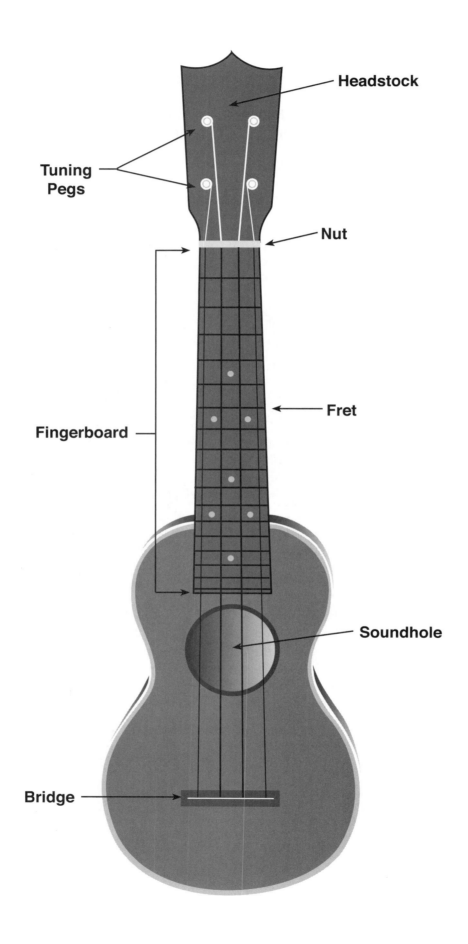

Headstock

Tuning
Pegs

Nut

Fret

Fingerboard

Soundhole

Bridge

HOW TO HOLD YOUR UKULELE

Standing

Cradle the ukulele with your right arm by gently holding it close to your body. Your right hand should be free to strum it. Keep your left wrist away from the fingerboard. This allows your fingers to be in a better position to finger the chords.

Sitting

Rest the ukulele gently on your thigh.

VIDEO EXAMPLE

THE RIGHT HAND: STRUMMING THE STRINGS

To *strum* means to play the strings with your right hand by brushing quickly across them. There are two common ways of strumming the strings. One is with a pick, and the other is with your fingers.

Strumming with a Pick
Hold the pick between your thumb and index finger. Hold it firmly, but don't squeeze it too hard.

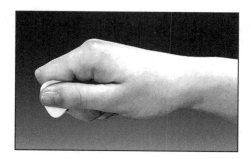

Strum from the 4th string (closest to the ceiling) to the 1st string (closest to the floor).

Important: Always strum by mostly moving your wrist, not just your arm. Use as little motion as possible. Start as close to the top strings as you can, and never let your hand move past the edge of the ukulele.

Start near the top string.

Move mostly your wrist, not just your arm.
Finish near the bottom string.

Strumming with Your Fingers
Decide if you feel more comfortable strumming with the side of your thumb or the nail of your index finger. The strumming motion is the same with the thumb or finger as it is when using the pick. Strum from the 4th string to the 1st string.

Strumming with the thumb.

Strumming with the index finger.

O EXAMPLE

USING YOUR LEFT HAND

Hand Position

Learning to use your left-hand fingers easily starts with a good hand position. Place your hand so your thumb rests comfortably in the middle of the back of the neck. Position your fingers on the front of the neck as if you are gently squeezing a ball between them and your thumb. Keep your elbow in and your fingers curved.

Placing a Finger on a String

When you press a string with a left-hand finger, make sure you press firmly with the tip of your finger and as close to the fret wire as you can without actually being right on it. Short fingernails are important! This will create a clean, bright tone.

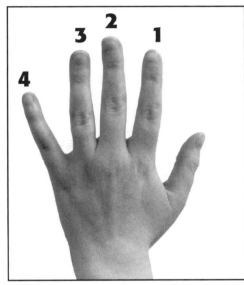

Finger numbers.

Keep elbow in and fingers curved.

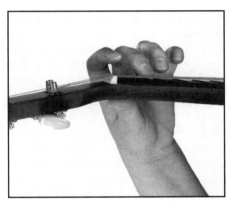

Like gently squeezing a ball between your fingers and thumb.

RIGHT
Your finger presses the string down near the fret without actually being on it.

WRONG
If your finger is too far from the fret wire the tone is "buzzy" and indefinite.

WRONG
If your finger is on top of the fret wire the tone is muffled and unclear.

VIDEO EXAMPLE

HOW TO TUNE YOUR UKULELE

Make sure your strings are wound properly around the tuning pegs. They should go from the inside to the outside, as in the picture.

Tuning a tuning peg clockwise makes the pitch lower. Turning a tuning peg counter-clockwise makes the pitch higher. Be sure not to tune the strings too high because they could break!

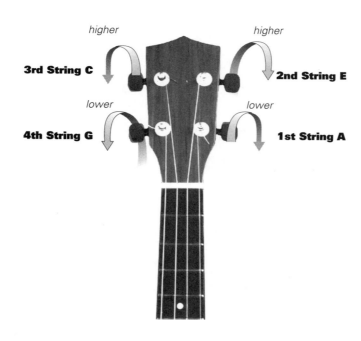

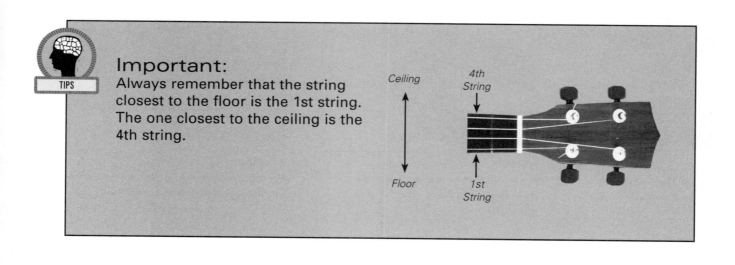

TIPS

Important:
Always remember that the string closest to the floor is the 1st string. The one closest to the ceiling is the 4th string.

Tuning with the MP3 Audio or the DVD

To tune using the MP3 audio (see page 4), play track 1. Listen to the directions and match each of your ukulele's strings to the corresponding pitches.

To use the DVD, go to the "Scene Selection" menu and click "How To Tune Your Ukulele." Follow the directions, and listen carefully to get your ukulele in tune.

Tuning the Ukulele to Itself

When your 1st string is in tune, you can tune the rest of the strings just using the ukulele alone.

If you have a piano, or keyboard, available, then tune the 1st string to A on the piano, and then follow the instructions below to get the ukulele in tune.

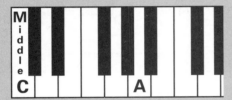

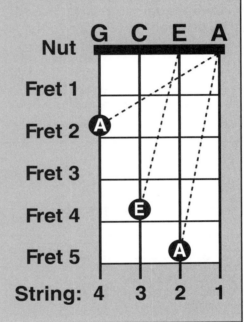

Press fret 5 of string 2 and tune it to the pitch of string 1 (A).

Press fret 4 of string 3 and tune it to the pitch of string 2 (E).

Press fret 2 of string 4 and tune it to the pitch of string 1 (A).

Pitch Pipes and Electronic Tuners

If you don't have a piano available, buying an electronic tuner or pitch pipe is recommended. The salesperson at your local music store can show you how to use them.

GETTING ACQUAINTED WITH MUSIC

Musical sounds are indicated by symbols called *notes*. Their time value is determined by their color (white or black) and by stems or flags attached to the note.

The Staff

The notes are named after the first seven letters of the alphabet (A–G), repeated to embrace the entire range of musical sound. The name and pitch of the note is determined by its position on five horizontal lines, and the spaces between, called the *staff*.

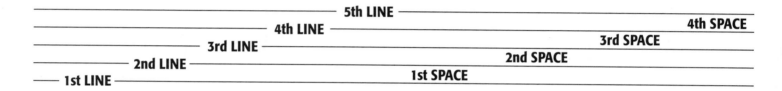

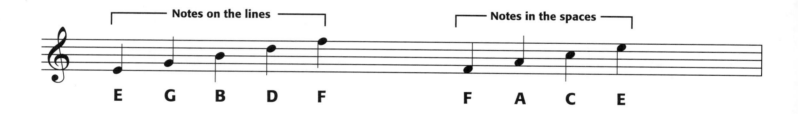

Measures

Music is divided into equal parts called *measures*.
One measure is divided from another by a *bar line*.

Clefs

During the evolution of musical notation, the staff had from 2 to 20 lines, and symbols were invented to locate certain lines and the pitch of the note on that line. These symbols are called *clefs*.

Music for ukulele is written in the *G clef* or *treble clef*.
Originally, the Gothic letter G was used on a four-line staff to establish the pitch of G.

This grew into the modern notation:

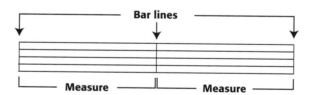

READING TAB AND CHORD DIAGRAMS

O EXAMPLE

Reading TAB

All the music in this book is written two ways: in standard music notation and TAB.

Below each standard music staff you'll find a four-line TAB staff. Each line represents a string of the ukulele, with the 1st string at the top and the 4th string at the bottom.

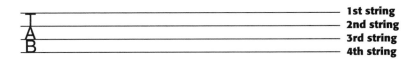

1st string
2nd string
3rd string
4th string

Numbers placed on the TAB lines tell you which fret to play. An 0 means to play the string open (not fingered).

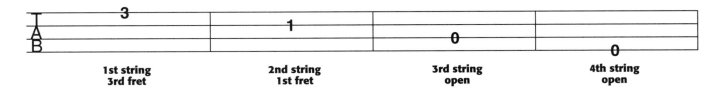

| 1st string
3rd fret | 2nd string
1st fret | 3rd string
open | 4th string
open |

By glancing at the TAB, you can immediately tell where to play a note. Although you can't tell exactly what the rhythm is from the TAB, the horizontal spacing of the numbers gives you a strong hint about how long or short the notes are to be played.

Chord Diagrams

Chord diagrams are used to indicate fingering for chords. The example here means to place your 1st finger on the 1st fret, 1st string, then strum all four strings. The o symbols on the 2nd, 3rd, and 4th strings indicate to play them open (not fingered).

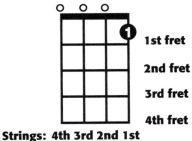

1st fret
2nd fret
3rd fret
4th fret

Strings: 4th 3rd 2nd 1st

VIDEO EXAMPLE

THE FIRST STRING A

OPEN STRING
(not fingered)

AUDIO EXAMPLE

A

2nd FRET

B

2nd FRET

C

Play slowly and evenly. Use only down-strokes, indicated by ⊓.
Remember, the symbol ○ over a note means *open string*. Do not finger.

First String Exercise

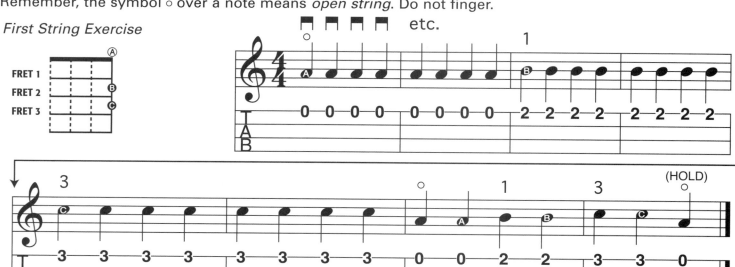

etc.

Playing with A, B, and C

AUDIO EXAMPLE

EXTRA CREDIT

TIPS

Make sure to place your left-hand fingers as close to the fret wires as possible without touching them. When you play the B on the 2nd fret and follow it with the C on the 3rd fret, keep your 2nd finger down. You will only hear the C, but when you go back to the B, it will sound smooth.

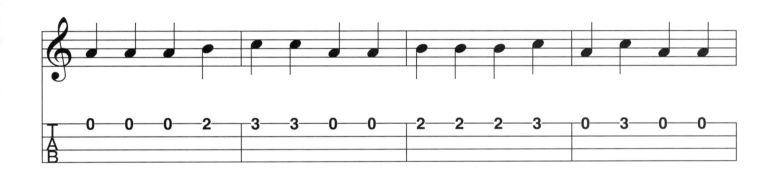

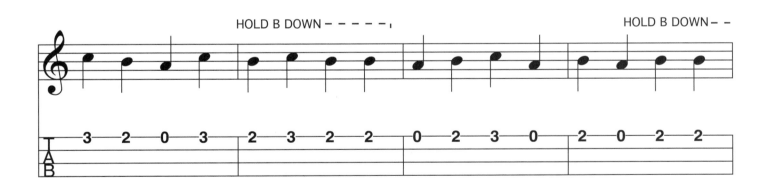

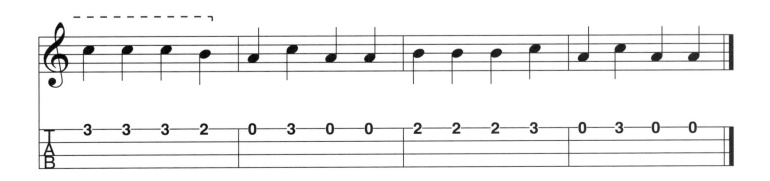

VIDEO EXAMPLE

SOUND-OFF: HOW TO COUNT TIME

4 Kinds of Notes

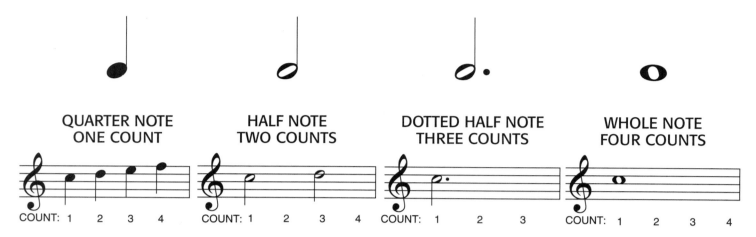

QUARTER NOTE
ONE COUNT

HALF NOTE
TWO COUNTS

DOTTED HALF NOTE
THREE COUNTS

WHOLE NOTE
FOUR COUNTS

COUNT: 1 2 3 4   COUNT: 1 2 3 4   COUNT: 1 2 3   COUNT: 1 2 3 4

Time Signatures

Each piece of music has numbers at the beginning called a *time signature*. These numbers tell us how to count time. The TOP NUMBER tells us how many counts are in each measure. The BOTTOM NUMBER tells us what kind of note gets one count.

Important: Go back and fill in the missing time signatures of the songs already learned.

FOUR COUNTS TO A MEASURE

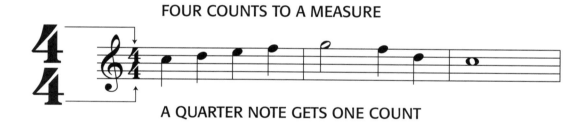

A QUARTER NOTE GETS ONE COUNT

THREE COUNTS TO A MEASURE

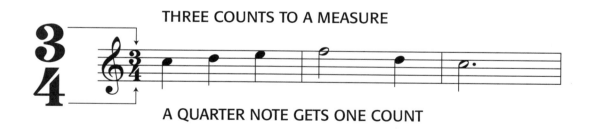

A QUARTER NOTE GETS ONE COUNT

TWO COUNTS TO A MEASURE

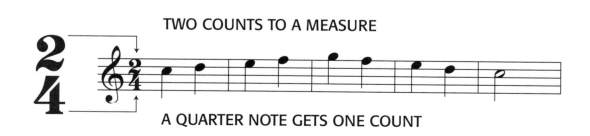

A QUARTER NOTE GETS ONE COUNT

REPEAT SIGNS

This music uses *repeat signs*. The double dots inside the double bars tell you that everything in between those double bars is to be repeated.

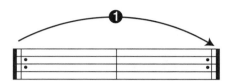 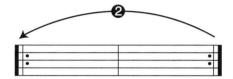 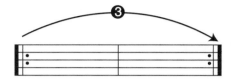

The best way to learn all the songs and exercises is to listen to the recording first so that you can hear exactly what is going to happen. Follow along in the music as you listen. Then, enjoy playing along.

First String Blues

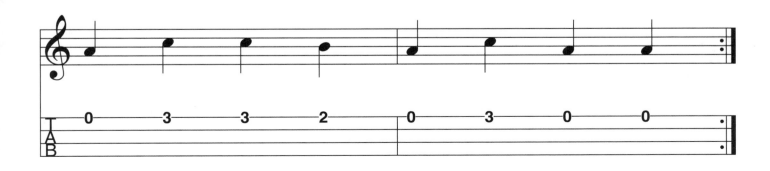

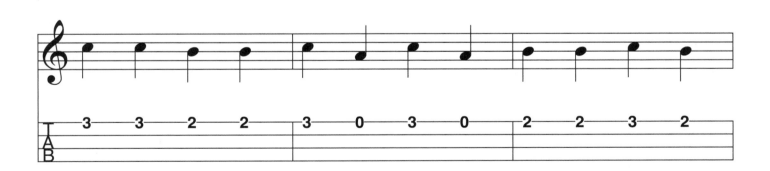

THE SECOND STRING E

OPEN STRING

O

E

1st FRET

①

F

3rd FRET

③

G

Second String Exercise

FRET 1 Ⓕ
FRET 2
FRET 3 Ⓖ

Ⓔ

Count: 1 2 3 4   1 2 3 4   (etc.)

Jammin' on Two Strings

Count: 1 2 3 4   (etc.)

Hot Cross Buns

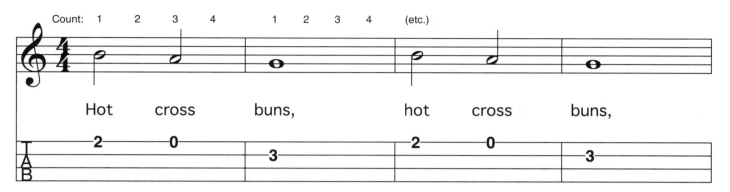

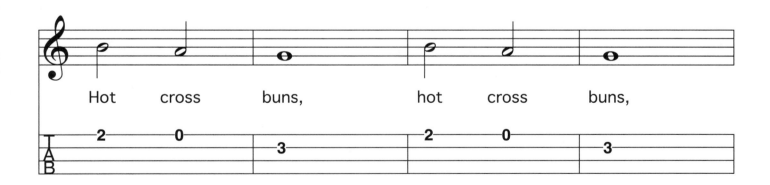

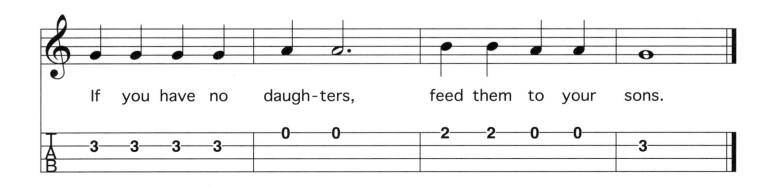

AUDIO EXAMPLE

Blues in C

If you have a friend or teacher and he or she wants to play along with you, the chord symbols above each staff may be used for a teacher-student duet. These chords are not to be played by the student.

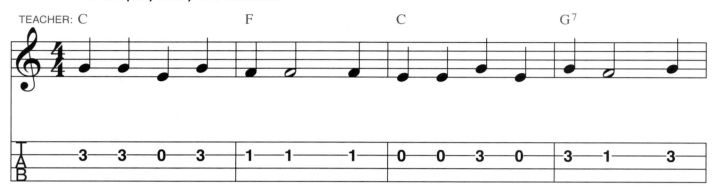

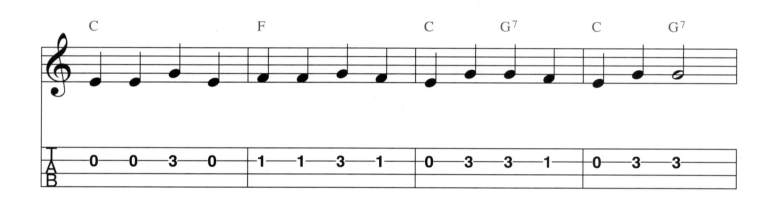

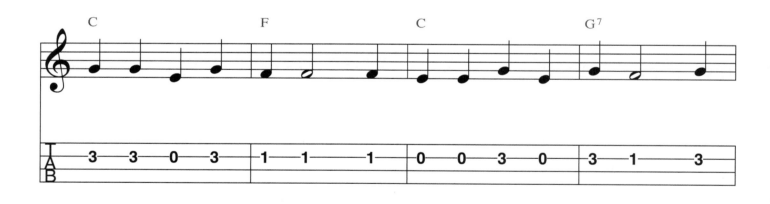

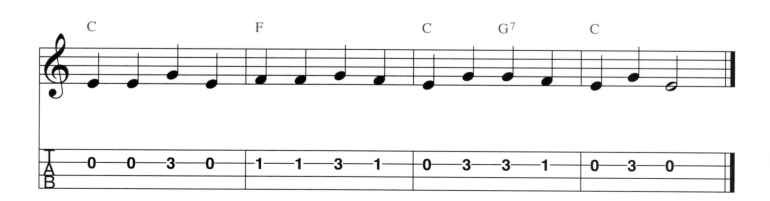

Rockin' Uke

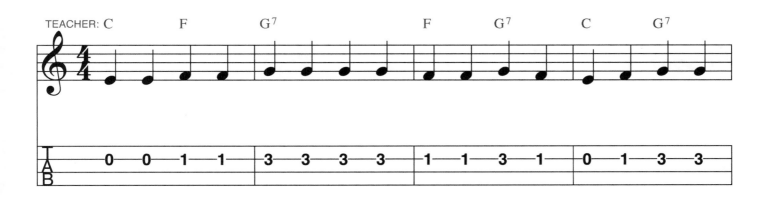

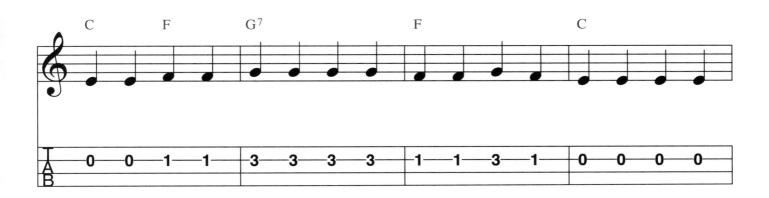

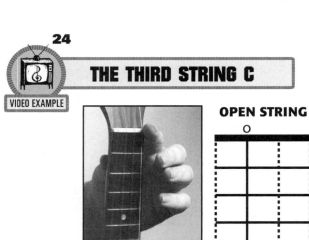

THE THIRD STRING C

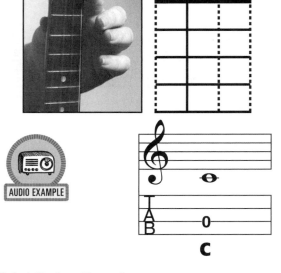

OPEN STRING

C

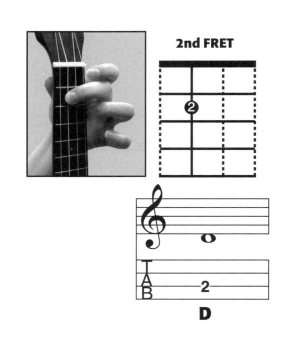

2nd FRET

D

Third String Exercise

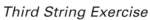

Jammin' on Three Strings

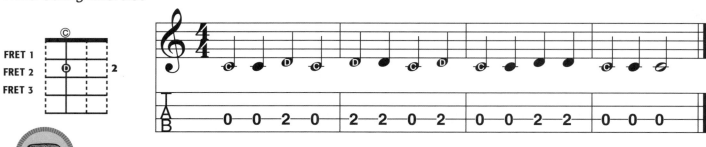

TEACHER: C   C⁷

Largo
(from the *New World Symphony*)

Antonin Dvořák

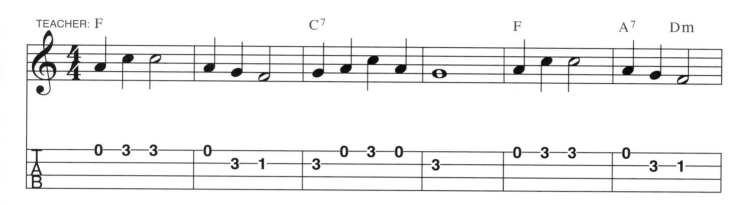

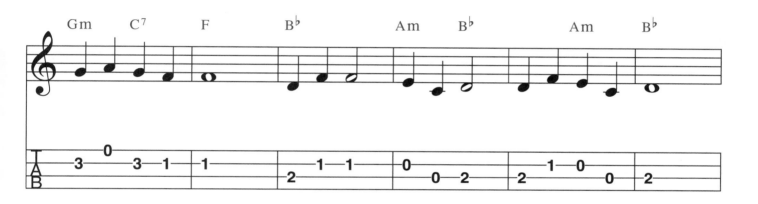

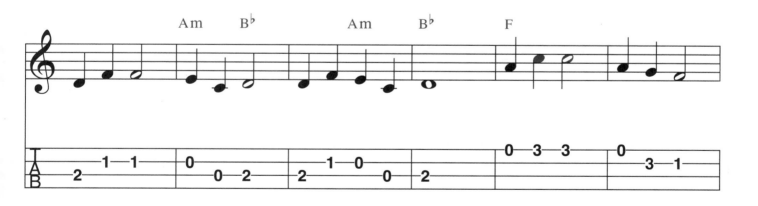

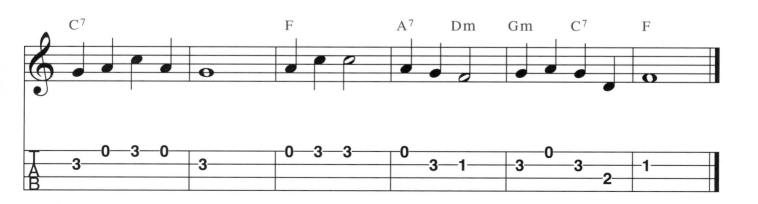

Jingle Bells

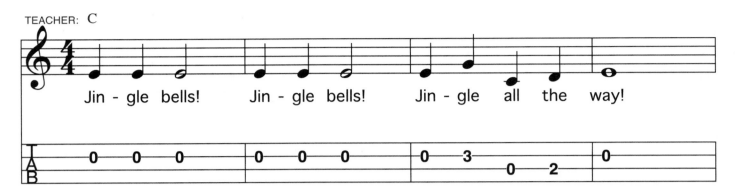

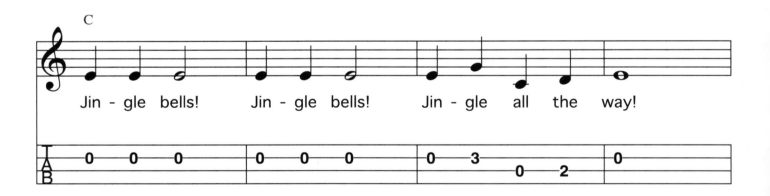

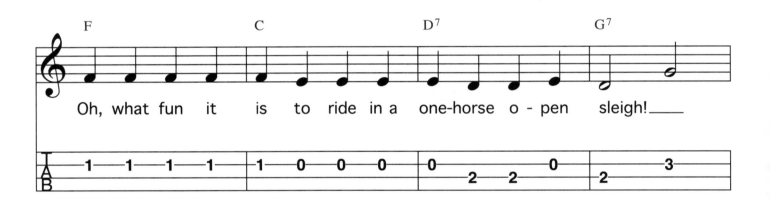

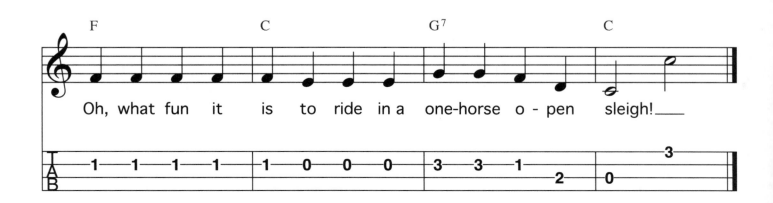

AUDIO EXAMPLE

Beautiful Brown Eyes

TEACHER: C

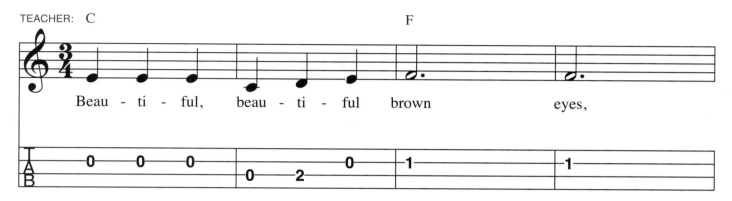

Beau - ti - ful, beau - ti - ful brown eyes,

smil - ing right in - to my heart. But now

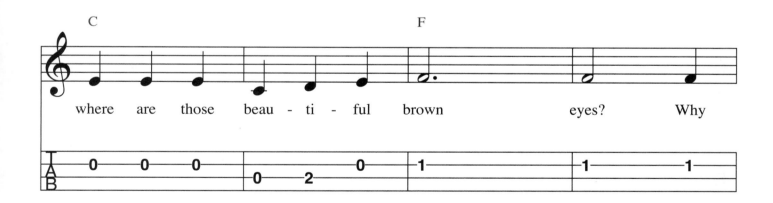

where are those beau - ti - ful brown eyes? Why

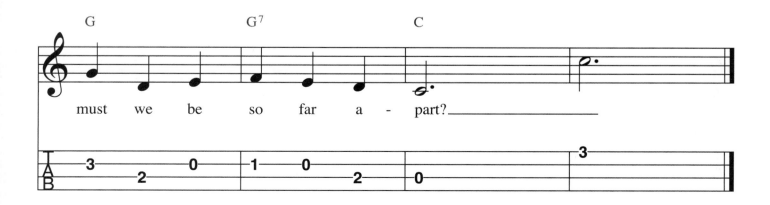

must we be so far a - part?

INTRODUCING B-FLAT

A *flat* ♭ lowers a note a half step. B♭ is played one fret lower than the note B. When a flat note appears in a measure, it is still flat until the end of that measure.

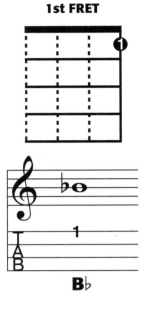

1st FRET

B♭

Aura Lee

DID YOU KNOW? This old American folk song was later recorded by Elvis Presley and called "Love Me Tender."

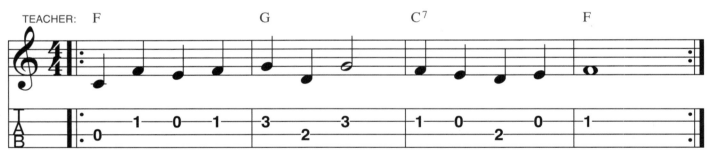

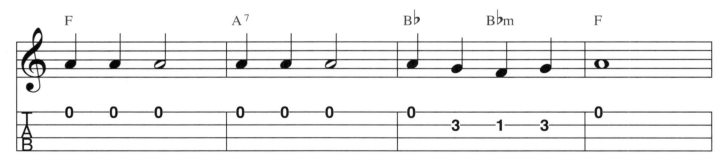

New Note B♭

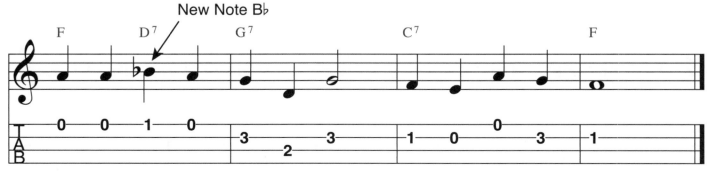

Three-String Boogie

This song uses all the notes you have learned. Don't forget to listen to the MP3 audio or DVD first!

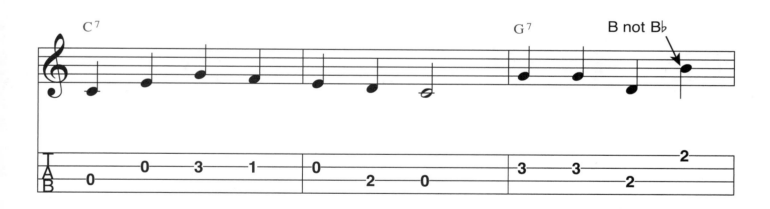

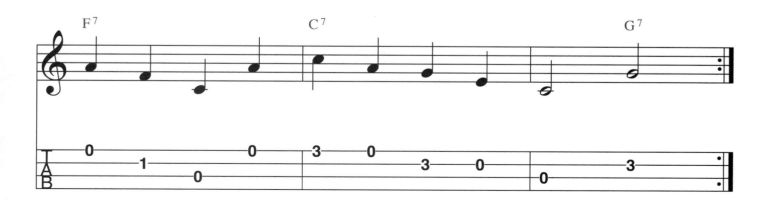

TEMPO SIGNS

VIDEO EXAMPLE

A *tempo sign* tells you how fast to play the music. Below are the three most common tempo signs, which are Italian words. In some music, you will see tempo signs written in English.

Andante ("ahn-DAHN-teh") means to play slow.

Moderato ("moh-deh-RAH-toh") means to play moderately.

Allegro ("ah-LAY-groh") means to play fast.

Quarter Rest
This sign indicates silence for one count. For a clearer effect, you may stop the sound of the strings by touching the strings lightly with the heel of the right hand.

AUDIO EXAMPLE

Three-Tempo Rockin' Uke

Play three times: first time **Andante**, second time **Moderato**, third time **Allegro**.

THE C7 CHORD

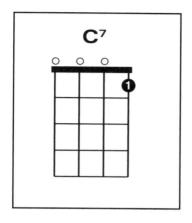 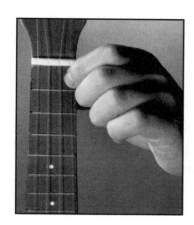

o = open string

- - - - - - - - - = string is not played

Place your 1st finger in position, then play one string at a time.

Play all four strings together:

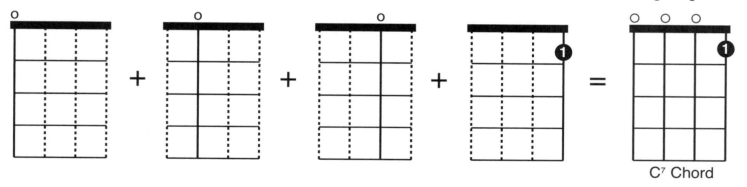

C7 Chord

Play slowly and evenly. Each slash mark ╱ means to repeat the previous chord. Strum downward for each chord name and slash mark. Use your finger or a pick. The chord name is repeated in each measure.

C7 Chord Exercises

THE F CHORD

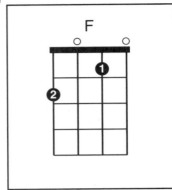

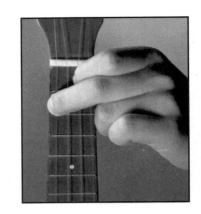

Place your 1st and 2nd fingers in position, then play one string at a time.

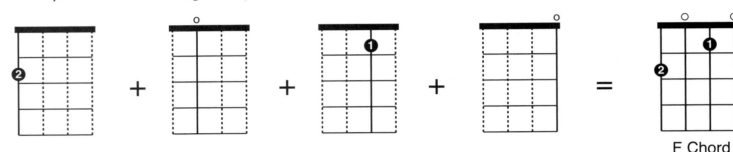

F Chord Exercises

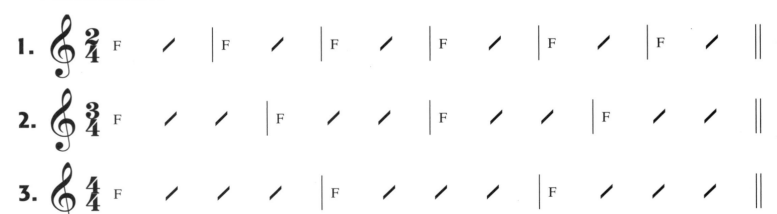

Once you can play both the F and C7 chords clearly, try combining them as in the following exercises.

F and C7 Chord Exercises

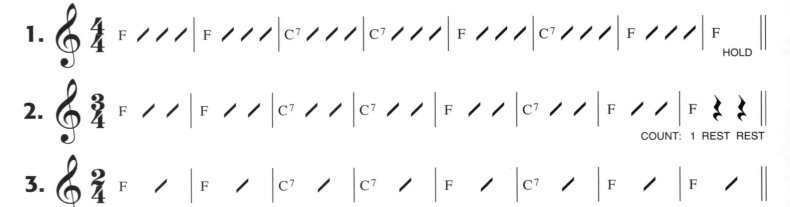

Good Night Ladies

For this song and most of the rest of the songs in this book, you can play either the melody or chords. Your teacher can play the part you aren't playing, or you can play along with the MP3 audio or DVD.

Moderato

Good night, la-dies, Good night, la-dies,

Good night, la-dies, We're going to leave you now.

Mer-ri-ly we roll a-long, Roll a-long, roll a-long.

Mer-ri-ly we roll a-long O'er the deep blue sea.

COUNT: 1 2 3 (REST)

KEY SIGNATURES

The *key signature* at the beginning of a piece tells you when a note is played as a flat note throughout the piece. In "Down in the Valley," each B is played as B-flat.

Ties

This curved line is called a *tie*. It connects two or more notes and ties them together. Play or sing the note once and hold it for the value of both (or more) tied notes.

In TAB, a tied note is shown as a number in parentheses. Do not pick the note again.

Down in the Valley

Key Signature: remember to play each B one half step lower.

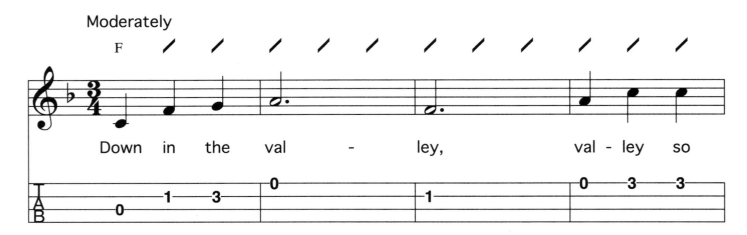

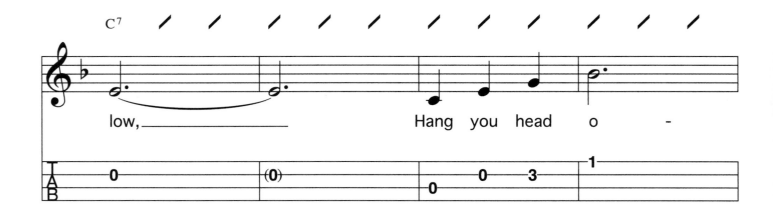

Ode to Joy

Theme from Beethoven's *Ninth Symphony*

Moderato

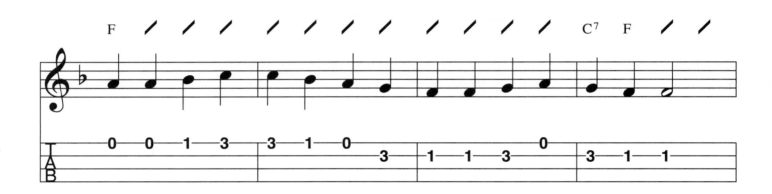

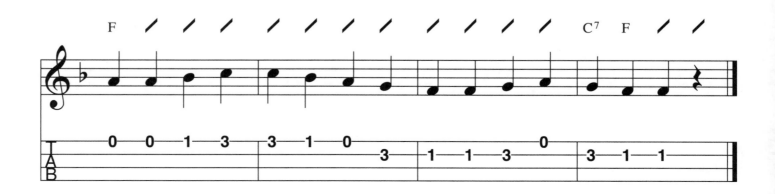

THE C CHORD

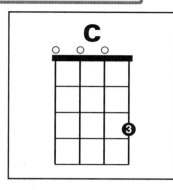

C

Place your 3rd finger in position, then play one string at a time.

Play all four strings together:

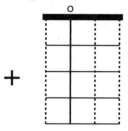 + 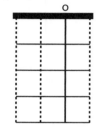 + + 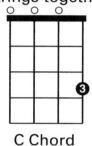 =

C Chord

 Play slowly and evenly.

C Chord Exercises

1. 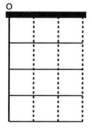 $\frac{2}{4}$ C / | C / | C / | C / | C / | C / ‖

2. $\frac{3}{4}$ C / / | C / / | C / / | C / / ‖

3. $\frac{4}{4}$ C / / / | C / / / | C / / / ‖

 Now try these exercise. They combine all the chords you know.

More C Chord Exercises

1. $\frac{2}{4}$ C / | C / | C⁷ / | C⁷ / | F / | F / | C / | C / ‖

2. $\frac{3}{4}$ F / / | C / / | F / / | C⁷ / / | F / / | F ‰ ‰ ‖

3. $\frac{4}{4}$ C / / / | C⁷ / / / | F / / / | C / / / | F / / / | C / / / | C / / / ‖

38

INCOMPLETE MEASURES

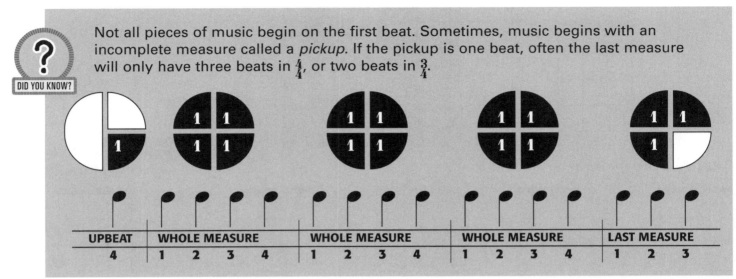

Not all pieces of music begin on the first beat. Sometimes, music begins with an incomplete measure called a *pickup*. If the pickup is one beat, often the last measure will only have three beats in $\frac{4}{4}$, or two beats in $\frac{3}{4}$.

A-Tisket, A-Tasket

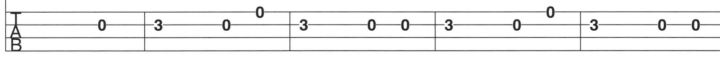

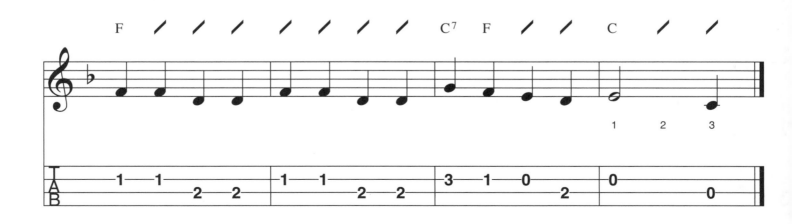

EIGHTH NOTES

Eighth notes are black notes that have a flag added to the stem: ♪ or ♩.

Two or more eighth notes are written with a *beam*: ♫ or ⌐⌐. Each eighth note receives one half beat.

Use alternating down-strokes ⊓ and up-strokes ∨ on eighth notes.

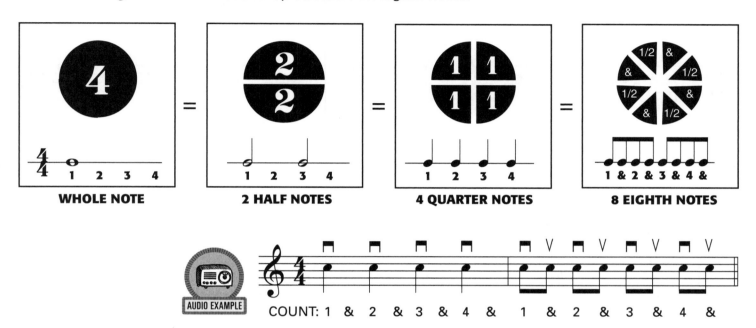

| WHOLE NOTE | 2 HALF NOTES | 4 QUARTER NOTES | 8 EIGHTH NOTES |

COUNT: 1 & 2 & 3 & 4 & 1 & 2 & 3 & 4 &

Jammin' with Eighth Notes

*Allegro moderato means moderately fast.

DOTTED QUARTER NOTES

A DOT INCREASES THE LENGTH OF A NOTE BY ONE HALF

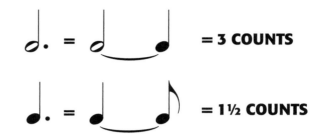

PREPARATORY DRILL

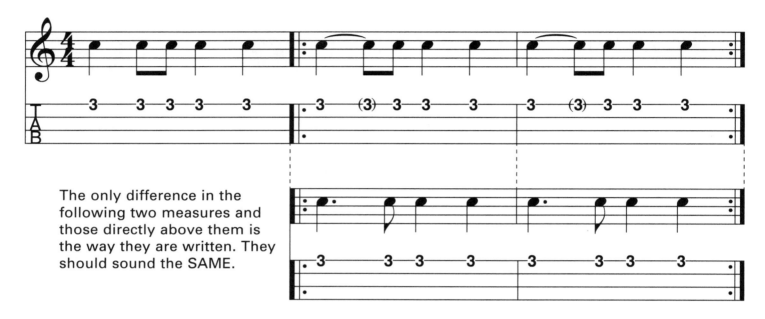

The only difference in the following two measures and those directly above them is the way they are written. They should sound the SAME.

AUDIO EXAMPLE

Cockles and Mussels

Moderately

In Dub-lin's fair cit-y, where girls are so pretty, I first set my eyes on sweet Mol-ly Ma-lone, As she

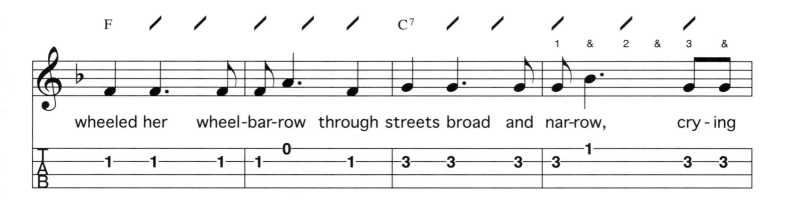

wheeled her   wheel-bar-row through streets broad and nar-row,   cry-ing

Cock - les   and   Mus-sels!   A - live,   a - live,   oh!

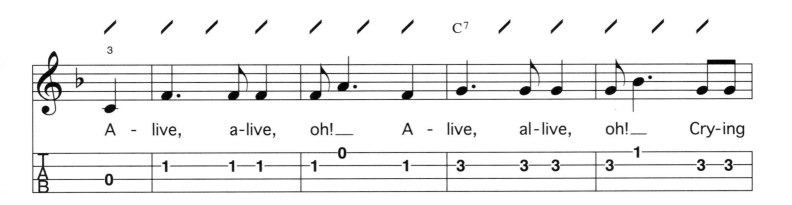

A - live,   a-live,   oh!__   A - live,   al-live,   oh!__   Cry-ing

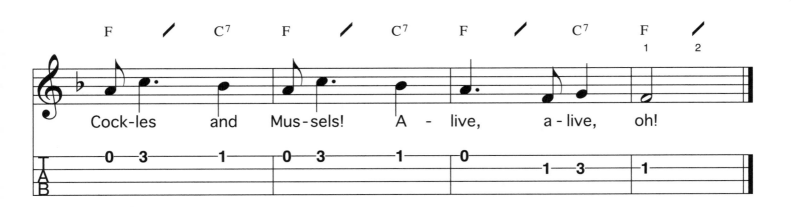

Cock-les   and   Mus-sels!   A - live,   a - live,   oh!

Clementine

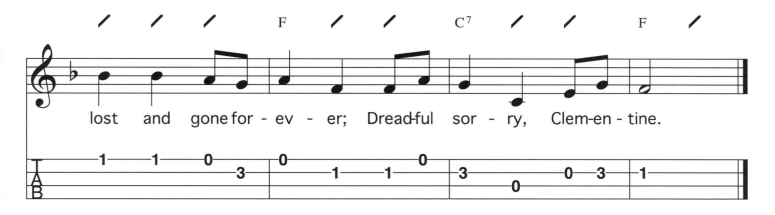

lost and gone for - ev - er; Dread-ful sor - ry, Clem-en - tine.

ADDITIONAL VERSES

VERSE 2:
LIGHT SHE WAS AND LIKE FAIRY,
AND HER SHOWS WERE NUMBER NINE,
HERRING BOXES WITHOUT TOPSES,
SANDALS WERE FOR CLEMENTINE.

CHORUS:
OH MY DARLING, OH MY DARLING,
OH MY DARLING, CLEMENTINE!
THOU ART LOST AND GONE FOREVER
DREADFUL SORRY, CLEMENTINE.

VERSE 3:
DROVE SHE DUCKLINGS TO THE WATER
EVERY MORNING JUST AT NINE,
HIT HER FOOT AGAINST A SPLINTER,
FELL INTO THE FOAMING BRINE.

CHORUS:
OH MY DARLING, OH MY DARLING
OH MY DARLING, CLEMENTINE!
THOU ART LOST AND GONE FOREVER
DREADFUL SORRY, CLEMENTINE.

VERSE 4:
RUBY LIPS ABOVE THE WATER,
BLOWING BUBBLES SOFT AND FINE,
BUT ALAS, I WAS NO SWIMMER,
SO I LOST MY CLEMENTINE.

CHORUS:
OH MY DARLING, OH MY DARLING
OH MY DARLING, CLEMENTINE
THOU ART LOST AND GONE FOREVER,
DREADFUL SORRY, CLEMENTINE.

THE G7 CHORD

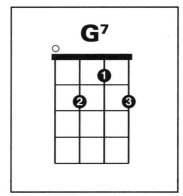

Place your 1st, 2nd, and 3rd fingers in position, then play one string at a time.

Play all four strings together:

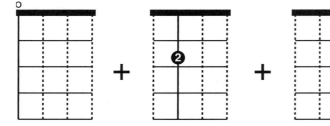 + 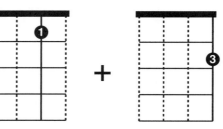 + 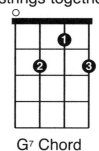 =

G7 Chord

Play slowly and evenly.

G7 Chord Exercises

1. 𝄞 **4/4** G⁷ / / / | C / / / | G⁷ / / / | C / / / |

2. 𝄞 **3/4** C / / | G⁷ / / | C / / | G⁷ / / | C / / | C 𝄽 𝄽 ‖

3. 𝄞 **2/4** G⁷ / | C / | G⁷ / | C / | F / | C / | G⁷ / | C / ‖

4. 𝄞 **4/4** C / / / | F / / / | C / / / | G⁷ / / / | C / / / | C / / 𝄽 ‖

5. 𝄞 **3/4** C / / | C⁷ / / | F / / | C / / | F / / | F / / | C / / | C / / |

G⁷ / / | G⁷ / / | C / / | F / / | C / / | C 𝄽 𝄽 ‖

Aloha 'Oe (Strummimng)

(Farewell to Thee)

To get used to playing the G7 chord, play this version of "Aloha 'Oe" (pronounced "oy") with just chords. Sing along with the melody.

This arrangement uses quarter note slashes ⌐ that indicate to play one strum on each quarter note.

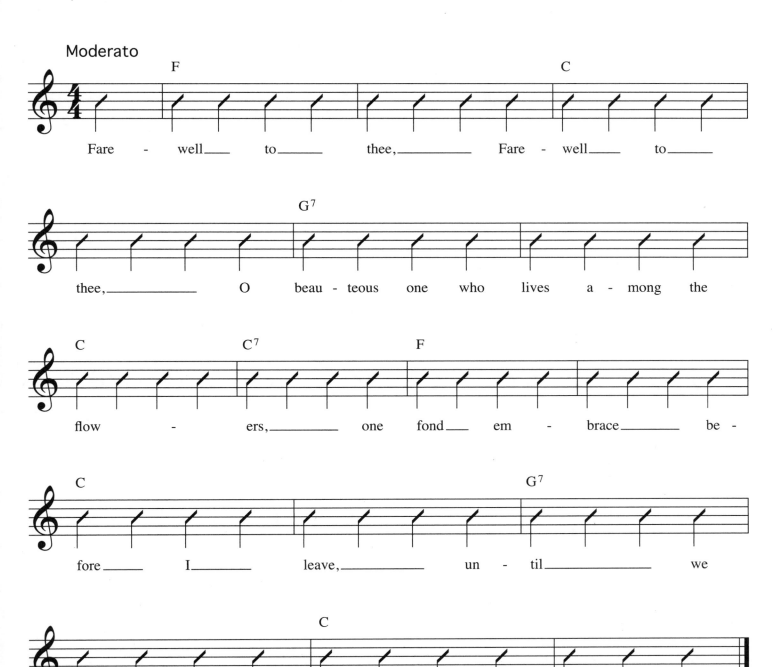

When the Saints Go Marching In

Love Somebody

The Streets of Laredo

Moderately

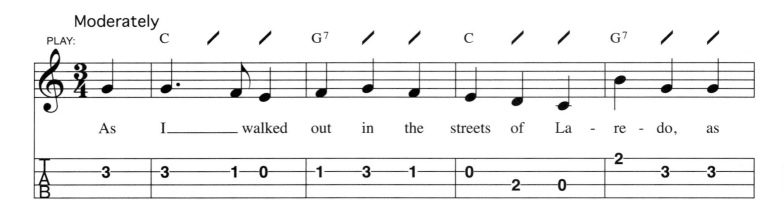

As I _____ walked out in the streets of La - re - do, as

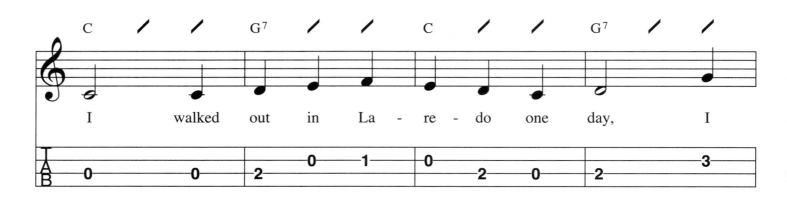

I walked out in La - re - do one day, I

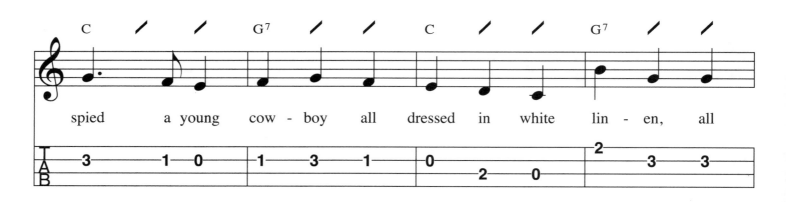

spied a young cow - boy all dressed in white lin - en, all

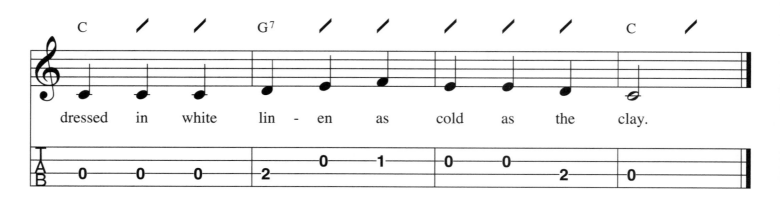

dressed in white lin - en as cold as the clay.

THE DOWN-AND-UP STROKE

You can make your accompaniment of waltz songs in $\frac{3}{4}$ like "The Streets of Laredo" more interesting by replacing the second beat of the measure with a down-stroke followed by an up-stroke. Together, the down-and-up strokes are played in the same time as a regular strum.

Try the following exercise to work on just the rhythm.

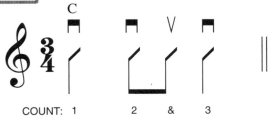

Now practice changing from C to G7.

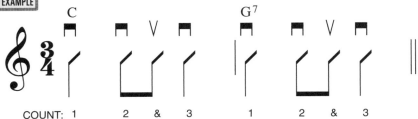

Now practice changing back and forth from C to G7 and back. When you can do it smoothly, go back to page 48 and use it to accompany "The Streets of Laredo."

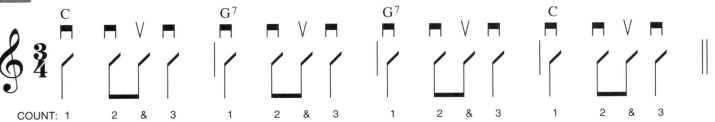

THE G CHORD

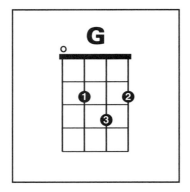

Place your 1st, 2nd, and 3rd fingers in position, then play one string at a time.

Play all four strings together:

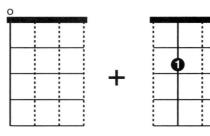 + 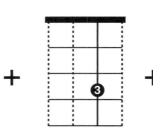 + 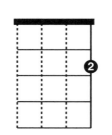 + 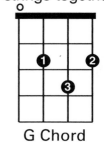 =

G Chord

THE D7 CHORD

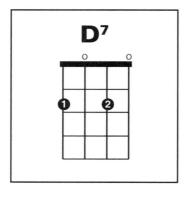

Place your 1st and 2nd fingers in position, then play one string at a time.

Play all four strings together:

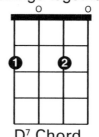

D7 Chord

Calypso Strum

The calypso strum is used to accompany Caribbean songs like "Mary Ann," "Jamaica Farewell," and "The Sloop John B." The rhythm is a little tricky, so make sure you can play the exercises on this page before trying the song on the following page.

Play a steady four-to-the-bar pattern on a C chord. Use only down-strokes.

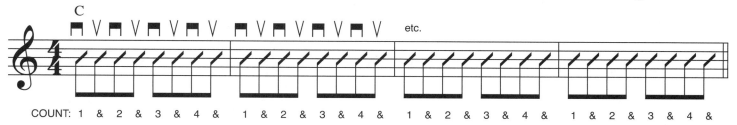

COUNT: 1   2   3   4   1   2   3   4   etc.

Now add an eighth note up-stroke after each down-stroke. Notice how the count has changed.

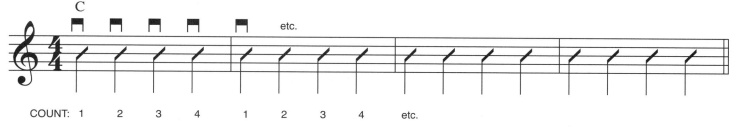

COUNT: 1 & 2 & 3 & 4 &   1 & 2 & 3 & 4 &   1 & 2 & 3 & 4 &   1 & 2 & 3 & 4 &

Now leave out the down-stroke on beat 3 and replace it with an eighth rest (𝄾). Notice that you now have two up-strokes in a row on the "and" of 2 and the "and" of 3.

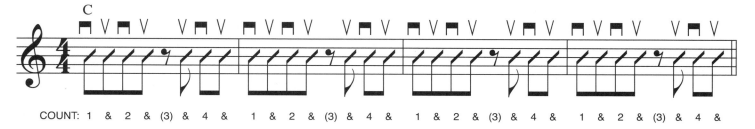

COUNT: 1 & 2 & (3) & 4 &   1 & 2 & (3) & 4 &   1 & 2 & (3) & 4 &   1 & 2 & (3) & 4 &

This whole pattern represents one measure of the calypso strum. As soon as you can do it without missing a beat, try "The Sloop John B."

INTRODUCING THE F SHARP

A *sharp* ♯ raises a note a half step. F♯ is played one fret higher than the note F. When a sharp note appears in a measure, it is still sharp until the end of that measure.

Notice "The Sloop John B." on page 52 uses a key signature with one sharp. Key signatures can use either sharps or flats.

2nd FRET

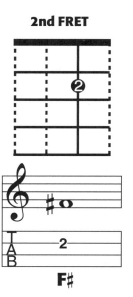

F♯

The Sloop John B.

Start this song with the calypso strum to get into the rhythm of it.
Then start singing.

MORE CHORDS

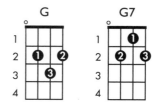

INTRODUCING G, D, D7, A, AND A7

Let's review the G7 and G chords. Coincidentally, G looks like G7 upside down on the fretboard.

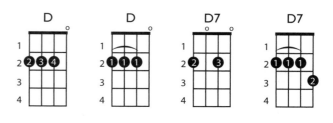

The D chord is shown with two fingerings. Many chords can be played in different ways depending on the needs of the situation. Start with a fingering that works for you, then learn other fingerings later. The second fingering of D uses the 1st finger across three strings to make a *barre*. To make a barre, you have to use the flat underside of your finger instead of the tip. D7 is also shown with two fingerings.

To the right are the A and A7 chords. A7 has two fingerings. As with D7 above, the two fingerings actually produce different arrangements of the notes in an A7 chord, so they are referred to as different *voicings*.

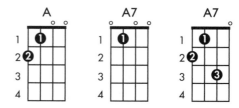

Here's a practice song you can use to work on your new chords. This song uses D, G, A, and A7, and is in the key of D. Notice how the music comes to rest on the tonic chord of D at the end. You can also try using the alternate fingerings for D or A7 shown above.

My Dear, Dear Mama From Madeira

Key: D

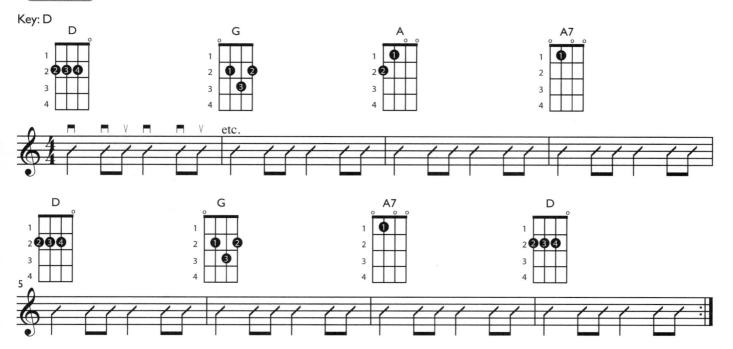

Below are the chords for the traditional Hawaiian song "Wai O Ke Aniani (Crystal Water)." It is popular with players of the *Hawaiian slack-key guitar style*, which involves special tunings and fingerstyle techniques and is sometimes accompanied by ukulele. Slack-key master Gabby Pahinui recorded this song in the 1940s, and many other artists have recorded it since then. "Wai O Ke Aniani" has different melodies for the verse and chorus but the chord progression is the same.

Wai O Ke Aniani (Crystal Water)

Traditional Hawaiian

Israel "IZ" Kamakawiwo'ole (1959–1997) was known to his fans as "Bruddah Iz." He inspired new interest in ukulele music with his 1993 interpretation of "Over the Rainbow/What a Wonderful World," which became a worldwide hit in the 2000s. In 1976, Iz co-founded the Makaha Sons of Ni'ihau, a band focused on bringing traditional Hawaiian music to a modern audience. Iz was much beloved for his tenor voice and tireless devotion to preserving Hawaiian cultural memory and independence through music.

MINOR CHORDS

VIDEO EXAMPLE

The chords you have learned so far are called "major" chords. They can be described as having a bright, happy sound because of the way the notes relate to each other. As you have seen, chord symbols for major chords are simply the letter name of the root. Any chord that is marked *min* is a *minor* chord. Minor chords have a darker or sadder emotional quality. You will learn more about the structures that create these sounds later.

Below are the minor chords that can be played in *open position* on the ukulele. (Open position refers to the open strings plus the first four frets.) In the case of Cmin, the first fingering is more common; the second fingering is shown if you have trouble barring your finger at first. To play the second fingering for Cmin, you have to mute the 2nd string (indicated by the "x"). You can do this by leaning your 2nd finger at a slight angle so that part of the finger touches the 2nd string to keep it from ringing. Use whichever Cmin works best for you.

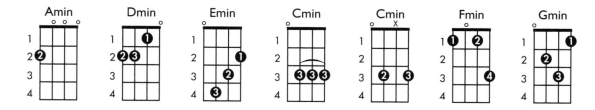

Try "It's Only a Minor Inconvenience" to get familiar with Amin, Dmin, and Emin. You'll notice a couple of new things.

- The chord diagrams are not shown. Many chord charts for songs only show the names of the chords. It's time to make sure you are memorizing new chords so that you know them whether or not the diagram is shown!

- There is a new strum pattern to try: three quarter notes and two eighths (down, down, down, down-up).

IT'S ONLY A MINOR INCONVENIENCE

AUDIO EXAMPLE

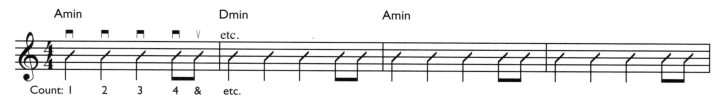

SUPER UKE TIP: IT'S OK TO LEAVE EARLY!

Have you noticed that when you're strumming, it's hard to change to a new chord on time? This is especially true if the strum pattern has an eighth note at the end (on the "&" of 4). Experienced strummers have a way to deal with this. You can lift your left-hand fingers up on the last upstroke in the strum pattern and move toward the new chord. That way you will be able to place your fingers on the new chord at the next downstroke. You will hear your upstroke striking the open strings as your fingers move. This may sound a little strange all by itself, but in the flow of the rhythm it's so short that it becomes masked by the sound of the real chords. You may want to strum a little lighter on that last upstroke so that the open strings don't get as much emphasis.

Here's what it would look like if we added a diagram for the open chord in the strum. Think of it not as a distinct chord (technically it's a C6) but as a transition chord.

Leaving Early Ex. 1

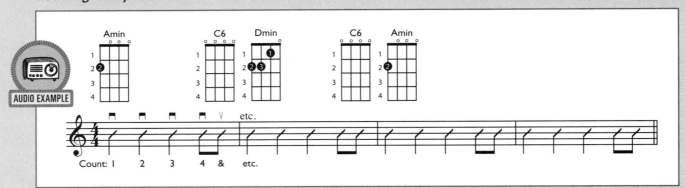

The rule to remember is this: It is more important to get to the next chord on time than it is to hold the current chord through the last eighth note. Of course, if you can do both, that's even better!

Here's one more progression to try using Cmin, Gmin, Dmin, and Fmin. Don't forget your new trick (above) for switching chords on time.

Leaving Early Ex. 2

Waltz time is another name for $\frac{3}{4}$ time. This means there are three beats in every measure and the quarter note gets one beat. First, familiarize yourself with the feel of three beats per measure by counting and tapping your foot for a few bars.

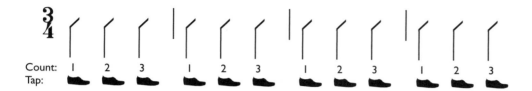

There are a variety of ways to strum in $\frac{3}{4}$ time.

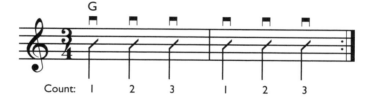

Waltz Strum No. 1:

Waltz Strum No. 2:

Waltz Strum No. 3:

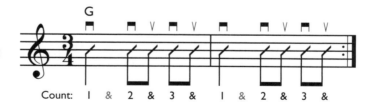

The gentle roll of waltz time can be particularly beautiful and lyrical. One of the most famous songs in ¾ is "Amazing Grace." Practice the chords using any of the strums on the previous page. You can also try the melody, which is shown in standard notation and TAB. You may have any easier time learning the melody if you go back and review the section on reading standard music notation, page 14. This arrangement of "Amazing Grace" is in the key of G. If you need to, you can simplify the chords by playing D instead of D7, and G instead of G7.

The melody of "Amazing Grace" has two eighth notes before the first full measure. This is a **pickup**, as we learned first on page 38. The two eighth notes that begin "Amazing Grace" are counted as beat 3 of an empty (or count-in) measure. The value of the pickup is then subtracted from the last measure. Sometimes it helps to count a waltz in with two measures. Count "1, 2, 3, 1, 2" and begin playing on beat 3. If you are strumming chords, wait until beat 1 of the first full measure (after the pickup notes) to come in with your strum pattern. Additionally, notice the dotted half notes (♩.) in measures 7 and 15. These last for three beats. For more on dotted half notes, see page 18.

AMAZING GRACE

RIGHT-HAND TOOLS AND TECHNIQUES

Now that you've had some experience playing the ukulele, it's time to look at the tools we can use to produce different sounds. Here are the main options used by most players:

Fingerstyle.

Thumbpick and fingerpicks.

- Index finger (usually labeled i)—using downstrokes and upstrokes

- Thumb (labeled T)—using downstrokes and upstrokes

- Combination of i and T.

- Fingerstyle—using thumb (T), index (i), middle (m), and ring (a) fingers.

- Pick—either a guitar-style plastic pick, or a hardened felt ukulele pick. Other materials are available, like wood and leather.

- Some fingerstyle players use a thumbpick and/or fingerpicks so they can get the brightness and volume of picks with the agility of fingerstyle.

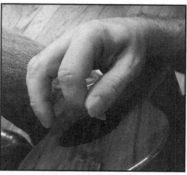
Guitar-style pick.

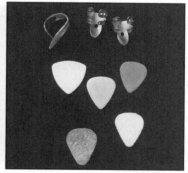
Thumbpick, fingerpicks, guitar picks, and felt ukulele picks.

HOW TO HOLD A PICK

Place your right-hand thumb across the top of the pick, with the point at a 90-degree angle from your thumb. Then, curve your index finger behind the pick, holding it between your thumb and the side of the first joint of your index finger. Your other fingers can curl into your palm or hang loosely. Just keep them relaxed. If the pick moves around too much when you play, hold it a little closer to the point.

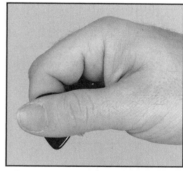
The correct way to hold a pick.

REST STROKES AND FREE STROKES

There are two main ways to strike a string with the thumb, fingers, or pick. Strumming is usually done with free strokes, while melodies can be played with either free or rest strokes.

Free strokes are the type of strokes you probably have already been using (whether you know it or not). The pick, thumb, or finger strikes the string (or strings) in an uninterrupted motion, either with a downstroke or upstroke. With a free stroke, the string vibrates in a more lateral motion*, roughly parallel to the top.

With a *rest stroke*, the thumb, finger, or pick strikes the string and then comes to rest on the next string that falls in its path (or simulates this motion if there is no string to rest on). Rest strokes cause the strings to vibrate in a motion that is more perpendicular to the top. This transmits more vibration to the bridge and creates a full, round, and sometimes louder tone. Rest strokes with the thumb are used by traditional Hawaiian thumb-style players to get an amazing tone out of the tiny ukulele.

* Technically, the string vibrates in an elliptical or oval pattern that is wider near the middle of the string.

Try any technique you are exposed to. You will find different techniques and tools have different applications in the music you play. Following are the pros and cons of some of the tools discussed in this lesson. Most of this book will work with most styles, though some techniques are more specific.

TOOL	PROS	CONS
Index finger only	• Easy to keep track of • The fingernail gives the downstroke brightness and definition • Can be easily blended with thumb techniques and fingerpicking • Bright sound that projects well	• Can get fatiguing in long, loud jam sessions if you're not careful • Downstroke and upstroke have different tonal qualities due to the fingernail
Thumb only	• Gives a softer, mellower sound with a big, round tone • Thumbnail can add brightness • Easily blended with finger techniques	• Downstroke and upstroke have different tonal qualities due to the thumbnail
Index finger and thumb, or fingerstyle: thumb, index, middle, and ring	• Provides a variety of tonal combinations • Experienced players are able to play with a great deal of speed using the combination of index and thumb • New techniques like triple strums and rolls become possible • See page 110 for more info	• Takes more practice and coordination to get used to • Sacrifices some of the volume and projection that is possible with a pick (in order to gain more tonal color and nuance)
Pick (see below for specific types)	• Easy to strum for long periods of time with a steady, even tone • Upstrokes and downstrokes have very similar tone and projection • Ample volume and bright tone	• More difficult to integrate with finger techniques • Some specialized uke techniques are not possible with a pick
Guitar-style pick (hard plastic or similar)	• Brightest and loudest tone • Readily available • Many shapes, sizes, varieties, and thicknesses • Thin picks make a softer, brighter tone; thick picks make a fuller, louder tone	• Tone may be more brittle or thin sounding than finger/thumb techniques, especially on single notes
Felt "uke" picks	• Made of thick, rigid felt • Softer tone than guitar picks • Over time, the felt becomes more flexible and develops a sound that is similar to strumming with the index finger	• Harder to find in music stores, though still widely available • New picks need some break-in time (keep track of your "good one!")
Thumbpick and/or fingerpicks	• Adds the volume, crisp tone and agility of a pick to the thumb technique • Thumbpick with bare fingers is a good compromise between the pick style and fingerstyle	• Requires quite a bit of practice to become proficient • Fingerpicks, especially the more common metal ones, can sound too bright and harsh on nylon strings

MORE ON SHARPS AND FLATS

ACCIDENTALS

Once you have become familiar with reading the natural notes, adding the accidentals (flats, see page 28. sharps, see page 51) is simple. Here's a quick review:

Symbol	Name	Description
♯	Sharp	Raises a natural note by one half step (one fret).
♭	Flat	Lowers a natural note by one half step (one fret).
♮	Natural	Cancels a sharp or flat—play the natural note.

In written music, a sharp, flat, or natural will appear just before the note it affects. When you say the note name out loud, say the letter first.

Say: "A-sharp   G-flat   A-natural"

ACCIDENTALS LAST FOR THE REST OF THE MEASURE
When a sharp or flat appears on a note, that note remains affected by the sharp or flat until the end of the measure. In other words, a sharp or flat can be canceled only by a natural or a bar line.

TIPS

Here's a tune that will give you a chance to practice reading accidentals. You may need a little help finding the new notes at first so the TAB is also shown.

Raised by Gypsies

ACCIDENTALS IN A KEY SIGNATURE

VIDEO EXAMPLE

Most pieces of music have a *key*. The key is named after the *tonal center* or *tonic* note. The tonic note is the first note of the scale for the key and the note that gives the strongest feeling of resolution or completion. Every major scale has its own unique set of notes, some of which may be sharp or flat. The *key signature* allows us to easily show which sharps or flats are in the key without cluttering the piece with accidentals.

A key signature appears just after the clef sign at the beginning of each line of music. It is a set of sharps or flats (never both). You were introduced to key signatures on page 34 but let's learn more about where key signatures come from and which keys they represent. If you see no key signature, it just means that the notes of the piece will all be natural notes, as in the key of C Major.

Reading a key signature is very simple. Look just to the right of the clef sign. Any sharps or flats that appear will affect that pitch throughout the entire piece of music. For instance, the key signature in the example to the right has an F♯ (F-sharp) and a C♯ (C-sharp). This means that *all* of the F notes and *all* of the C notes will be sharped unless marked with other accidentals.

IMPORTANT NOTE

TIPS

Accidentals in key signatures affect the notes in every octave, not just the line or space on which the accidental appears.

Try reading through the classic cowboy song "Red River Valley," below. The key signature contains one flat, B♭ (B-flat), which is the signature of F Major. The notes affected by the key signature have been circled to remind you that they are flatted, but this is just to help you out this one time! TAB is also included.

Red River Valley

AUDIO EXAMPLE

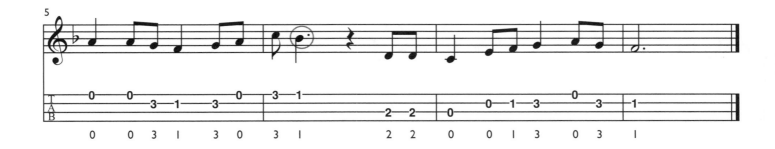

NAVIGATING A MUSICAL MAP

The following short piece contains some devices that allow a longer musical idea to fit into a shorter space on the page. The repeat sign at the end of the fourth bar tells you to repeat from the beginning. The *first ending* (measures 3 and 4) indicates the music you should play on the first time through. The *second ending* indicates that on the second time through, you should play the second ending instead of the first ending.

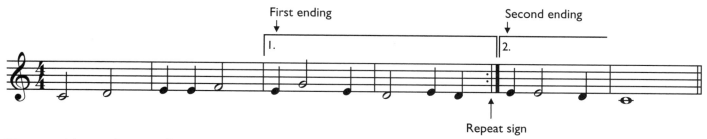

The markings above tell you to follow these steps:

1. Play measures 1 through 4 as normal.

2. Repeat from the beginning, playing measures 1 and 2.

3. At measure 3, skip over both measures 3 and 4 (the first ending), and, instead, play the second ending (the last two measures of the tune).

Following are a few other markings you might see as you become more advanced. They are provided as a reference. Like many musical markings, they originate in Italian terms.

D.C.	D.C. stands for *Da Capo*, Italian for "from the head." It tells you to repeat the whole piece of music from the beginning.
D.S. 𝄋	D.S. stands for *Dal Segno* (pronounced "sane-yo"), meaning "from the sign." *D.S.* tells you to look for the special sign (shown at left) earlier in the music and repeat the music from that point.
al Fine	*Fine* (pronounced "fee-nay") means "the end." *Al Fine* can be added to *D.C.* or *D.S.* Repeat the piece as indicated by *D.C.* or *D.S.*, but end your second pass through the piece at the end of the measure marked "*Fine.*"
al Coda ⊕	A *coda* (meaning "tail") is new music added to the end of a piece. *Al Coda* can be added to *D.C.* or *D.S.* Repeat the piece as indicated by *D.C.* or *D.S.* up until you see the first coda symbol (shown at left). At this point, jump to a later point in the music marked with the second coda symbol and begin again from there.

The markings above all require you to jump from one section of the written music to another without interrupting the flow of the music. Always check out a piece of music before you start playing it, looking for repeats, endings, and other similar directions. You may need to plan out where the "jumps" are, and even highlight them on the music so you know where to go ahead of time.

PART 2: MORE ADVANCED PLAYING

THE MAJOR SCALE IS YOUR MEASURING STICK

TWO FOUNDATIONS:
THE CHROMATIC SCALE AND THE MAJOR SCALE

The foundations of music theory in the Western, or European, tradition are the chromatic scale and major scale. The chromatic scale gives us the 12 tones in each octave on our instrument. If you're still shaky on the chromatic scale, go back and learn it by heart before proceeding.

The major scale gives us a very common set of notes and relationships we can use to make music. We also use the major scale as a "standard of measurement" to compare all the other scales to, much like we would compare a prize-winning giant cucumber to a ruler to see how long it was. Below is a C Major scale. The notes can be numbered 1–7, with the 8th note being the same as note number 1 in the next octave. These numbers are called *scale degrees*.

Note:	C	D	E	F	G	A	B	C
Scale Degree:	1	2	3	4	5	6	7	8(1)

```
T ------------------------------------0----2----3---
A ------------------0----1----3----------------------
B ----0----2-----------------------------------------
```

```
0    2    0    1    3    0    2    3
```

THE SECRET FORMULA

The C Major scale is made by playing the natural notes C–D–E–F–G–A–B–C. There is a half step between E and F. All of the other letters are a whole step apart. In terms of scale degrees, the half steps are between notes 3 and 4, and between notes 7 and 8 (which could also be called note 1). This gives us the series of whole steps and half steps that make every major scale. To the right is the C Major scale with the intervals and scale degrees shown.

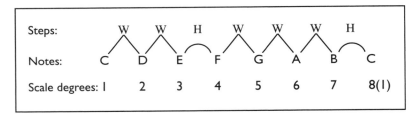

With careful use of the formula, you can *spell* (apply the formula of whole steps and half steps) the major scale starting on any note. Just start with the key note (1st scale degree) and then follow the formula, using each letter only once.

The D Major scale is shown below. Notice that to make E to F a whole step, as the formula requires, we must raise the F a half step to F♯. Try spelling the A and B♭ Major scales (the correct answers are underneath the Tips box below).

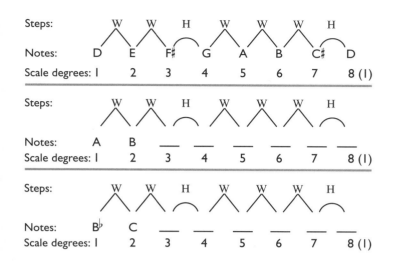

Steps:		W		W		H		W		W		W		H	
Notes:	D		E		F♯		G		A		B		C♯		D
Scale degrees:	1		2		3		4		5		6		7		8 (1)

Steps:		W		W		H		W		W		W		H	
Notes:	A		B		__		__		__		__		__		__
Scale degrees:	1		2		3		4		5		6		7		8 (1)

Steps:		W		W		H		W		W		W		H	
Notes:	B♭		C		__		__		__		__		__		__
Scale degrees:	1		2		3		4		5		6		7		8 (1)

TIPS

1. Use every letter in the musical alphabet once, in alphabetical order.

2. The last note is the same as the first.

3. You will need to use either sharps or flats (never both) to make the notes fit the formula.

Answers:

Notes:	B♭	C	D	E♭	F	G	A	B♭
Scale degrees:	1	2	3	4	5	6	7	8 (1)

Notes:	A	B	C♯	D	E	F♯	G♯	A
Scale degrees:	1	2	3	4	5	6	7	8 (1)

Try playing the A Major scale by going up the 1st string. Playing the scale on a single string makes it easy to see the whole steps and half steps. When you get comfortable with it, try going backwards! You will learn other fingerings for major scales in different keys later in this book.

Note:	A	B	C♯	D	E	F♯	G♯	A
Scale Degree:	1	2	3	4	5	6	7	8(1)
	0	2	4	5	7	9	11	12
	0	1	3	4	1	3	4	4

THE CIRCLE OF 5THS

The *circle of 5ths* is like the "secret agent decoder ring" of music theory. A *5th* is the distance between the 1st and 5th degrees of a scale. To make a circle of 5ths, just take the keys and arrange them in a circle so that the next keynote (going clockwise) is the 5th degree of the last scale. For example, the 5th degree of a D Major scale is A, so the next key in the circle is A.

The circle of 5ths makes it easy to learn the key signature for each key. The "sharp keys" (clockwise on the circle) add one sharp for each new key. The new sharp is always the 7th scale degree of that key. The "flat keys" (counterclockwise) add one new flat for each key. That new flat is always the 4th scale degree of the key.

Notice that the keys of G♭ and F♯ are in the same position in the circle. The two scales are played on exactly the same strings and frets and sound exactly the same. When two notes have the same sound but different names, they are *enharmonic equivalents*.

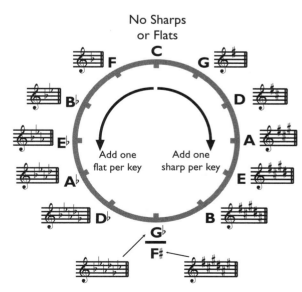

No Sharps or Flats

Add one flat per key

Add one sharp per key

INTERVALS ARE YOUR BUILDING BLOCKS

Along with the music alphabet and the major scale, *intervals* are a fundamental element of music theory. An interval is the distance between two notes, measured in steps. You've already worked with a couple of intervals: the half step (known in interval lingo as a *minor 2nd*) and the whole step (*major 2nd*).

HOW INTERVALS ARE NAMED

Interval names include a number (like 2nd or 3rd) and a word that describes the interval's *quality* (major, minor, augmented, diminished, or perfect). The number describes how many steps, or letters in the music alphabet, are spanned by the interval. The quality helps describe the interval more precisely. The distance in an interval is always calculated from the lower of the two pitches to the higher.

THE INTERVALS IN ONE OCTAVE AND HOW TO PLAY THEM

Because of its unique reentrant tuning, there are many ways to play the various intervals on the ukulele. You will encounter many of them as your learning progresses. The important thing right now is that you become familiar with the naming system for intervals and their sounds. A simple way to do this is to use the 4th string (G) as a constant root note and making the intervals above G on the 2nd and 1st strings. Here are all the intervals in one octave using G as the lowest note (or root). The note names are shown above the music. You can play the intervals *harmonically* (together, as shown) or *melodically* (one note after the other). After you have tried them out, you will learn about the different types.

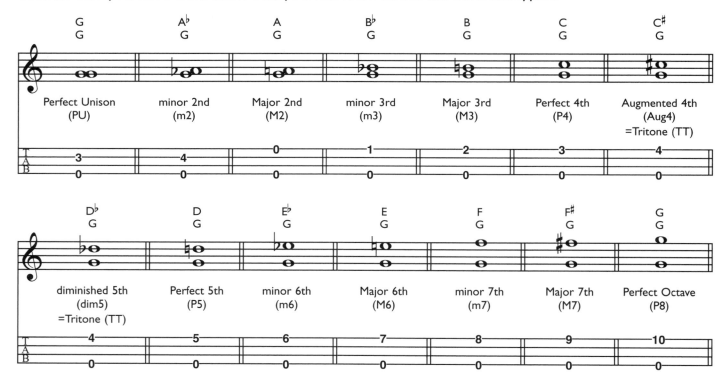

THEORY TIP

The intervals shown above are arranged from the smallest to the largest, with the augmented 4th and diminished 5th producing the enharmonic names of the same note (C♯ and D♭). It's a great idea to memorize the names of the intervals in ascending order as well as their half steps. The chart on the next page shows the intervals and half steps.

The chart to the right shows the intervals and their abbreviations from smallest to largest by half steps.

Interval	Abbreviation	Half Steps
Perfect Unison	PU	0
minor 2nd	m2	1
Major 2nd	M2	2
minor 3rd	m3	3
Major 3rd	M3	4
Perfect 4th	P4	5
Augmented 4th (or Tritone)	Aug4 or TT	6
Diminished 5th (or Tritone)	dim5 or TT	6
Perfect 5th	P5	7
minor 6th	m6	8
Major 6th	M6	9
minor 7th	m7	10
Major 7th	M7	11
Perfect Octave	P8	12

PERFECT INTERVALS
There are only four intervals in an octave that are described as *perfect*. They are the unison, the 4th, the 5th, and the octave (or PU, P4, P5, and P8). These intervals do not come in major and minor versions (see below). When the two notes of a perfect interval are played together on a well tuned instrument, they resonate with great clarity, like a camera lens that is in perfect focus.

MAJOR AND MINOR INTERVALS
The following intervals come in major or minor versions: 2nds, 3rds, 6ths, and 7ths. In the case of any one of these intervals, the *major* interval is larger, or farther apart, by one half step. The *minor* interval is smaller, or closer together, by one half step. The abbreviations for major intervals use an uppercase "M," while the minor intervals use a lower case "m." The major and perfect intervals correspond to the steps in the major scale (see below).

AUGMENTED AND DIMINISHED INTERVALS
All types of intervals can be augmented or diminished. To augment means to add to or make bigger. An *augmented* interval is one half step larger than a major or perfect interval. To diminish means to make smaller. A *diminished* interval is one half step smaller than a minor or perfect interval.

THE TRITONE (AUGMENTED 4TH/DIMINISHED 5TH)
Between the perfect 4th and perfect 5th is an interval called a *tritone* (abbreviated TT). "Tone" is another word for whole step, so, a tritone equals three whole steps (equivalent to six half steps). In the interval naming system, a tritone is either an augmented 4th (one half step larger than a perfect 4th) or a diminished 5th (one half step smaller than a perfect 5th). Both the augmented 4th and the diminished 5th refer to the same distance of six half steps.

INTERVALS OF THE MAJOR SCALE
You can use the major scale as a reference for your intervals. To make a major scale, use only the perfect and major intervals. You can then find the minor intervals by lowering any major interval by one half step. Below are the intervals of the G Major scale. The upper notes show the scale, while the lower note remains G throughout to show the interval distances from the tonic.

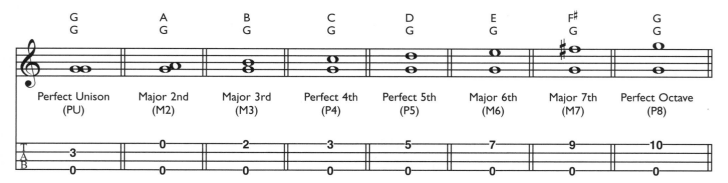

HARMONY AND CHORDS

Remember, a chord is any three or more notes played together. The subject of chords and how they behave is called *harmony*. The most basic kind of chord is called a *triad*. A triad is a three-note chord, generally made by stacking one interval of a 3rd on top of another. You have already learned several major and minor chords, and some 6th and 7th chords. The major and minor chords are triads (sometimes with a note repeated if you are strumming all four strings). The 6th and 7th chords have four notes.

Below is a C Major scale that has been *harmonized*. This means that 3rds have been stacked above each note of the scale to form triads. The harmony notes are all within the scale—no sharps or flats have been added or changed. This is called *diatonic harmony*, or harmony within the key. TAB has been included so it will be easy for you to hear what the harmonized scale sounds like. You can also play the chords using any other familiar fingerings. You will find three types of triads: major, minor, and diminished, which are all discussed below.

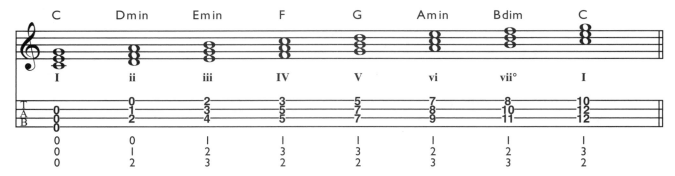

Notice that the chords have been designated with Roman numerals. This allows for a distinction between scale degrees and chord numbers. The Roman numerals also show the quality of the chord (uppercase for major chords, and lowercase for minor and diminished chords). Diminished chords are also labeled with a small superscript circle (as in B°).

ROMAN NUMERAL REVIEW

I or i.......... 1	V or v 5
II or ii 2	VI or vi 6
III or iii 3	VII or vii ... 7
IV or iv 4	

THREE KINDS OF TRIADS

The three types of triads that result from harmonizing the major scale are all made with different combinations of major and minor 3rds.

- A *major triad* is a major 3rd with a minor 3rd on top. Its structure is root–3rd–5th.

- A *minor triad* is a minor 3rd with a major 3rd on top. Its structure is root–♭3rd–5th.

- A *diminished triad* is a minor 3rd with another minor 3rd on top. Its structure is root–♭3rd–♭5th.

TRIAD STRUCTURE
The bottom note of the triad is the *root*. The root is always the note the chord is named for. The middle note, which is a 3rd above the root, is called the *3rd*. The top note, which is a 3rd above the 3rd and a 5th above the root, is called the *5th*.

For comparison, this example shows the three types of triads, all built on a C root.

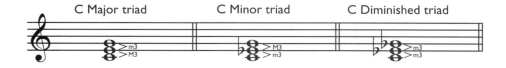

THREE PRIMARY CHORDS

The *primary chords* in every major key are the I, IV, and V (one, four, and five) chords.

Here is a C Major scale with the roots of the I, IV, and V chords circled.

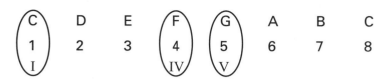

Bellow is a chord progression using I, IV, and V. The key of C Major is indicated. Also try it in D and G. Use any chord fingerings or strum patterns you like.

Key of C Major

Key of D Major

Fill in the blanks. The answers are at the bottom of the page.

Key of G Major

Fill in the blanks. The answers are at the bottom of the page.

MORE ABOUT THE CIRCLE OF 5THS

The circle of 5ths can be used to show basic harmonic movement. Instead of keys, these are major chords. Box or circle any three adjacent chords. The one in the middle is I. The one going clockwise is V. The one going counterclockwise is IV.

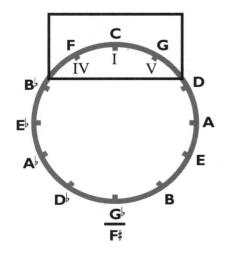

ANSWERS:

Key of D: D G A   Key of G: G C D
I IV V   I IV V

OLD-TIME UKULELE AND BACKING UP FIDDLE TUNES

Old-time music is an American traditional style based on fiddle tunes and songs that were played for dances and parties in the late 1800s and early 1900s. The roots of the music are in tunes that have been played for hundreds of years in Europe and the British Isles, mixed with influences from Africa, Native Americans, and immigrant cultures. Old-time music is one of the roots of more recent styles like bluegrass and Americana.

Old-time music is a community music and lots of fun to play along with. Sometimes a picking session is just a few people, but some jams can get very large with many fiddles, banjos, and guitars. The portability and unique voice of the uke have made it an adopted member of the old-time family. The banjo uke is a particular favorite in old-time jams because it is louder and more percussive than wooden ukes, but you can play with any type of uke.

The role of the uke in an old-time jam is generally as part of the rhythm section (along with guitars and upright basses). Since the uke is high pitched and has little sustain, it projects best when strumming chords in a steady rhythm. The constant, repetitive groove made by the rhythm section provides a foundation for the fiddles, banjos, and mandolins to play syncopated melodies against.

THE COMMON FIDDLE KEYS

The fiddle is a central instrument in old-time music. The keys of C, G, D, and A allow the fiddle to make use of its open strings for extra harmony notes, and so these keys have become the most common keys for tunes. It's a good idea to memorize the primary chords (I, IV, and V) for these common keys. That way, when someone tells you the key for a tune, you'll have at least an idea of what some of the chords might be. The chart to the right shows what you need to know.

KEY	I	IV	V
C	C	F	G or G7
G	G	C	D or D7
D	D	G	A or A7
A	A	D	E or E7

DID YOU KNOW?

Photo by Joe Del Tufo

Jeff Claus—of the Ithaca, New York band The Horse Flies—helped spark new interest in using the banjo uke to accompany old-time music starting in the mid-1980s. The Horse Flies play traditional acoustic fiddle tunes with drive and momentum, but they are also known for using echo and wah effects to create minimalist soundscapes reminiscent of composer Steve Reich, and for their influences of punk, indie, and new wave.

STRUM PATTERNS AND A TUNE IN G

You can use your index finger to strum old-time music. Let your strumming motion come from a loose, relaxed wrist and fingers. Many uke players who play old-time music like to use a pick instead. A long high-energy jam can really wear down your fingernail if you're not careful. See page 59 for more on picks. Here are a couple of strums that work well for old-time uke. The first one ought to be pretty familiar by now! Try each one many times over using different chords.

Below are the chords to a classic old-time and bluegrass song also known as "Nine Pound Hammer" or "Roll On, Buddy." Try it with the second strum shown above, or mix up the strum patterns. Stay loose, because these tunes can get pretty fast in jam situations! This tune is in the key of G. The chords are G (I), C (IV), and D (V).

This Hammer's Too Heavy

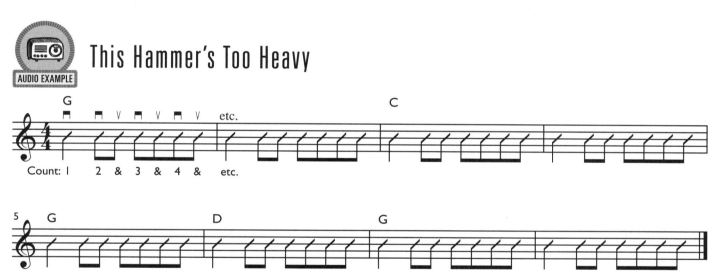

C TUNING OR D TUNING?

You can ignore this box and lead a happy uke life, but if you're curious about tunings, read on. This book is written for ukuleles tuned G–C–E–A, also known as C or C6 tuning. Some players like to tune a whole step higher to A–D–F♯–B. This is known as D or D6 tuning. Here's where it helps to know the I, IV, and V chords in common keys. In D tuning, just transpose the chord shapes for each key down a whole step from what you normally use in C tuning.

For example, if you were playing in the key of D in standard C tuning, your chord shapes would be D (I), G (IV), and A (V). If you were playing in the key of D in D tuning, your chord shapes would be fingered like C, F, and G in C tuning. The D tuning is a whole step higher, so the corresponding chord shapes are a whole step lower.

You can simulate this on a standard tuned uke by placing a *capo* (a device that clamps the strings down to a fret) at the 2nd fret. Some players also like the D tuning because it puts more tension on the strings, giving the uke an even brighter, snappier tone when strummed.

ACCENTING THE BACKBEAT, THE E AND E7 CHORDS, AND "SALLY ANN" IN A

One way to inject more propulsion into the old-time groove is to accent the backbeat. An *accent* (>) is a musical symbol that tells you to play a note or chord louder than the surrounding notes. Many grooves in blues, jazz, rock, bluegrass, and old-time are based on a four-beat rhythm pattern: bass note or kick drum on beats 1 and 3, and a high-pitched sound like a snare drum or guitar chord on 2 and 4. Beats 2 and 4 in this rhythm are called the *backbeat*. This rhythm has its roots in the basic foot-stomp and handclap rhythm that accompanied spirituals and work songs sung by Africans in America during the era of slavery. The backbeat rhythm became the heartbeat of many styles of music.

Try the following strum using a medium volume for most of the strokes and a louder strum on beats 2 and 4. You can achieve this with a stronger snap of the wrist, or by flicking your finger a little more forcefully. If you're using a pick, hold the pick a little tighter on the accent beats and you'll hear them pop out.

Accenting the Backbeat

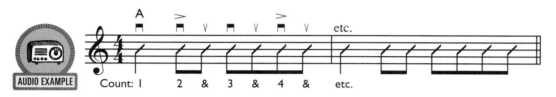

Here are the chords to "Sally Ann" in the key of A, using the accented backbeat strum. "Sally Ann" has two sections, the A part and the B part. Each part is repeated, and the whole tune can be played many times. Note the *right-facing repeat* at the start of the B part; it tells you that the repeat at the end of the B part (*left-facing*) begins here.

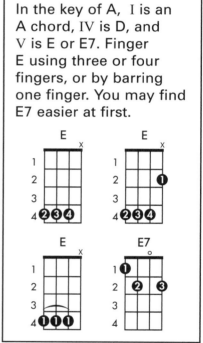

In the key of A, I is an A chord, IV is D, and V is E or E7. Finger E using three or four fingers, or by barring one finger. You may find E7 easier at first.

Sally Ann

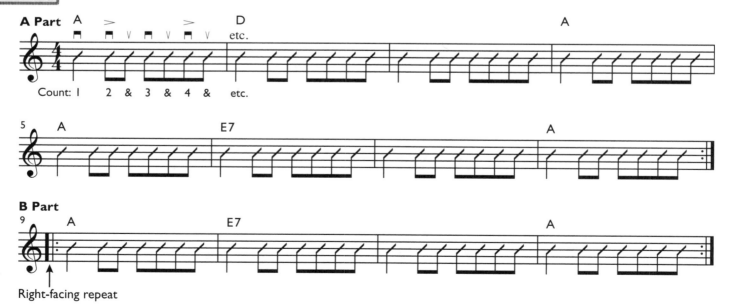

FIDDLE-TUNE FORM AND SOLDIER'S JOY IN D

Form is the internal structure that repeats (or cycles through a series of sections) to form a piece of music. One of the most common forms in old-time music is the *two-part fiddle tune*. This form is known in classical theory as a *binary form*. The two main sections of the tune are labeled the A part and the B part. Each part is repeated before moving on. The basic form of the tune can be described as "A A B B." This form is then repeated over and over for as long as the group wants to jam on it.

One of the oldest and most popular tunes in the repertoire is "Soldier's Joy" in the key of D. The I, IV, and V chords are D, G, and A respectively. Don't forget to repeat both the A part and the B part. The melody is a little tricky to play on the uke, but a simplified version is shown with TAB if you want to try it (pay close attention to the fingering shown below the TAB!). On the video, you'll hear the melody played by the fiddle, as well as a bass line to give you the feel of a real jam. Use any of the patterns from the last several pages to strum.

Soldier's Joy

OLD SCHOOL: THE SWINGIN' UKULELE

The first big wave of international popularity for the ukulele came in the early decades of the 1900s. During this same period, various streams of popular music—including parlor songs of the 1800s, ragtime, marching band music, and blues—were combining and evolving into jazz. The jazz and swing band music heard on the radio and in dance halls was sophisticated and virtuosic, requiring experienced musicians and a lot of practice. When the ukulele came along, it offered the average person an accessible way to capture some of the energy and rhythm of a swing band. The uke was relatively inexpensive and you could carry it to the college pep rally in the pocket of your oversize fur coat (an essential fashion item of the time).

TIN PAN ALLEY AND HAPA HAOLE

The fad of the ukulele and Hawaiian music (or semi-Hawaiian music) took over the 1920s, and many modern uke enthusiasts still play the songs and styles that evolved during this era. A major source of material in this period were the writers and publishers of sheet music for popular songs. This industry was based in New York City and is referred to as "Tin Pan Alley." The Tin Pan Alley writers worked night and day to create new songs that could be sold to a public that was hungry to join whatever fad was hot at the moment. They created hundreds of songs that combined Hawaiian words, fake Hawaiian-sounding language, and humorous or romantic themes in English set to the popular swing rhythms of the day. These mixed-language songs became known as *hapa haole* songs, where *hapa* (pronounced HAH-pah) means half, and *haole* (pronounced HOW-leh) means non-native or Caucasian.

HOW TO SWING

The basis of swing and jazz music is a way of counting and feeling the underlying beat of the music. You have already played music with eighth notes, so you know that eighth notes divide the beat into two equal pieces. This type of eighth notes is called *straight eighths*.

There is another way to count eighth notes called *swing eighths*. In swing eighths, the onbeat is given longer emphasis while the offbeat ("&") is made shorter. In straight eighths the beat is divided into two equal pieces. In the swing feel, the pulse of the beat is divided into three pieces, or eighth-note triplets. To count triplets, try saying this aloud to a steady beat: "Trip-pul-let, trip-pul-let."

In swing eighths, the first two notes of the triplet are tied together, so that you don't hear an individual note on the second eighth. In the swing feel, this rhythm happens so much that it becomes unwieldy to write and count full triplets all the time. Instead, the swing-eighths rhythm is counted as if it were eighth notes with an onbeat that is twice as long as the offbeat.

Swing eighths are designated at the beginning of a piece of music in one of two ways (see right). If you see either designation, it means all eighth notes in the piece are to be "swung."

Grab a C chord on your ukulele and try strumming and counting some swing eighths. This next example introduces a new symbol called the *simile mark*. It looks like a slash with a dot on either side. The simile mark tells you to duplicate whatever you were doing in the previous measure. In the following examples, it tells you to continue the same strumming pattern.

Swing Eighths Ex. 1

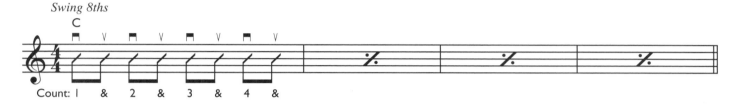

Now try your trusty quarter-and-two-eighths strum using the swing-eighths feel. This makes a great strum for swing tunes. Try it with different chords or make up some progressions.

Swing Eighths Ex. 2

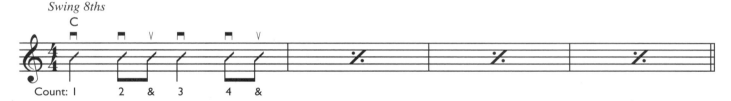

I SEE YOU'VE GONE STACCATO

Here's a nifty way to put a little jump in your swing strum. Remember, legato means the notes are held for their full duration, which is the normal, or "default," way that we play notes and chords. Staccato means the sustain of the note or chord is cut off early, resulting in a "clipped" sound for that beat. You can play a staccato chord by relaxing the pressure of the fretting fingers just after you strum the chord. Don't take them all the way off the strings. Technically, this is not full staccato, because the open strings in the chord will still be ringing, but it is enough to give a nice texture to the groove.

Try the following strum on a G chord with staccato chords on beats 1, 2 and 3. Staccato is indicated with a dot above or below the note head, opposite the stem. Use the squeezing and relaxing pressure of your left-hand fingers to create the staccato. You can also throw in staccato notes to other strum patterns.

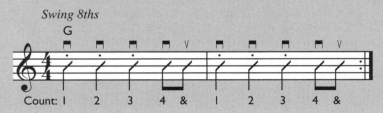

JAZZY PROGRESSIONS NEED JAZZY CHORDS

One of the most recognizable characteristics of jazz and swing is the use of chords that move beyond the three notes of the triad. As soon as a fourth note is added to a chord, it becomes more colorful and complex.

6TH CHORDS

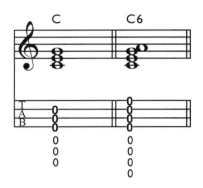

As you have learned, a major triad consists of a root, 3rd, and 5th, corresponding to the first, third, and fifth notes of a major scale. If you add the sixth note of the major scale to the triad, you get a *major 6th chord*. An example (shown on the right) is the C6 chord, which contains the notes C, E, G, and A (root, 3rd, 5th, and 6th).

Below are fingerings for 6th chords based on the major chords you have learned. As you learn each one, try alternating the 6th chord with the corresponding major chord. This will help you see the similarity and hear the difference between them.

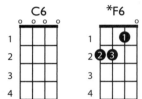 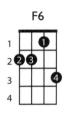 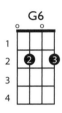 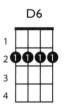 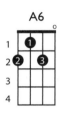 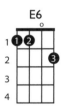

Try the progression below. It may look difficult to switch chords every two beats, but if you look carefully you will notice that you only have to move one or two fingers in each bar to make the change. It's very common to use 6th chords alternating with major or 7th chords to give melodic motion within one basic chord. Remember that you can lift on the last upstroke of the bar in order to move to the next chord in time.

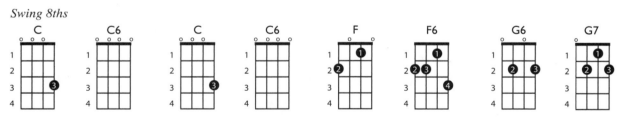

6th Chords Ex. 1

* This F6 should remind you of Dmin, because it has the same notes! A full F6 chord contains F, A, C, and D. This fingering only contains F, A, and D, which also make up a Dmin chord. This fingering for F6 is shown here because it is easy to get to from the familiar two-finger F chord. On the uke, it is not uncommon to have chord voicings that leave out a note or two from the full versions of the chords. The next F6 contains all of the notes in the chord.

The next progression gives you a chance to try out D6, A6, and E6 from the previous page. If D6 gives you trouble as a one-finger barre chord (see page 88 for tips), you can try fingering the normal three-finger D chord you've been using and add the 4th finger on the 2nd fret of the 1st string to make it D6. This progression uses the staccato strum you learned in the previous lesson. It works well here because these chords have few open strings, making it easier to hear the staccato notes cut off as you relax the pressure of your fingers.

6th Chords Ex. 2

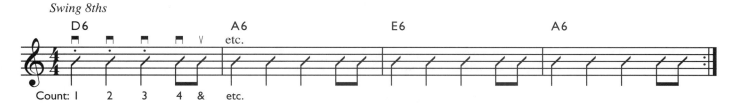

DOMINANT 7TH CHORDS

A *7th chord* is made by stacking another 3rd on top of a triad (root–3rd–5th–7th). There are several types of 7th chords. The type you are going to learn first is called a *dominant 7th chord*. The dominant 7th chord is a major triad with a minor 7th ($\flat$7) added. The chord symbol for a dominant 7th chord consists of a root note followed by the number 7 (as in G7). For example, the G7 chord contains the notes G–B–D–F (root–3rd–5th–$\flat$7th).

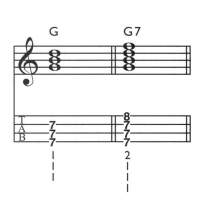

You have learned many of these dominant 7th chords already, but here they are for review. A few have multiple fingering/voicing options. You'll be using some of these dominant 7ths in the next lesson, so make sure you can do at least one fingering for each.

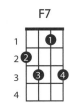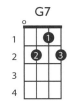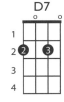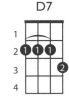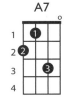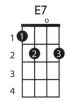

"DOMINANT" IS ANOTHER WORD FOR THE V CHORD

The name *dominant* refers to the 5th note (or V chord) of a major scale. The dominant 7th chord is the type of 7th chord that occurs on the V chord in a major key. For example, the G7 chord discussed above is the V chord of the key of C Major, and all of its notes are found in the C Major scale.

Dominant 7th chords can be used as the V chord of a major key, but they can also be used to add additional color to major triads. Sometimes it sounds great, other times it adds too much color to the chord. The best approach is to try it and see if you like it. Here's a tip if you're overwhelmed by learning lots of chords at once: In any situation that calls for a 6th chord or dominant 7th chord, you can play the plain major chord instead. The major triad is part of each of these chords, so all you would be doing is leaving a note out. No problem!

THE CIRCLE OF 5THS PROGRESSION

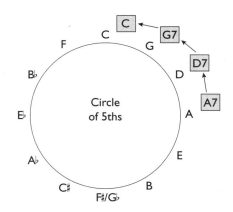

The roots of jazz are in *ragtime*, a popular form of music in the late 1800s and early 1900s. Ragtime was known for its syncopated rhythms, catchy tunes, and virtuosic performers. One of the most common progressions to come out of ragtime is the *circle of 5ths progression*. This progression creates an unusual sound because it does not follow all of the diatonic chord qualities of the major scale.

Imagine that the circle of 5ths shown on the right represents major chords. If you follow the circle counterclockwise, each chord is the V chord of the next chord in the circle. When we use V chords that belong to chords other than the I chord of the key, they are called *secondary dominants*.

A circle of 5ths progression usually follows four chords around the circle (going counterclockwise), with the last chord being the I chord of the key. The other three chords can be played as dominant 7ths to increase the sense of each chord being a V chord to the next; for example, the progression shown in the highlighted chords in the illustration above goes A7–D7–G7–C. This is a circle of 5ths progression in C Major.

You can play circle of 5ths progressions by following any set of four adjacent chords counterclockwise around the circle. Try it with major chords and with dominant 7ths. To get you started, here's a progression in C that begins on C (the I chord), then jumps to A7 and follows the circle of 5ths counterclockwise back to C. There are probably thousands of songs that include this progression or something like it!

Cycle of 5ths Progression Ex. 1

Photo by William P. Gottlieb

Cliff Edwards (1895–1971), known by his nickname "Ukulele Ike," was a prolific recording artist and performer during the uke heyday of the '20s and '30s. The massive popularity of his records, including a #1 hit recording of "Singin' in the Rain," helped inspire the sale of vast numbers of ukuleles and Tin Pan Alley songs in sheet music. Edwards appeared in movies as an actor/singer and as a voice actor for animated films. His most known role was as the voice of Jiminy Cricket in the 1940 Disney movie *Pinnochio*.

Here, we move the same progression to the key of F. Can you find the chords on the circle of 5ths?

Cycle of 5ths Progression Ex. 2

The next example moves the progression to the key of G, then follows with a typical ragtime treatment. The strums are shown to give you some rhythm ideas. The third line has a new *syncopated* rhythm like the horn section might play in a big band. In syncopated rhythms, emphasis is placed on the offbeats rather than the onbeats (for more on syncopation, see page 84).

HOW WILL I EVER LEARN TO CHARLESTON IF I CAN'T EVEN TIE MY OWN SHOES?

THE TRIPLE STRUM

The ukulele is one of the easiest instruments to play for simple song accompaniment. It is also capable of fun and somewhat acrobatic special effects, especially in the form of unique strums. So far, your strums have involved just two strokes: the downstroke and upstroke. The *triple strum* (also called a *triple stroke* or just a *triple*) adds an extra stroke to the mix, creating a three-stroke pattern that can be placed in the rhythm in various ways.

The triple strum works best using a combination of thumb and fingers. You can simulate the motion with a pick, but you may have a hard time getting as much speed as you can with the thumb and finger. There are several ways to execute a triple. Here, you will learn the "down-down-up" technique.

The triple strum is not synonymous with a rhythmic triplet. Though triple strums can be played in a triplet rhythm, they can also be adapted to a variety of other rhythms.

TRIPLE STRUM: DOWN-DOWN-UP

The following photos show the unused fingers curled up into the palm. This is just so you can see the motion of the active fingers better. In reality, you can either curl your unused fingers under or let them hang out extended. Stay relaxed and loose!

1. Downstroke with index finger.

2. Downstroke with thumb.

3. Upstroke with index finger.

Below are several bars of the triple strum in ¾ time so you can practice giving each stroke equal time and emphasis. Try the triple strum on lots of different chords.

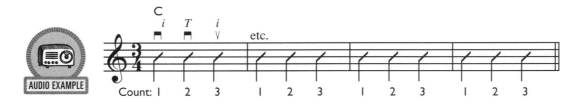

SUPER UKE TIP: BE PATIENT WITH NEW SKILLS
Specialized techniques like triple strums rely on muscle memory. In other words, your hand needs to have practiced the same sequence of motions so many times that you can do it with just one thought. At first you will think "down index, down thumb, up index." Later on, you'll just think "triple strum" and your hand will do it. It may take a lot of repetitions over many practice sessions before you can execute the triple strum smoothly. Be patient and practice the move for a few minutes every session, along with other things you're working on. If you stay relaxed and look for small improvements over time, you won't get frustrated. Like learning to swim or ride a bicycle, it may take longer to get it right than you hoped. But once you get it, you'll have it forever!

TWO TRIPLES AND A DOUBLE IN ONE BAR, OR, 3+3+2

While this may sound like a lovely evening out after a hard day at work, it's actually just a way to include triples into a measure of eighth notes.

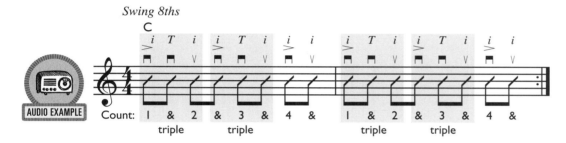

THE TRIPLE AS A TRIPLET

Here, the triple strum is used to play triplet eighth notes on the last beat of the measure. Remember, the eighth notes are swung, so the triplet feel is already present in the rhythm. All you have to do is insert the thumb downstroke between the normal downstroke and upstroke on the fourth beat.

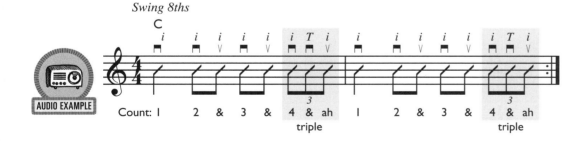

On the next page, you'll put these patterns into practice. You can also use them to strum through the progressions earlier in this book, or just sprinkle them into another pattern to spice things up.

The following exercise uses the 3+3+2 strum in the first four measures, then the triplet triple strum in the next three measures. This exercise also contains a four-finger version of F7 in measure four that you might not have tried yet. If you're having trouble getting the triple strums together, try strumming through this progression a few times with simple swing eighths using the regular down-up alternating motion. Practice the triple strum patterns separately and then try plugging them into the progression as they get easier.

The Secret Handshake Rag

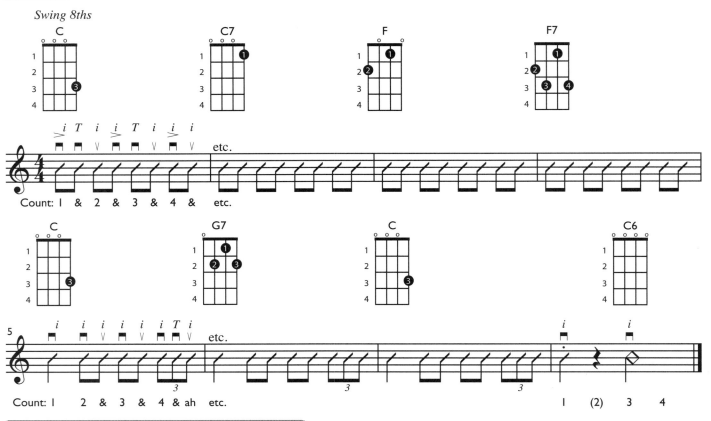

THE TRIPLE BURST STRUM

You have learned how to incorporate the triple strum into regular eighth-note strumming. You can also learn to do triples very fast and use them as a flourish to accentuate a normal rhythm. These types of flourishes are sometimes called *bursts*, *rolls*, or *shakes* after both the sound and the quick movement of the hand.

INTRODUCING THE SIXTEENTH-NOTE TRIPLET

The triple burst is shown as a *sixteenth-note triplet*. *Sixteenth notes* look like eighth notes, but with a double beam, or a double flag for single sixteenths. Normal sixteenth notes divide a quarter note into four pieces, counted "1-e-&-a."

Triplet sixteenths, like all triplets, allow you to fit three notes where there are normally two. Normal sixteenths are *two* equal notes in the space of an eighth note. Triplet sixteenths are *three* equal notes in the space of one eighth note. One common way to count two sets of sixteenth-note triplets (one full beat's worth) is "1-la-li-&-la-li." This can be a tongue twister if the tempos are fast, so an alternative is "1-a-la-&-a-la."

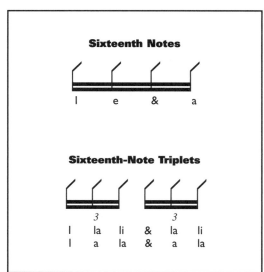

A *triple burst* is a sixteenth-note triplet followed by an accented downstroke. The triplet falls on the "&" of the beat before the accented downbeat. The end result should sound like a burst of four strums (kind of like a machine-gun burst), with the last strum falling on a strong downbeat. To get an idea of how it fits in the rhythm, try saying this out loud "gimme a BEAT!" In that phrase, "gimme a" is the triplet, and "BEAT!" is the accented downbeat.

Here is a triple burst consisting of a down-down-up (*i-T-i*) triple strum immediately followed by an accented downstroke of the *i* finger.

When you practice this, try holding your index finger and thumb in a "U" shape as you start the triple motion. This will help the thumb follow right behind the index in a single hand motion.

You can also do triple bursts using just downstrokes and upstrokes of the index finger or pick. The tricky thing is that the final accented beat will fall on an upstroke instead of a normal downstroke.

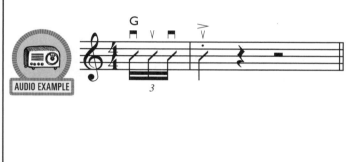

The example below contains a lot of information, but it's not too difficult if you think it through. The basic strum is a staccato quarter note followed by eighth notes. On the last eighth of the measure (the "&" of 4), do a triplet sixteenth-note burst into the accented first beat of the next bar. Don't forget to swing the eighths!

HITCH IN MY GIT-ALONG RAG

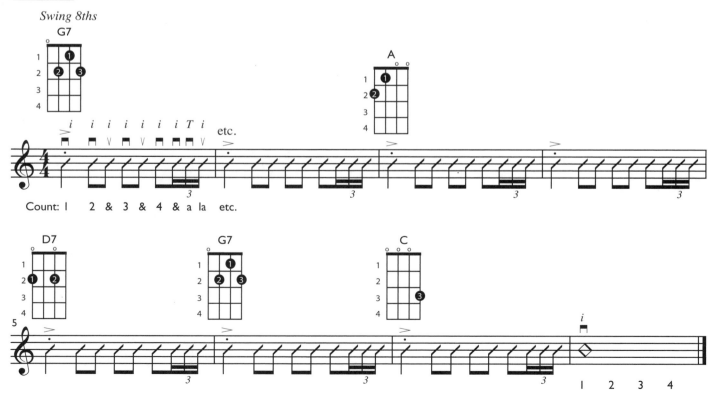

ROCKING OUT THE UKE

In recent years, the uke has come to be a symbol for musicians who are a little different, who don't travel the well-worn path. The uke has snuck into punk clubs, songwriter listening rooms, and major pop hits like "Hey, Soul Sister" by Train. Nowhere has the uke blossomed more than on Internet video sites like YouTube. It fits easily in a Webcam close-up, sounds okay through a cheap computer mic and speakers, and is simple enough to allow just about anyone to share their own song with the whole world. This section will help you learn some new strums and chords so you can join the new pop ukulele revolution.

THE SYNCOPATED STRUM

Syncopation means to shift the emphasis to the offbeat. To show syncopation in written music, dotted rhythms, rests, and ties are sometimes used.

The strum shown below is the Swiss Army knife of strum patterns. It is the universal folk-rock-alternative-swing-funk-punk-campfire strum. This one is good at any speed, fast or slow, swinging or straight. Note the tie that connects the "&" of beat 2 to beat 3, creating a syncopation. Be sure to tap your foot and count out loud.

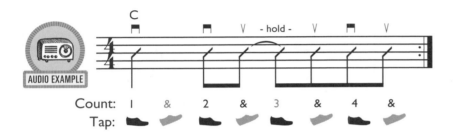

If you find this rhythm a little confusing, break it down into one- or two-beat segments:

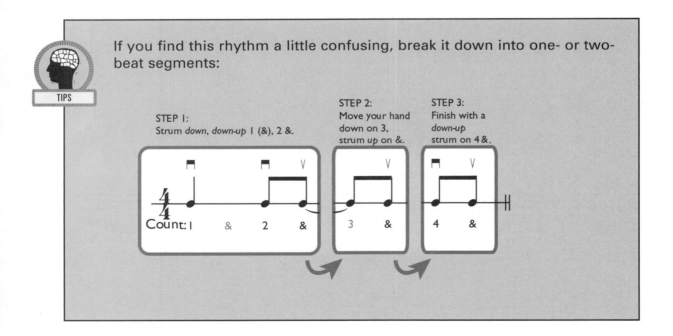

To practice the syncopated strum, here are some exercises that follow the same progression as parts of Train's "Hey, Soul Sister." This progression of diatonic chords goes I-V-vi-IV, a progression that can be heard in countless songs. Remember that in a major key, I, IV, and V are major, while vi is minor. Here it is in the key of C.

MY FEET HURT (OY! SOLE BLISTERS!)

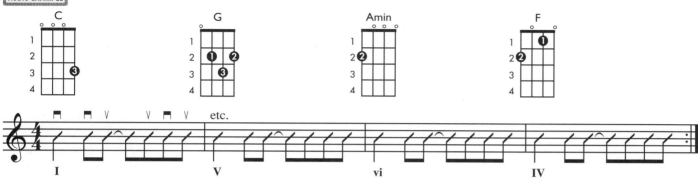

Now try it in G. The vi chord is Emin, which you haven't had a chance to play very much.

AUTOHARP SALE (REPLACE OLD ZITHERS!)

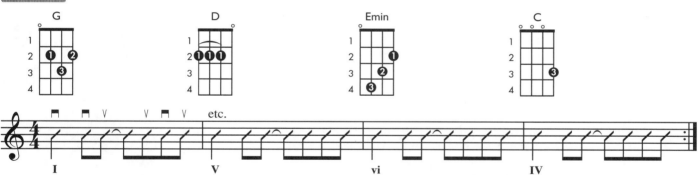

Here's one more I-V-vi-IV progression. This time, the rhythm is in swing eighths and the strum has a slight variation (leaving out the upstroke on the "&" of beat 2). The key is F.

DREAMS OF SUMMER ON A GLOOMY DAY (HAZE, COLD, MISTERS)

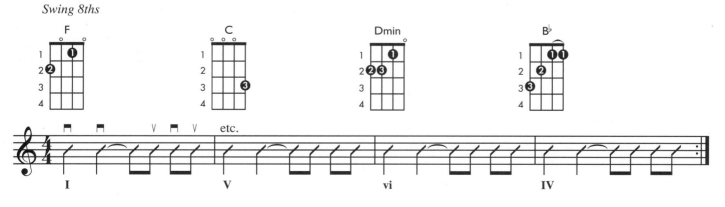

ADDING PERCUSSION WITH MUTE STROKES

A *mute stroke* is a downstroke where the strings have been muted or damped. All you hear is the percussive snap of the downstroke, but none of the notes of the chord. You can mute the strings with either the right or left hand. Mute strokes allow you to introduce a new texture into your strumming so that you can play more sophisticated grooves. You can even create the impression of more than one instrument playing!

THE RIGHT-HAND MUTE STROKE

By muting the strings with the right hand as you strum down, you can create the loudest form of mute stroke. The right-hand mute stroke works great even if you are strumming chords with open strings. These steps will show you how to do it.

1. First, make sure your left hand is not fingering a chord or touching the strings while you learn how to do the stroke.

2. Now, holding your uke in playing position, place your right-hand palm on the strings, fingers stretched out, covering up the soundhole. Keep your wrist fairly straight so that your hand falls across the strings at a natural angle. (See photo to the right.)

Step 2.

3. Rock your hand backward on the strings so that your thumb sticks up at about a 45 degree angle to the top. The other side of your hand should still be touching the strings. Think of this as the "karate chop" part of your hand. This is the part that mutes the strings. (See photo.)

4. Now that your fingers have some room to move, you should be able to perform a downstroke with your index finger while keeping the strings muted with the "karate chop" part of your hand (see photo). You should hear just a percussive sound. If you hear notes, the muting part of your hand is not doing its job!

Step 3.

5. Repeat the downstroke several times so that you get used to the sound and feel of it. You're not done yet, though!

6. The tricky part is that you need to execute the mute at the same time you are performing a normal downstroke. First, lift your hand off the strings and perform a normal downstroke. Now try it again in slow motion, but this time turn your hand to the right so that the "karate chop" part contacts the strings a fraction before the index finger does the downstroke. It will take some practice to get the timing just right. Repeat it over and over so that you can do it in one fluid motion.

Step 4.

7. You can do the right-hand mute stroke with the index finger downstroke or with a pick. The motion and basic sound is the same.

MUTE STROKES ON THE BACKBEAT

Remember the backbeat? The backbeat is beats 2 and 4 of a measure of 4 beats (see page 72). In a rock or blues drum pattern, these are the beats where the loud crack of the snare drum is heard. You can use mute strokes (shown with an X on the note head) to simulate the snare drum in a rock beat. Remember, on the mute stroke, you should hear *no notes, only percussion*!

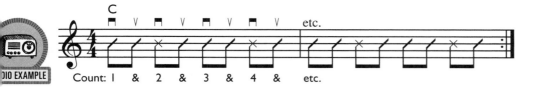

The strum pattern shown above is reminiscent of the guitar grooves used by John Fogerty of Creedence Clearwater Revival. This groove has its roots in Tex-Mex, a Texas hybrid of Mexican traditional music and Texas blues and rock. Following is a progression to practice using your new strum.

TRY IT WITH A SWING

If you use the mute stroke with a swing-eighths feel, you get a Jamaican reggae kind of groove. Try the above progression with swing eighths. Then try the one below. It has an additional challenge of switching chords within the measure on bars 2 and 4. You may need to practice these separately before trying the whole progression.

THE LEFT-HAND MUTE STROKE

You can also use your left-hand fingers to create mute strokes. To do this, strum normally and relax the pressure of your fretting fingers on the beats you want muted. This works best on chords that have few open strings, like D and G. You'll be able to use this approach a lot more with the moveable chord forms in the next lesson. Try it with the progressions on this page to hear which chords work better.

MOVEABLE CHORD FORMS

When you learned your first chords, you were told "here's how to play a C chord; any time you see a C chord in the music, play it like this." You can play a ton of great music just using simple open position major and minor chords. But if you really want to take the lid off of your capabilities, you need *moveable chord forms*.

Moveable chord forms are based on the interval structures and shapes of open-position chords. As these structures move up the neck, they no longer have open strings. When you take open strings out of the equation, you can move any shape to any fret position and get the same type of chord and sound on a new root note.

PASSING THE BARRE EXAM

To take advantage of moveable chord forms, you're going to need to be able to play multiple strings with one finger (usually your 1st finger). This is called a *barre*. You may have to barre two, three, or four strings.

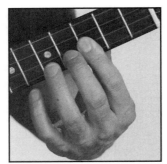
2-string barre.

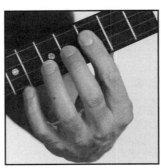
3-string barre.

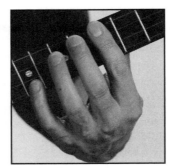
4-string barre.

You have had opportunities to try barres and partial barres throughout this book. If you've been avoiding them or felt like you couldn't make them work, now is the time to prevail! Here are a few tips:

- *The goal of the barre is to get the strings down to the fret!* It doesn't matter how hard you press or how much you grit your teeth if the strings aren't getting to the fret. It shouldn't take too much physical effort, but you need to be aware of what is happening with the strings.

- A barre requires a different finger placement than a normal note. Don't use the tip of your finger, instead use the flat part where your fingerprint is.

- You may need to straighten out your finger and use two joints to cover the strings. Be careful that the little dip at the finger joint doesn't get placed on a string, or that string might not get pressed down.

- You may also need to shift your finger up or down, or roll your finger slightly to one side or another to get the notes to sound.

- Above all, be patient and persistent. Try practicing barres for a few minutes every day. It's amazing what you can do if you give things time to develop!

THE A FORM MOVEABLE CHORDS

Let's start your exploration of moveable forms with forms based on open A chords. Below are the variations of A chords you have worked with so far: A Major, A Minor, and two fingerings of A7. Underneath each diagram, the chord tones are labeled.

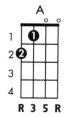
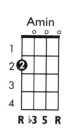
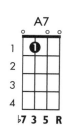
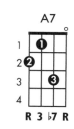

R =	root
3 =	3rd (major 3rd)
♭3 =	minor 3rd
5 =	5th
♭7 =	minor 7th

Following are the same chord forms moved up one half step (one position) to form chords in B♭. Look at the first chord (B♭ Major) and compare it with A Major above. Each note on the 3rd and 4th string have been moved up one half step, with the fingering changed to the 3rd and 2nd finger. This frees up the 1st finger to barre strings 1 and 2 at the 1st fret. These notes were open in the A Major chord but need to be on the 1st fret in the B♭ chord. The structure of roots, 3rds, and 5ths is identical. Try learning and comparing all the fingerings.

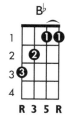
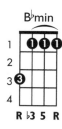
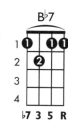
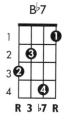

We'll call these fingerings the *A form* chords because they are based on the structures used for the open A chords. The fingerings for the B♭ chords can continue to be moved up the neck to make new chords based on the A forms. You can follow the root notes up the A string (1st string) to find all of the new chords (see chart below). For example, if you put your 1st finger at the 5th fret and build the minor chord fingering shown above, you'll have a D Minor chord.

The A Form Chords by Position (Root on String 1)

Here are the chords you get by moving the A form up the neck. The fret positions indicate the position of the barre finger. If you use the minor shape, you get minor chords. If you use the dominant 7th shapes, you get dominant 7th chords. Try starting at the 1st fret with any fingering, and name the chords as you move up one fret at a time.

Fret position:	Open	1st	2nd	3rd	4th	5th	6th	7th	8th	9th	10th	11th
Chord:	A	A#/B♭	B	C	C#/D♭	D	D#/E♭	E	F	F#/G♭	G	G#/A♭

Note: Depending on how many frets your uke has, you may not be able to move the position past the 9th or 10th fret.

THE C FORM MOVEABLE CHORDS

Below are the open C and C7 chords, with the chord tones shown underneath. Since the 3rd of the chord is on the open 2nd string, and therefore can't be lowered to a minor 3rd, we won't have a minor fingering in this set. To the right of the C chords are the corresponding D chords you get by moving the C chords up one whole step. The barred 1st finger replaces the notes that were open in the C chords.

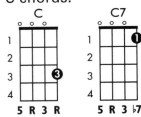
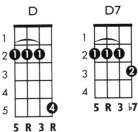

The C Form Chords by Position (Root on String 3)

Here are the chords you get by moving the C form up the neck. The root of this form is on the 3rd string.

Fret position:	Open	1st	2nd	3rd	4th	5th	6th	7th	8th	9th	10th	11th
Chord:	C	C#/Db	D	D#/Eb	E	F	F#/Gb	G	G#/Ab	A	A#/Bb	B

THE F FORM MOVEABLE CHORDS

Now, let's look at the F forms. Below is the open F chord plus two fingerings of F7. F Minor can be played in open position but it requires a few changes to the structure so we'll leave it out for now. Compare the F chord fingerings to the G chords you get by moving the F chords up one whole step.

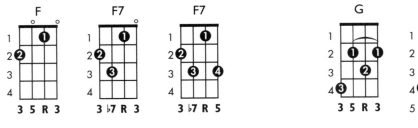
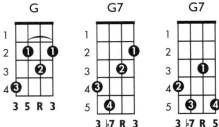

The F Form Chords by Position (Root on String 2)

Here are the chords you get by moving the F form up the neck. The fret positions indicate the position of the root note on the 2nd string. Note that this form has notes that are lower on the neck than the position of the root note, so the root note position does not equal the position of the barre.

Fret position:	1st	2nd	3rd	4th	5th	6th	7th	8th	9th	10th	11th	12th
Chord:	F	F#/Gb	G	G#/Ab	A	A#/Bb	B	C	C#/Db	D	D#/Eb	E

THE G FORM MOVEABLE CHORDS

Here are fingerings for G, G Minor, and G7, followed by the moveable fingerings you get if you move the G chords up one whole step.

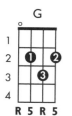
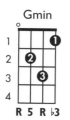
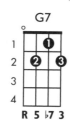
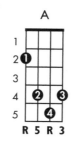
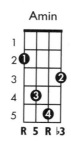
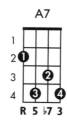

SUPER UKE TIP

Sometimes, we don't play or finger all of the available notes in a chord. For example, it would be very common (and easier) to finger and play only the first three strings of the A chords shown. You have to remember where your root is!

The G Form Chords by Position (Root on String 4)

Here are the chords you get by moving the G form up the neck. The root of these forms is on the 4th string.

Fret position:	Open	1st	2nd	3rd	4th	5th	6th	7th	8th	9th	10th	11th
Chord:	G	G#/Ab	A	A#/Bb	B	C	C#/Db	D	D#/Eb	E	F	F#/Gb

THE D FORM MOVEABLE CHORDS

The last form we'll look at is based on D chords. Here are D, D Minor, and D7, followed by E, E Minor, and E7 with the same structures moved up a whole step. You may remember another fingering for D7 that appeared with the C form chords. Some of the forms do overlap in parts of their shapes.

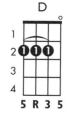
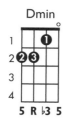
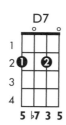
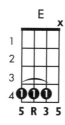
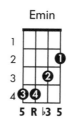
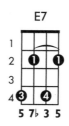

The D Form Chords by Position (Root on String 2)

Here are the chords you get by moving the D form up the neck. The root for the D and D Minor forms is on the 2nd string. The D7 form is tricky, because it doesn't have the root in this fingering. The best way to keep track is to visualize the D Major form to find the position of the chord you are looking for, then make the necessary fingering changes to get the dominant 7th form of that chord.

Fret position:	2nd	3rd	4th	5th	6th	7th	8th	9th	10th	11th	12th	13th
Chord:	D	D#/Eb	E	F	F#/Gb	G	G#/Ab	A	A#/Bb	B	C	C#/Db

USING MOVEABLE CHORDS, LEFT-HAND MUTE STROKES, REGGAE, AND SOUL

This lesson will make use of your new moveable chord shapes and recombine some of your strumming techniques to get new grooves.

THE REGGAE BEAT, SCRATCHING, AND SQUEEZING

Reggae music originated in Jamaica in the 1960s and became a worldwide phenomenon in the 1970s with artists like Bob Marley, Peter Tosh, and Jimmy Cliff. Reggae's influence continues both as a vehicle for political expression and in the laid-back grooves of artists like Jack Johnson and Jason Mraz.

The rhythm guitar of Bob Marley established one of the most imitated grooves of all time. The trick is to use moveable chord forms so there are no open strings. The mute strokes (indicated by an "X" on the note head) are made by relaxing the finger pressure of the left hand without lifting the fingers off the strings. The mute strokes are "scratching." The following groove scratches on beats 1 and 3, while squeezing the chord on beats 2 and 4. Think "scratch, squeeze, scratch, squeeze." Don't forget to swing the eighths!

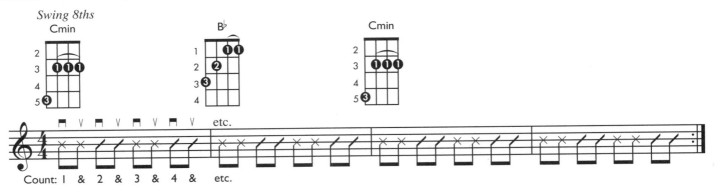

Here's another chance to work with the reggae groove. You'll be playing in the key of B♭, using chord shapes from the A form and D form. The E♭ and F chords shown might give you trouble depending on your particular fingers. It's perfectly okay to just play strings 2, 3, and 4 on these chords, leaving the 1st string muted so you can focus your effort on the 3rd-finger barre. Note that in measures 2, 4, and 6, you have to change chords within the measure—but you're just moving the same form up or down two frets.

WHO WANTS A COOL BEVERAGE?

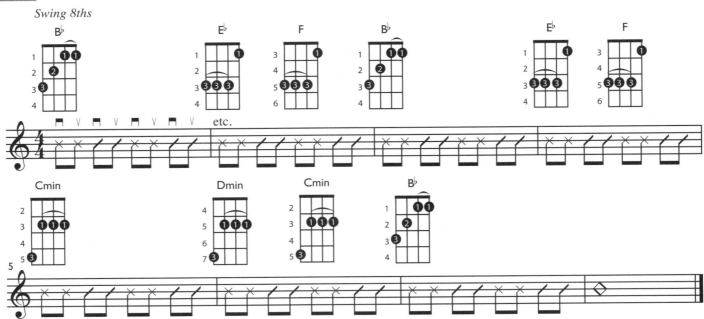

The next exercise uses scratch strokes in a different part of the groove. This strum pattern has more space in it, beginning with a half note followed by a staccato quarter note, then eighth-note mute strokes. The eighth notes are straight (not swung) and the groove has an old-school gospel/soul feel like the music of Curtis Mayfield. The groove changes up to a simple strum on the third line. "Uke Got Soul" is in the key of D Major and uses moveable chord shapes from the C form, A form, F form, and G form. Note that the G form chords in the third line leave off the note on the 4th string. This makes them much easier to finger and move.

UKE GOT SOUL

TAKING IT HOME: ISLAND STYLE

The Hawaiian style of ukulele is full of variety and continues to evolve in the present through young modern players like Herb Ohta, Jr. and Daniel Ho. Hawaiian music comes in many flavors and rhythms, from the swing-influenced Hapa Haole songs of the '20s and '30s to the rolling fingerpicked guitar style known as "slack-key." If you dig deep into the Hawaiian repertoire, you will find that songs are often presented in many different styles and tempos. Overall, the Hawaiian ukulele style prizes beautiful tone, delicately textured rhythms, and a sense of ebb and flow that recalls the natural beauty of the islands and the surrounding ocean.

If you were to only learn one Hawaiian song, a good choice is "Aloha 'Oe," composed in 1878 by Queen Lili'uokalani, the last monarch of Hawaii. The melody shows the influence of Christian hymns brought to the islands by missionaries in the 1800s. The lyrics tell of a parting embrace, which has come to symbolize longing for loved ones and for homeland. There are countless recordings, from Hawaiian steel guitarists to Elvis.

The following arrangement in the key of F shows both the melody and the chords. Try strumming it first in a slow walking tempo with straight-eighth notes, using the rhythm you learned on page 51. Also, try it using swing eighths or with other strum patterns you have used. You can use the standard notation or the TAB to learn the melody, which consists of a 16-measure verse and a 16-measure chorus. The phrase marks (page 114) show that the verse and chorus each consist of four phrases of about 4 bars each. Here are the chord shapes you'll need:

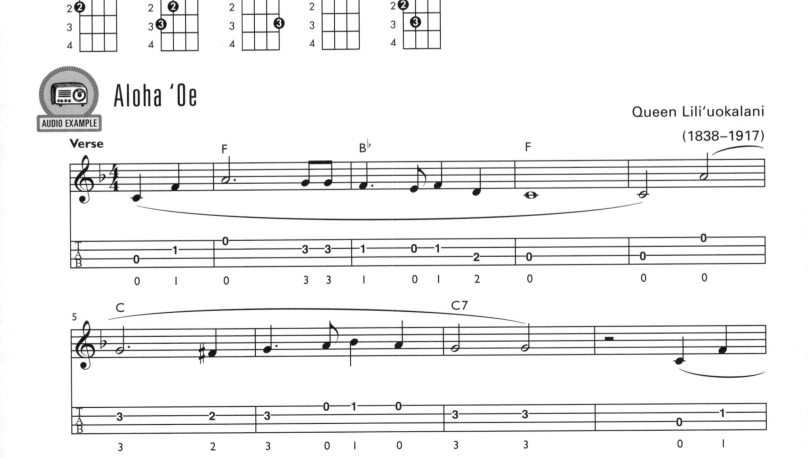

Aloha 'Oe

Queen Lili'uokalani
(1838–1917)

NEW STRUMS

In this lesson, you will learn a few new strums that fit nicely with a swing-eighths groove for Hawaiian-style songs. First, start by strumming and counting basic swing eighths with the index finger. Take notice of the "&" of beats 2 and 4 (marked with *). You'll be doing something special with these soon.

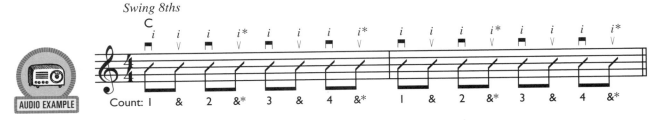

ROLLING WITH A RAKE

One technique that adds texture is to *roll* the chord on certain beats within the pattern. Each normal stroke should sound like all the strings are hit at once but a roll sounds like the notes of the chord come out very quickly one after the other. There are many ways to accomplish this effect. The simplest way to roll the chord is called a *rake*. This is done by dragging the finger through the strings so that they sound one at a time but still quickly enough that they ring together as a chord on the beat. A rake can be a downstroke or an upstroke depending on the beat on which it falls. Try adding a rake on the "&" of 2 and the "&" of 4 in your strum pattern. These will be upstroke rakes.

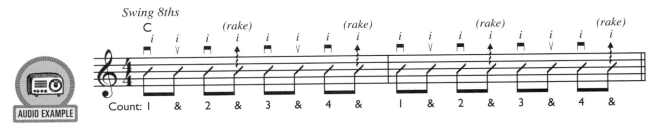

THE ALTERNATING TRIPLE STRUM

Another strumming groove for swing eighths incorporates one of the triple strums you learned on page 80. Here, the triple strum produces a triplet rhythm on beats 2 and 4. This triple strum is a downstroke with *i*, followed by another downstroke with the thumb (*T*), and then an upstroke with *i*.

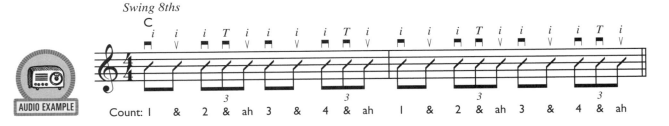

ALTERNATING TRIPLE WITH A RAKE

Once you're very comfortable with the above strums, try adding rakes to the alternating triple strum. Go slowly and count the beats. This strum was inspired by some advanced strums used by ukulele player and falsetto singing master Richard Ho'opi'i and other players.

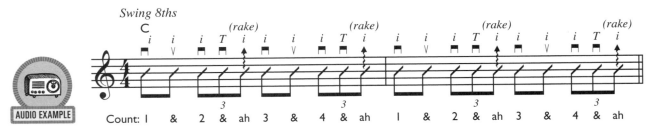

Here's a short strumming tune that pays tribute to the style of Richard Ho'opi'i (pronounced Ho-OH-pee-ee). The song is in the key of C and begins with a two-bar vamp of D7, G7, and C. The *vamp* is a common introduction for songs that accompany traditional Hawaiian hula dancing. It can be repeated as many times as desired before the rest of the song starts. The eight beats of the vamp match up with the eight counts of the hula dance step called the *kaholo*, used at the introduction of hula dances.

This song will introduce you to some new chords, such as Csus4 (an abbreviation for the full name "C suspended fourth"), F Minor (Fmin), and new voicings for D7 and G7. You can try all of the new techniques as shown, or use simpler strums and familiar voicings of the chords.

HULA FOR HO'OPI'I

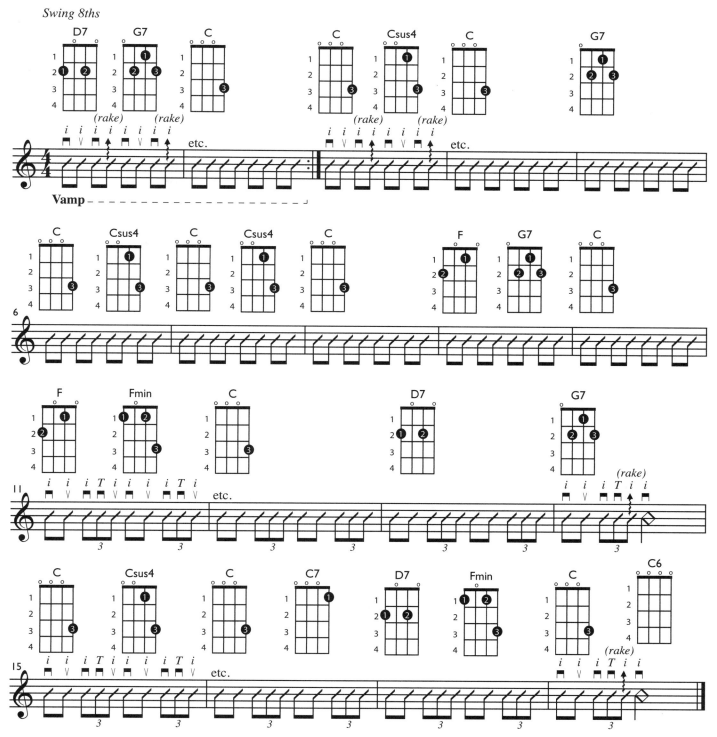

UKULELE BLUES

The blues is so much a part of American music that its influence is felt in nearly every style. Far more than just the feeling of "good times that done gone bad," the blues is:

- A musical style
- A form of poetry
- A type of scale
- An attitude
- A specific musical form and chord progression
- An incurable, infectious human condition that is both miserable and joyful at the same time

THE 12 BAR-BLUES

THE FORM

The *12-bar blues* is one of the most basic song *forms*. Remember, the form is the organization, or structure, of a piece. The 12-bar blues derives its name from the number of measures (bars) in the form. Below is a common version of the 12-bar blues in the key of A. Included are chord symbols and Roman numerals indicating the analysis of the harmony. Try it with either simple downstrokes or one of the swing-eighths strums you learned on page 75. You can play this progression using the simple major chords shown, or you can replace each chord with dominant 7ths (A7, D7, E7). The blues progression is unusual in that it sounds good to use dominant 7ths on all chords, not just the V chord. Fingerings for these chords are on page 77.

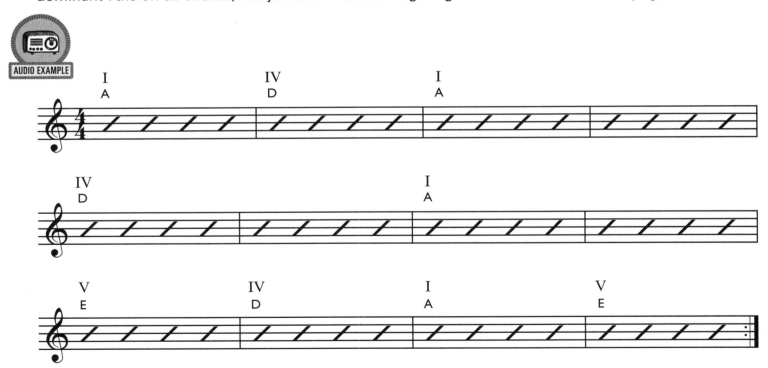

MEMORIZING THE 12-BAR BLUES

There may be times when you want to play with other people who don't know the same songs you do. The 12-bar blues is widely known by musicians at all levels of experience. A working knowledge of how to play through the progression, as well as improvising on it, can give you an "ace up your sleeve" in those difficult situations when you can't decide what to jam on.

BLUES POETRY

The 12-bar blues is organized in three lines of four measures each. This mirrors the poetic form of many blues lyrics. A common form of blues lyric consists of a statement (line 1), a repetition of the statement (line 2), and a sort of "clincher" (line 3). Check out these common blues verses:

My baby just left me, and man I feel so bad

My baby just left me, and man I feel so bad

Since my baby left me, I lost everything I had

I'd rather drink muddy water, sleep in a hollow log

I'd rather drink muddy water, sleep in a hollow log

Than stay in this city, treated like a dirty dog

PLAY BY NUMBERS

You may have noticed that the blues contains the three primary chords discussed on page 69. These are the I, IV, and V chords. In the key of A, these would be:

I = A   IV = D   V = E

Try to memorize the progression using these numbers. That way, you will learn its structure without being limited to the key of A. Soon, you will be able play the blues in any key, as long as you know what the I, IV and V chords are for that key. To make it easier, memorize one line at a time.

PLAY IT IN YOUR SLEEP

To get the most out of learning the blues, try to memorize the progression. Be able to play it over and over without losing your place in the form. This will make it much easier to jam with other players. You will be able to enjoy the musical interaction of the moment without worrying about whether you brought your music or whether you are on bar 10 or bar 6.

In addition, you should know there are many possible variations on the 12-bar blues form. Some have more chords, some have fewer, and some have different chords substituted for the common ones. By burning a specific, basic version of the pattern into your brain through repetition and study, you will have an easier time compensating for slight variations from song to song.

THE BLUES SHUFFLE RHYTHM

The blues progression can be played to just about any rhythm you can imagine. One of the classic rhythms, particularly associated with Chicago blues, is the *shuffle*. In music, the word shuffle can mean different things to different people. For example, to a fiddler, a shuffle is a particular type of bowing pattern. To a blues player, a shuffle is a type of groove played in the swing-eighths feel. There is, of course, an exception. A "straight shuffle" uses the same patterns you are learning here but with a straight-eighths (un-swung) feel.

PLAYING THE SHUFFLE

The following shuffle pattern is based on patterns you hear from rhythm guitar players or the left hand of a blues piano player. This type of shuffle starts with a major chord on the first two eighth notes, then moves the 5th of the chord up a whole step to the 6th for two eighth notes.

Below, the shuffle pattern is shown for each chord you will need in the key of A. Practice each pattern separately for several bars. In blues rhythm, chords can be played as full triads, or as just the root with the 5th (alternating with the 6th), as is shown for the D and E chords. To give it a more authoritative sound, use all downstrokes instead of alternating down-up.

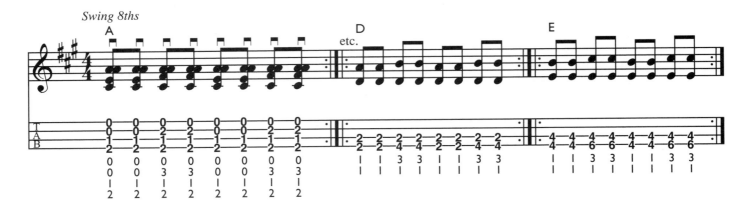

Here are a few more tidbits about playing the shuffle:

- These shuffle patterns above represent the concept of *playing a pattern that represents a single chord.* Even though, technically, you are alternating between, say, A and A6, the pattern functions in the same way as an unchanging A chord. Sometimes in the blues, single-note riffs or even tiny progressions are used to represent each chord.

- When you are playing the D and E shuffles, you have to press down both the 3rd and 4th strings with your 1st finger. To do this, remember to use the flat part of your finger (where your fingerprint is) instead of the tip.

- On the D and E chords, you can use the 2nd finger instead of the 3rd if it works better for you.

Here is the whole 12-bar blues form in the key of A, using the shuffle patterns you just learned. The chord analysis (I, IV, V) is shown under the standard notation. Remember, if you get tired of the shuffle rhythm, you can play any versions of A, A7, D, D7, E ,or E7 in place of the shuffle pattern for those chords.

GIVE IT A TRY

WHY DOESN'T IT END ON THE I CHORD?

This 12-bar blues progression ends on the E chord (the V). The V chord doesn't sound like a final resting place for the progression. Rather, the V chord makes it sound like it should repeat. When you have jammed through the form as many times as you want to, you can add one more simple A chord after the 12th measure to give your blues a sense of "coming home to the I chord."

AUDIO EXAMPLE

Shufflin' Through the Blues in A

THE MINOR PENTATONIC SCALE

Many blues melodies and solos use the notes of the *minor pentatonic scale.* Unlike the major scale, which has seven different notes, the minor pentatonic scale has only five different notes (*penta* is the Greek word meaning "five"). Pentatonic scales are very common in folk and traditional music from many cultures around the world.

SCALE DEGREES OF THE MINOR PENTATONIC

Remember back on page 64 when you learned that the major scale can be used to help us understand other scales? Below is a comparison of the notes and scale degrees of an A Major scale and an A Minor Pentatonic scale. The notes and scale degrees show us the differences. The minor pentatonic scale leaves out scale degrees 2 and 6, and lowers the 3rd and 7th by one half step.

A Major Scale:	I A	2 B	3 C#	4 D	5 E	6 F#	7 G#
A Minor Pentatonic Scale:	I A		♭3* C	4 D	5 E		♭7* G

THE MINOR PENTATONIC SCALE IN A ON ONE STRING

Below is the A Minor pentatonic scale shown on the 1st string. You can use any fingering you like. Once you have learned to go up and down the scale, try making up melodies and riffs. Play long and short notes, repeat notes and groups of notes, skip around—do anything to make it sound like music. For fun, try improvising with these notes while the recording of "Shufflin' Through the Blues in A" from page 101 plays in the background.

Note:	A	C	D	E	G	A
Scale Degree:	I	♭3	4	5	♭7	8(I)

Tab: 0 — 3 — 5 — 7 — 10 — 12

Fingering: 0 — 3 — 4 — 1 — 3 — 4

BLUE NOTES

When a scale has a lowered 3rd degree (♭3), it is said to be a *minor scale.* The cool thing about the blues is that, while the chords are often major, the melody is often minor. This creates a funky, slightly *dissonant* (clashing) sound between the major chords and the minor melody, giving the blues its melancholy, expressive sound.

The minor pentatonic scale contains both the ♭3 and ♭7. These notes help us approximate the sound of old African scales that lie at the core of the blues. When these minor scale notes are played against major chords, they are called *blue notes.* Sometimes blue notes are "bent" out of tune a bit to make them even more expressive.

THE MINOR PENTATONIC SCALE IN A (OPEN POSITION)

The A Minor Pentatonic scale can also be played in open position. The only tricky thing is that our ukulele tuning only goes down to C, so we have to imagine the low A at the root of the scale. You can substitute the A an octave above (on the open 1st string, or 2nd fret, 4th string). Here are the notes and scale degrees, including an imaginary low A.

Note:	(A)	C	D	E	G	A	C
Scale Degree:	(1)	♭3	4	5	♭7	1	♭3

LEARNING TO IMPROVISE

The point of learning the minor pentatonic scale is to use it as a tool for improvising solos. Here are a few tips to get you going.

- When it's your time to solo, remember that you don't have to play a constant stream of notes. Leave some space and choose your moments.

- A *phrase* is like a musical sentence. It has a beginning, middle, and end. A phrase doesn't have to jump immediately into more notes. Imagine that you are inserting commas, periods, question marks, and exclamation points into your solo. This is called *phrasing* (for more, see page 114).

- Repetition is your friend. Repetition is your friend. Repetition creates something familiar for the listener so that when it changes, it has more meaning (like this sentence). You can repeat a note, a phrase, or a rhythmic idea.

- Your other best friend is the tonic note of the scale (note number 1). In the blues, the tonic note works with any of the chords. Even though it is not part of the V chord, it signals that the V chord is heading toward a chord with the tonic note in it. Any time you feel lost, go back and play the tonic note and let it hang for a moment. It's like a reset button for your solo. If you end phrases with a good strong tonic note, they will sound defined and resolved. Later on, you will learn how to creatively work with the other notes, but first, make friends with the tonic!

Here are a couple of short *licks* (mini-phrases) to get you started. Each one ends with the tonic note. Try these when you improvise over the blues progression. You can even try repeating licks like these over and over while the chords change underneath.

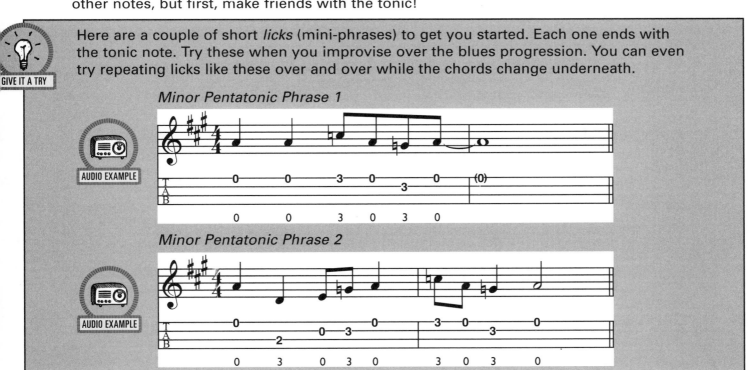

Minor Pentatonic Phrase 1

Minor Pentatonic Phrase 2

TRANSPOSITION

Transposing means changing the key of a song. You'll find a handy chart to help with transposing later in this book on pages 148 and 149.

WHY TRANSPOSE?

The most common reason for transposing a song to a new key is to better fit the vocal range of a singer. For example, imagine a song in the key of G Major. If this key is too low, you could transpose up to A or even B. Another reason to transpose is to make a melody or chord progression easier to play on the ukulele.

THE SUBSTITUTION METHOD

This method of transposition is the easiest to learn but not the most efficient. First, consider the following progression in G Major. Use simple downstrokes.

Transposition Ex. 1

Transposing from G Major to D Major

First, you must know how far the new key is from the original key. The key of D is a perfect 5th (P5, seven half steps, seven frets) higher than the key of G. To transpose the song, substitute each of the original chords with the chord a perfect 5th higher:

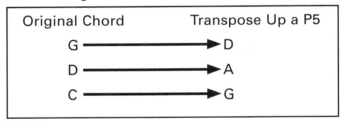

Here is the above progression transposed to D Major.

Transposition Ex. 2

Transposing from G Major to A Major

Try using this method yourself. The answers are at the end of the lesson on page 105.

Transposition Test 1

    1. How far above G is A?

    2. What is the new chord progression?

Transpose this example to the key of A (write in your answers):

THE CHORD ANALYSIS METHOD

At first, this method takes more practice and thought, but eventually you will be able to transpose songs without having to write out the new chords.

Here is an example progression in the key of D Major.

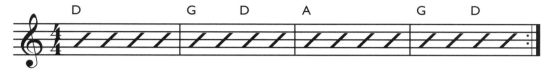

Transposing From D Major to G Major

First, analyze the chord progression with Roman numerals (page 68).

Now you are ready to transpose to any key. Try the key of G Major.

Key of G: I = G   IV = C   V = D

Transposition Ex. 3

Transposing from D Major to A Major

Try this one yourself (the correct answer is at the bottom of this page).

Transposition Test 2

1. What are the primary chords in the key of A Major?   I = ___   IV = ___   V = ___

Answers to Transposition Test 1 & 2:

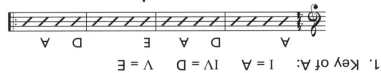

1. Key of A: I = A   IV = D   V = E

1. The key of A Major is one whole step higher than the key of G Major.

TRANSPOSING THE BLUES AND THE MINOR PENTATONIC SCALE

Now that you have learned some of the basics of transposition, you can apply them to the blues. By now, you should have the blues progression memorized by chord number (I, IV, and V). This is useful because you never know what key someone might want to play in when you're in a jamming situation.

Let's say you want to play a 12-bar blues in C. First, you need the I, IV, and V chords in the key of C. You can either name them by memory or find them by counting up the C Major scale.

Key: C Major I = C   IV = F V = G

You can plug those chords into the 12-bar blues formula you learned on page 98.

Now that you know what the chord progression is, you can choose the chord voicings and groove you might use to play it. Here are some options:

- The easiest option is to play the major chords in open position with simple downstrokes. Elegant and tasteful!

- You can use dominant 7th chords for each chord in the progression. Simply change C, F, and G to C7, F7, and G7.

- Try some of the different strum patterns, grooves, and swing-eighth/straight-eighth feels you have learned.

If you're up for a new challenge, try some moveable forms for dominant 7th chords. Give these fingerings a spin, then plug them into the 12-bar blues in C shown below with a staccato swing strum.

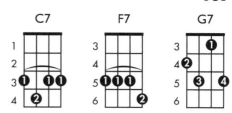

12-Bar Blues in C (A Bouncy C)

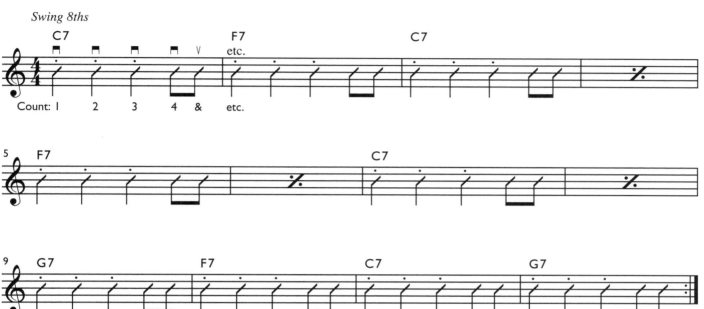

SUPER UKE TIP: MOVEABLE CHORDS MAKE FOR EASY TRANSPOSITION

If you learned the 12-bar blues in C using the moveable chords shown above, you can easily transpose to nearby keys by moving all the shapes up or down on the neck. For example, if you wanted to play the 12-bar blues in the key of D, just move the whole set of chords up one whole step (two frets).

You can also transpose the minor pentatonic scale to a new key. The easiest way to do this is to treat the scale fingering as a moveable shape. You learned the minor pentatonic scale in A. The key of C is a minor 3rd (three frets) higher than A. If you move all of the notes from the A Minor Pentatonic scale up three frets, you will have the C Minor Pentatonic scale. You get a bonus note in this key: the tonic note of C is available on the open 3rd string. Use this scale to improvise riffs and solos over "12-Bar Blues in C (A Bouncy C!)."

C Minor Pentatonic Scale

Note:	C	E♭	F	G	B♭	C	E♭
Scale Degree:	1	♭3	4	5	♭7	1	♭3

BLUES IN A MINOR KEY

THE NATURAL MINOR SCALE IN A

Technically, any scale that has a minor 3rd (♭3) is considered minor. There is one particular scale that is called the *natural minor scale*. Here it is in the key of A on the 1st string.

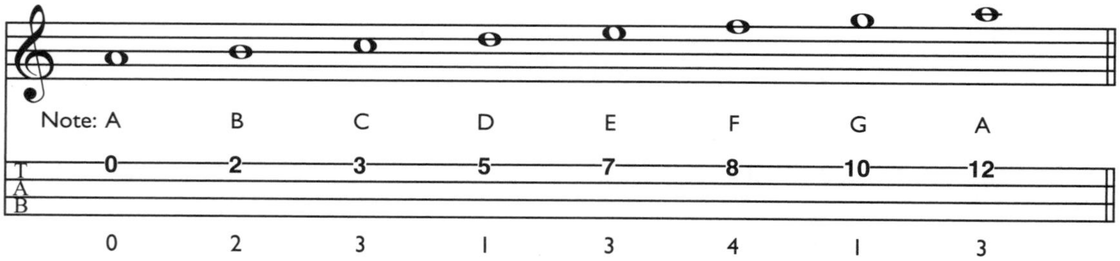

Following are a few things to notice about the natural minor scale.

Relative Minor (A Minor) and Relative Major (C Major)

In the key of A, the natural minor scale has no sharps and flats. It has the same notes and key signature as the key of C Major. We say that A Minor is the *relative minor* of C Major. The relative minor is always the scale whose root is the 6th note of the relative major.

Characteristic Notes: ♭3rd, ♭6th, and ♭7th

Let's compare the A Natural Minor scale with the A Major scale to see what is different. The 3rd, 6th, and 7th degrees are all a half step lower (♭3, ♭6, and ♭7).

A Major Scale:	A	B	C♯	D	E	F♯	G♯	A
Scale degrees:	1	2	3	4	5	6	7	8(1)
A Natural Minor Scale:	A	B	C	D	E	F	G	A
Scale degrees:	1	2	♭3	4	5	♭6	♭7	8(1)

The Primary Chords Are All Minor (i, iv, v)

If we build triads on the 1st, 4th, and 5th degrees using only the notes of the natural minor scale, we get i, iv, and v chords that are all minor. Fun fact: There are other minor scales that have different qualities on the IV and V chords, but those scales are also named differently.

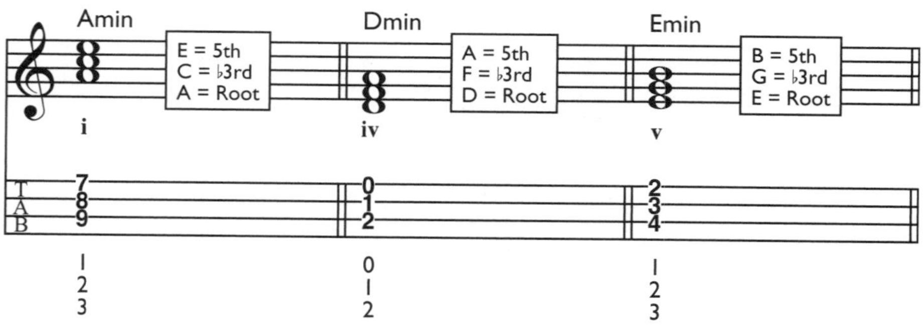

Here is a 12-bar blues progression in the key of A Minor. Note that the last measure stays on A Minor instead of going to the v chord of E Minor. Variations like this are common in blues progressions.

Nunmoor Blues: A 12-Bar Blues in A Minor

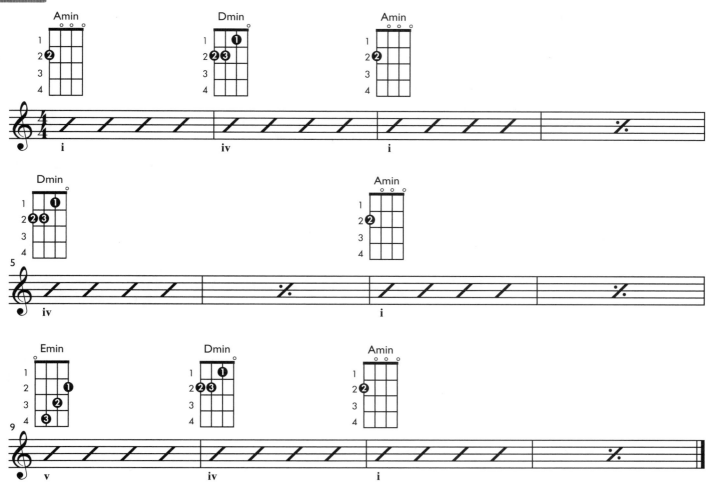

IMPROVISING ON A MINOR BLUES

The good news about playing in minor keys is that you can still use the minor pentatonic scale. In fact, it is more closely tied to the harmony of a minor key than it is to a major key. You can also fill in the missing 2nd and ♭6th degrees to make it a natural minor scale. Below is the A Minor pentatonic followed by the A Natural Minor in open position. Notice the imaginary low A and B notes that are needed to make the scale appear complete. These notes can be replaced with their counterparts an octave higher. Listen to the recording of the blues progression shown above and use it as a backing track to practice soloing.

INTRODUCTION TO FINGERSTYLE: THE RIGHT-HAND POSITION

Fingerstyle, or *fingerpicking*, means playing the ukulele with the right-hand fingers and thumb, using one digit per string. Many great ukulele players have incorporated fingerstyle into their playing. John King, for example, used classical techniques to bring the music of Bach to the uke. Others use fingerstyle to play folk, blues, or jazz.

RIGHT-HAND FINGERS

There are many stringed instruments played fingerstyle, so there are different systems for naming the right-hand fingers. Classical guitarists use abbreviations of the Spanish names for the fingers: *p, i, m, a* (*p* = thumb, *i* = index, *m* = middle, *a* = ring). The ukulele has many playing styles, including thumb style, which designates the thumb as *T*. Since we have already used *T* for the thumb, we will continue to use it throughout this method.

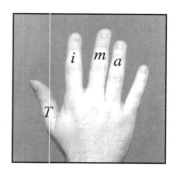

HOME POSITION

You will begin your exploration of fingerpicking by assigning each finger to one string. This may change later on, but it's a good place to start.

- *T* plays the 4th string.
- *i* plays the 3rd string.
- *m* plays the 2nd string.
- *a* plays the 1st string.

T = Thumb
i = index finger
m = middle finger
a = ring finger

Fingerstyle "home position."

THE RIGHT-HAND WRIST

To achieve the best technical fluency possible (to maximize tone and minimize stress), it is helpful to understand some basic terms regarding the wrist:

Arch
(up-and-down motion)

Rotation
(side-to-side motion)

Tilt
(Left-to-right motion from the elbow)

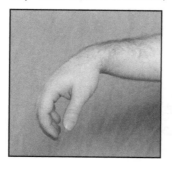

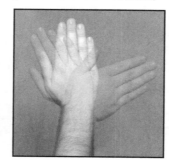

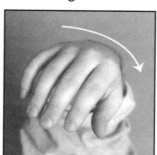

Your wrist should have a slight arch, little or no rotation, and perhaps a slight tilt in toward your thumb. Keep your fingers relaxed and avoid tension in your forearm. If you feel tension or tightness, stop and "shake it out."

BLUES IN A MINOR KEY

A good way to start fingerpicking is to learn a few repetitive patterns. These can be used with any chords you know. By placing your fingers in "home position," you can concentrate on which finger to play without worrying about which string to play.

If you find yourself getting tripped up, remove your hand from the ukulele. Hold it up in the air and practice moving the fingers to the pattern while saying the right-hand pattern aloud a few times (for example: *T–i–m–a, T–i–m–a,* etc.). Then go back to the uke and try again.

The pattern on this page is called an *arpeggio*. An arpeggio is the notes of a chord sounded one at a time. They can be played ascending, descending, or in a more complex pattern. The reentrant 4th string of the uke adds complexity to the sound of the arpeggio pattern, even though the finger pattern is very simple. The pattern you will play goes "thumb-index-middle-ring," or *T–i–m–a.* The progression shown uses C, F, and G7 chords, but you can try this pattern with any chord progression. You may want to practice the pattern with each chord individually for a while before putting the song together.

This progression comes from a Hawaiian song named "Hi'ilawe" (pronounced "he-ee-LAH-vey"), written in the 1880s. This song is a standard among slack-key guitarists. Slack-key master Gabby Pahinui (1921–1980) made "Hi'ilawe" one of his signature songs.

Hi'ilawe

Sam Li'a Kalainaina, Sr.

MIDDLE AND RING FINGERS TOGETHER

The pattern in this lesson goes "thumb-index-middle/ring-index," or *T–i–ma–i*. Your right-hand fingers will be in the same home position as the last lesson. The difference is that now your middle and ring fingers will play simultaneously. You can warm up for this pattern by tapping your fingers on a table. Try to get *m* and *a* to synchronize so they move as one. The following progression is in the key of G, but you can also try the pattern with other chords or the song from the previous lesson. The first iteration of the pattern has been highlighted to make it easier to see.

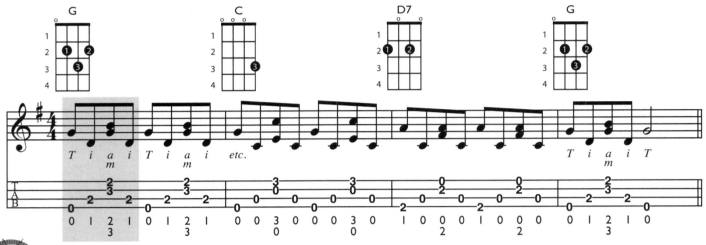

FINGERPICKING IN ¾

You can use a variation of the above pattern to fingerpick progressions in waltz time (¾). Since the last pattern was actually two beats long, all you have to do is add two extra eighth notes to make the pattern three beats long.

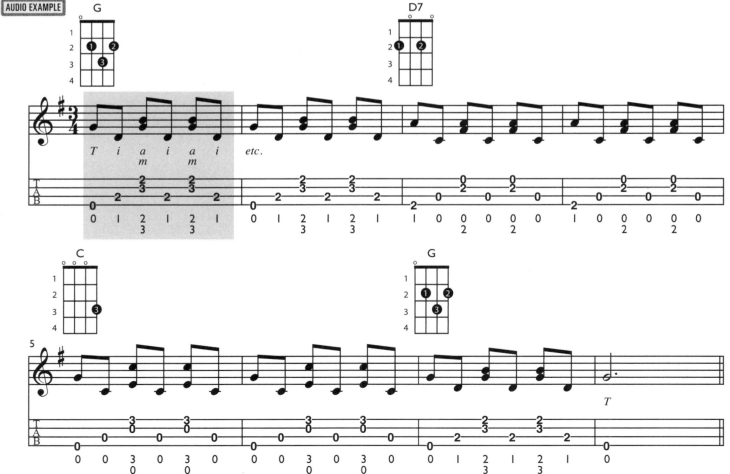

ALTERNATING-THUMB PATTERN T–i–T–m

A CHANGE IN HOME POSITION

In alternating-thumb patterns, the thumb moves back and forth between two strings. You will have to change your home position so that the thumb can be in charge of both the 3rd and 4th strings. The index finger will play string 2, and the middle finger will play string 1. The ring finger can go for drinks.

Here is the pattern slowed down to quarter notes to make it easier to learn. The chords alternate between C and C6.

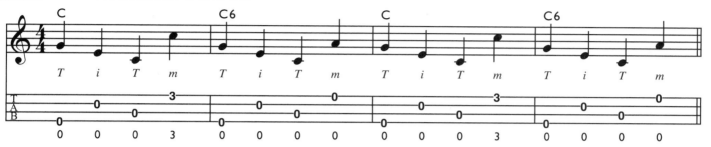

The fun thing about the alternating-thumb pattern is that when it combines with the reentrant tuning, it begins to play tricks on your ears. It's hard to tell where the pattern starts and stops. Try this solo fingerstyle piece. If you stay focused on the picking pattern, you won't get lost. There are a couple of new chords and voicings that give a sense of melody to the progression. Don't forget the repeats!

Ukaleidoscope

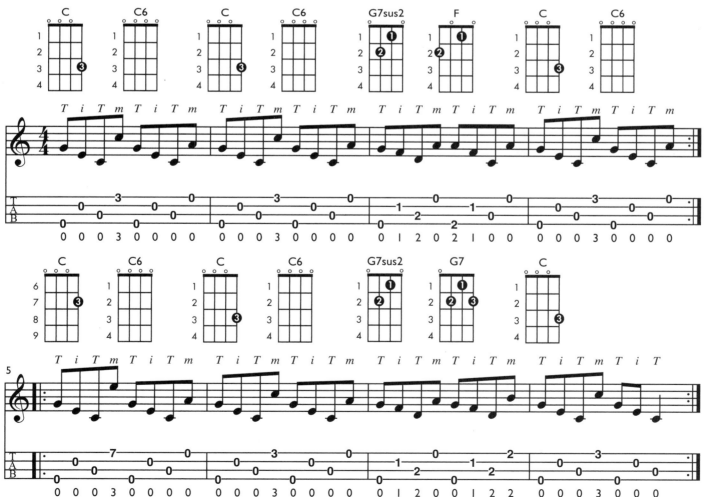

GETTING READY FOR THE NEXT LEVEL: MUSICAL EXPRESSION

EXPRESSION

Music is not just about keeping time and playing the right notes or chords. In order for music to have an emotional effect, it needs a sense of *expression*. Two very important elements of musical expression are *phrasing* and *dynamics*.

PHRASING

Phrasing is the way that touch, volume, and tempo are used to imply a sense of direction, movement, and rest in a piece of music. If notes are like words, then phrasing is the way that the words are made to sound like sentences, or complete thoughts.

Phrase Markings

Written music uses a number of markings and terms to communicate phrasing and expression to the performer. Many of these terms are in Italian. A quick tour of a few commonly used terms should give you some ideas for your own music. First, the *phrase mark* is a curved line that loosely connects a passage of music. It can be confused with a slur or a tie, but the phrase mark is usually shown above the staff and may have slurs or ties beneath it.

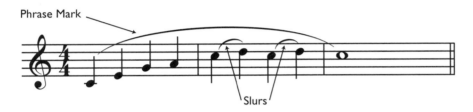

More About Phrases

- *Add your own phrase marks:* Phrase marks are sometimes shown in sheet music to give a detailed description of how the passage is to be expressed. You can also add your own phrase markings to help you break up a longer passage into smaller thoughts. This helps you learn it more quickly by working on smaller chunks of music at a time.

- *Common phrase lengths:* Musical phrases are very often two, four, or eight measures long. Four-bar phrases are probably the most common length, especially in vocal songs where four measures is the standard length for a line or two of lyrics.

- *Phrases don't always start on beat 1*: Sometimes phrases start on pickup notes before beat 1 (page 58). Often, if there are several phrases in a row, they may all have pickup notes.

- *Phrases create a sense of dialog:* Musical thoughts sometimes mirror the construction of speech. Two musical phrases might be paired together to form a musical "question and answer." Just as phrases are often two or four bars long, phrases themselves often appear in groups of two or four. Groups of phrases form larger sections of the form, like verses, choruses, and other types of sections.

OTHER PHRASING AND EXPRESSION TERMS

TERM	DEFINITION	MARKING
Legato	Notes are to be played in a smooth, connected fashion.	The word "Legato" marked above the music.
Staccato	Short, detached, unconnected notes.	The word "*Staccato*" marked above the music, or small dots above or below individual note heads.
Accent	A note played louder than the surrounding notes.	This sign > above or below the note head.

DYNAMICS

Dynamics define how loud or soft the notes or passages of music will sound. Dynamic expression and contrast are very important to imparting a sense of emotion in a piece of music.

	LOUD			**SOFT**	
Mark	*Term*	*Definition*	*Mark*	*Term*	*Definition*
mf	Mezzo Forte	Medium Loud	*mp*	Mezzo Piano	Medium soft
f	Forte	Loud	*p*	Piano	Soft
ff	Fortissimo	Very Loud	*pp*	Pianissimo	Very soft
fff	Fortississimo	Very, very loud	*ppp*	Pianississimo	Very, very soft
<	Crescendo	Gradually becoming louder	>	Decrescendo	Gradually becoming softer

THE DYNAMIC SCALE

Arranged from softest to loudest, the dynamic markings look like this:

Softest   *Loudest*

ppp   pp   p   mp   mf   ff   fff

THE "ARCH"

Often, a phrase or an entire piece of music will lend itself to a dynamic "arch" that begins at a softer dynamic, climaxes at a louder dynamic, then returns to a softer level. This is especially true if the melody moves from low notes up to high notes, then back down. Look for opportunities to place this kind of expression in your music. Also, look for spots where a "reverse arch" (loud to soft to loud) might work.

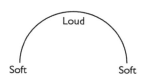

BUY A METRONOME

A *metronome* is an adjustable device (either wind-up or battery-powered) that generates a beat pulse for you to play along with. You can adjust the pulse from very slow to very fast. The speed is marked in beats-per-minute. A metronome speed of 60 is the same as one beat per second. The simplest metronomes make a ticking sound, while the more involved ones will make drum sounds and even mark measures for you.

When used regularly (and with a Zen-like patience), the metronome will help you learn to play with a steady rhythm. The only practice technique that is as valuable is to play with another person who has good rhythm—this can be difficult to do on a daily basis.

Don't let the metronome drive you crazy! At first, it may seem to be speeding up and slowing down while you play. Listen carefully—it's probably you. Pick a consistent, slow tempo to work with for the first few days and try the metronome with one favorite song. See how many measures you can play before you and the metronome have a parting of the ways. Gradually increase your endurance before you increase the speed.

RESOURCES FOR FURTHER STUDY

In addition to other players mentioned in this book, here are just a few more players to check out. Look for their Websites and videos, buy their recordings, and keep an eye out for the next generation of influences!

Ukulele Giants of the Past
Roy Smeck
Tessie O'Shea
Andy Cummings

Modern Players

Jason Arimoto	*Gordon Mark*	*Byron Yasui*
Jim Beloff	*Marcy Marxer*	*The Sweet Hollywaiians*
Benny Chong	*Brittni Paiva*	*The Ukulele Orchestra of Great Britain*
Andy Eastwood	*Lyle Ritz*	*The Wellington International Ukulele Orchestra*
Kimo Hussey	*Steven Sproat*	
Eddie Kamae	*Brian Tolentino*	

THE WORLD A'CHORDING TO UKE: THEORY AND MAJOR TRIAD INVERSIONS

In this section, we'll explore playing chords up the neck. We do this by playing *moveable chord inversions*. As you learned in the lesson starting on page 88, the term "moveable" refers to chords or scale shapes that do not use open strings. Because there are no open strings, you can move the shapes up and down the neck and retain the same chord qualities. (We'll learn about "inversions" below.) Once you learn these moveable shapes, you can use just a few chord shapes to play many different chords, moving each shape up the neck chromatically (or, the distance of one fret at a time). First, we'll review the theory of how these chords are constructed.

Let's start by taking a look at the harmonized major scale. Using only the notes of the C Major scale, we build triads on each note of the scale, skipping every other note. The chords built on I, IV, and V are *major triads* consisting of root, major 3rd, and 5th. These three major chords are the foundation of numerous songs in many styles. The chords built on ii, iii, and vi are *minor triads* consisting of root, ♭3rd, and 5th. And the chord built on vii is a *diminished triad* consisting of root, ♭3rd, and ♭5th. (Notice the "vii" underneath the staff below. The symbol beside it (○) means "diminished."

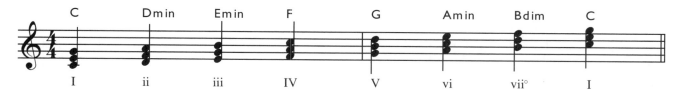

A chord inversion is created by placing any other note of the chord—beside the root—at the bottom. Below are three inversions of C, using one string for each note. The root-position chord is built root–3rd–5th; the 1st inversion is 3rd–5th–root; and the 2nd inversion is 5th–root–3rd. Notice in the example below we are going from the lowest position on the fretboard to the highest.

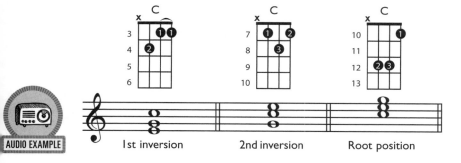

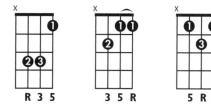

Below are three moveable inversion shapes. Move any of the above C shapes up two frets and the chord becomes a D. Move it down two frets and it becomes a B♭. Each of these three shapes can be moved to become any of the 12 major chords. Practice finding the locations for all of the G chords, F chords, D chords, etc.

R 3 5   3 5 R   5 R 3

By doubling one note of each inversion, we can create moveable chord shapes using all four strings. These shapes are particularly usable for strumming any chord, as there are no open strings. Below are four moveable inversions of C.

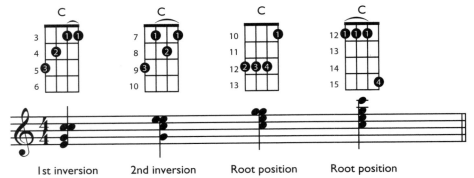

Using any C shape above, move up one fret for D♭, another fret for D, and so on. Again, practice finding different chords using all four shapes below.

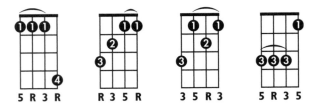

The moveable major shapes above are the basis for creating minor, diminished, and other types of chords, and will allow us to greatly expand our chord vocabularies.

MINOR TRIAD INVERSIONS

To build a moveable minor chord shape, simply flat the 3rd of the major chord.

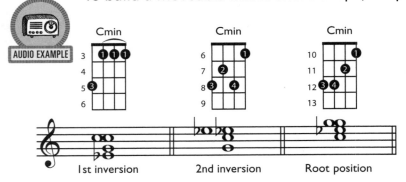

Below are the moveable minor shapes. Practice finding the locations of different minor chords all over the fretboard.

DIMINISHED AND AUGMENTED TRIAD INVERSIONS

To build a diminished triad, flat the 5th degree of the minor chord. An interesting aspect of the diminished triad is that the interval from the root to the 3rd is a minor 3rd, and so is the interval from the 3rd to the 5th. So, it is perfectly symmetrical.

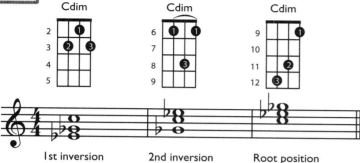

There is one more type of triad, which we didn't encounter in the harmonized major scale, and it is the augmented triad. The augmented triad is built by sharping the 5th of the major chord. As with the diminished triad, it is symmetrical; the interval from the root to the 3rd is a major 3rd, and so is the interval from the 3rd to the 5th. In addition, notice that all three augmented inversions are exactly the same shape. Three for the price of one!

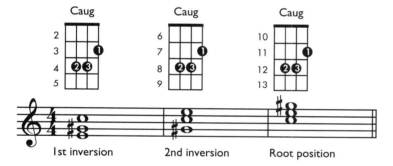

DOMINANT 7TH CHORD INVERSIONS

Now, we'll take a look at the most commonly used four-note chord—the dominant 7th. It's constructed by adding a fourth note to the V (dominant) chord of any scale. In the key of C, the dominant (V) chord is G. The notes of the G Major triad are G–B–D. We'll add one more note from the C scale, F, which is an interval of seven scale tones from G. The resulting four-note chord, G–B–D–F, is the dominant 7th chord called G7.

Important Note: The dominant 7th chord is so commonly used that it isn't generally called by its full name. So, if a piece of music says to play G7, we assume that it's a dominant 7th chord. If you encounter a major 7th or minor 7th, those are different types of chords, and we'll be exploring them in depth later in the book.

Another way to look at the dominant 7th chord is by comparing it to a G Major scale: G–A–B–C–D–E–F♯–G. If we take the seventh note of this scale and lower it by half a step, this note is considered a ♭7th. The formula for building any dominant 7th is root–3rd–5th–♭7th. We will now look at four moveable shapes of the dominant seventh chord containing all four of these notes. Below are the four moveable inversions in C. Notice there is a new inversion—3rd inversion—which has the 7th as the lowest note. Additionally, note that as we move up the neck, the melody note (on the 1st string) of the chord changes—from root to 3rd, then 5th, and then 7th.

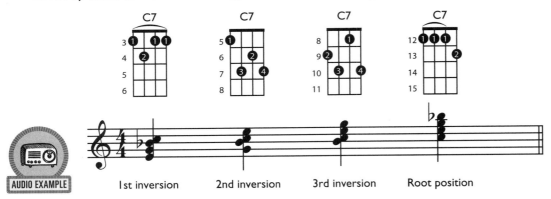

1st inversion   2nd inversion   3rd inversion   Root position

Try finding other 7th chords (G7, D7, A7, etc.) using these same shapes:

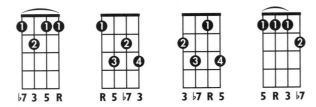

♭7 3 5 R   R 5 ♭7 3   3 ♭7 R 5   5 R 3 ♭7

DIMINISHED 7TH CHORD INVERSIONS

Another useful four-note chord is the diminished 7th chord. It is constructed by flatting (or diminishing) each note of a dominant 7th chord except the root. Its formula is root–♭3rd–b5th–♭♭7th. The double-flatted 7th, which lowers a note by two half steps, can also be enharmonically considered a 6th. As an example, take a C7 chord, C–E–G–B♭, and flat each note to get C–E♭–G♭–B♭♭(A).

Another way to look at the diminished 7th chord is as consecutively stacked minor 3rds. It is a symmetrical chord, and each of the four notes in the chord can be its name. (Note: this is also true of the diminished triad.) So, Cdim7 is also Ebdim7, Gbdim7 (or F♯dim7), and Adim7. To the right are the inversions of Cdim7. Notice that each new inversion is the exact same shape three frets higher.

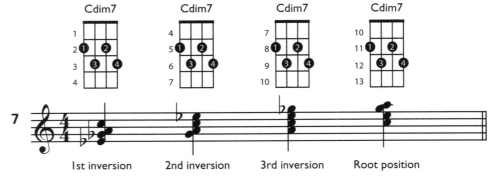

1st inversion   2nd inversion   3rd inversion   Root position

I–IV–V **PROGRESSIONS USING MOVEABLE SHAPES**

Now, we'll examine some ways to use the moveable chord shapes we've been covering. Our first example is "Louie's Wild Thing," a common I–IV–V rock progression in the key of C, using major triads. You'll notice some melodic movement on the A string using these inversions—this will be the basis for creating chord-melody arrangements later on.

Louie's Wild Thing

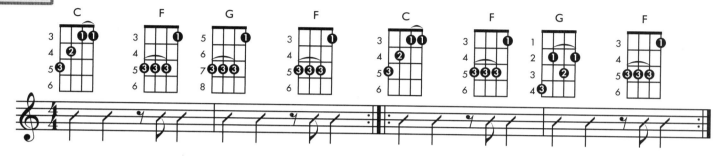

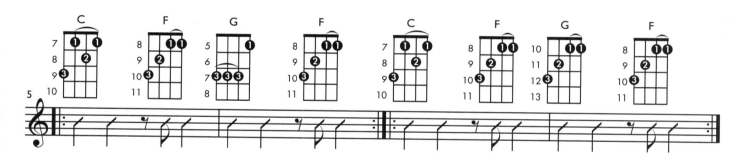

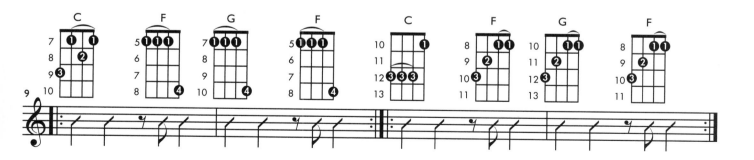

Now, we'll transpose a few of the examples from the preceding page into another key.
Note that we're still using the same shapes but at different frets, since we're in a new key.

Louie's Wild Thing in G

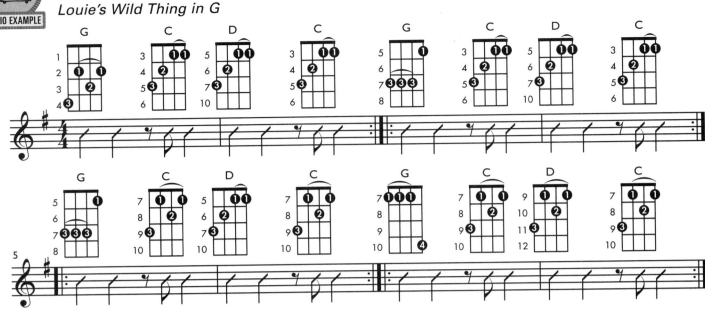

I–vi–ii–V

Our next chord progression was common for 1950s ballads and uses moveable major, minor, and dominant 7th chord shapes. "There Must Be Fifty Ways (to Leave the Fifties)" is a I–vi–ii–V progression in the key of C. The time signature $\frac{6}{8}$ means there are six beats per measure with the eighth note getting one beat. In $\frac{6}{8}$ time, there are usually two accented beats, 1 and 4, so you would count: ONE-two-three, FOUR-five-six. (For more about $\frac{6}{8}$ time, see page 129.)

There Must Be Fifty Ways (To Leave the Fifties)

Now, let's transpose the tune from the preceding page into the key of F. Notice that we're still using many of the same chord shapes but at different frets. Try transposing this same progression into other keys as well.

There Must Be Fifty Ways (To Leave the Fifties) in F

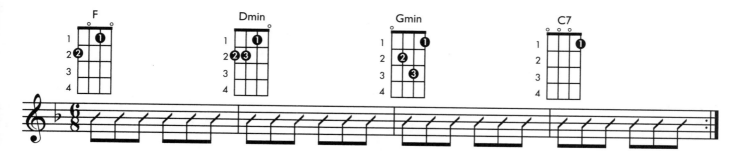

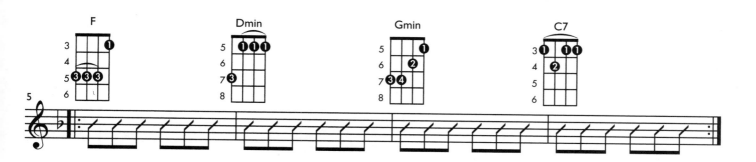

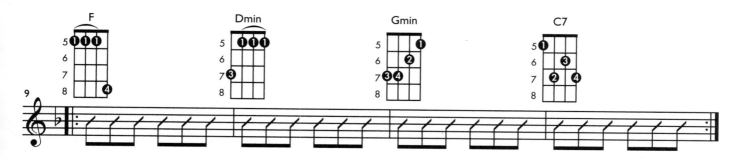

i–VII–VI

"All Along the Stairway" uses the progression of i–VII–VI–VII. In the key of Amin, the chords are Amin–G–F–G. You've heard this progression in songs by artists such as Bob Dylan and Led Zeppelin.

All Along the Stairway

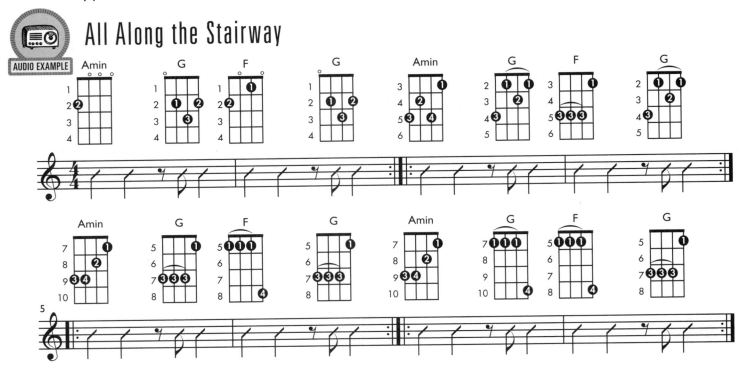

Now, we'll transpose "All Along the Stairway" into D Minor. Note that we're still using many of the same chord shapes but at different frets. Again, you can try transposing this progression into other keys or positions on the neck.

All Along the Stairway in D Minor

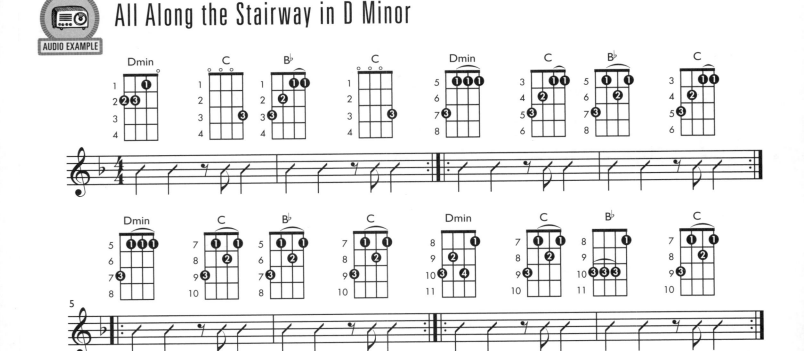

EXPANDING YOUR GROOVE PALETTE: GROOVE CONCEPTS

With a varied repertoire of more complex rhythm patterns and strums, you can make even the simplest chord progressions sound more interesting. In this section, we'll work on expanding your palette of strums.

To review a concept introduced on page 49, it's extremely important to align downstrums and upstrums with the correct beats (or parts of the beat), otherwise your strums won't have the right groove or feel for a song. There's a saying in real estate that there are three important things to consider when buying a house: location, location, location. For uke playing, the three most important things to remember are strum direction, strum direction, strum direction.

Although there are some exceptions to this rule, in general, when playing a $\frac{4}{4}$ rhythm, we'll use downstrums (toward the ground) on the downbeats (1, 2, 3, 4) and upstrums (toward the sky) on the offbeats, or upbeats, (the &'s). Notice that the names "downbeat" and "upbeat" are descriptive. If a rhythm has continuous eighth notes (1-&, 2-&, 3-&, 4-&), you'd play alternate strum directions (down-up, down-up, down-up, down-up). If a beat is left out, leave out its strum and use the appropriate direction for the next strum. So, you might end up with two upstrums or two downstrums in a row. For example, if the rhythm is 1, 2-&, 3-&, 4, you'd play down, down-up, down-up, down. Also, make it a point to tap your foot on the downbeats, as this will help you internalize where they should occur.

Sometimes, it's not what you play that makes a piece of music interesting, it's what you leave out. This next exercise demonstrates this concept. Play the first measure, repeating many times and getting a good groove going. Then, try the second measure, also repeating many times, leaving out the downbeat of beat 3, and accenting the up on the & of 2 (this produces a really energetic groove). Make sure to follow the downstrum and upstrum indications accurately. Next, do the same for measures 3 and 4. Also, try alternating the two measures, creating a two-measure strum pattern.

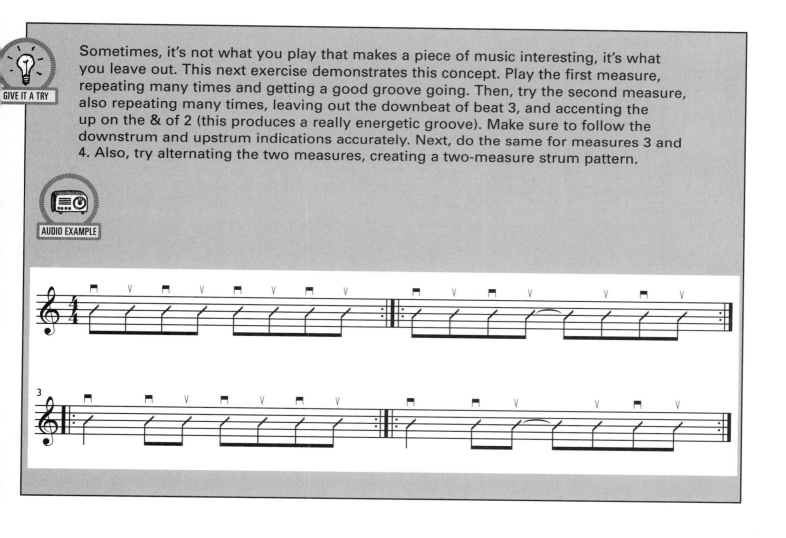

RHYTHMS USING TRIPLETS

Many blues rhythms use triplets, so we'll look at those now. When playing triplets, we're fitting three eighth notes into the space of two normal eighth notes. If we were to follow strict alternate strumming, 1-&-a would be down-up-down, and then the second beat would start on an upstrum. However, that doesn't result in a strong a groove, so we're going to modify this by starting beat 2 on a downstrum. We'll do the same for the third and fourth downbeats, playing down-up-down, down-up-down, down-up-down, down-up-down for our count of 1-&-a, 2-&-a, 3-&-a, 4-&-a.

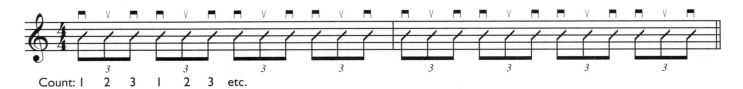

Count: 1 2 3 1 2 3 etc.

Triplet Rhythms with Duple Rhythms

Often, triplet rhythms are juxtaposed with duple rhythms, or rhythms where the beat is divisible by 2 rather than 3. Following are some examples combining triplets and duple rhythms. The first example is reminiscent of Robert Johnson's "Sweet Home Chicago" and "Dust My Broom." The second example is a common rhythm and the third example is a variation of it, adding an offbeat on the "&" of 4. The fourth example is the rhythm from Robert Johnson's "Terraplane Blues" and the last example is a variation on it, again adding an offbeat on the "&" of 4.

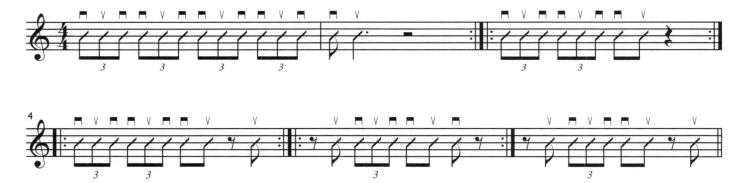

3+3+2

So far, many of our $\frac{4}{4}$ rhythms have had a duple, or two, feel, with emphasis placed on the number counts. To explain this in more depth, if we think of a $\frac{4}{4}$ measure as eight eighth notes, then we've been subdividing them into twos: ONE-two (i.e., 1-&), ONE-two (2-&), etc.

However, this isn't the only way to subdivide the beats. We can create groupings of three eighth notes. As you learned on page 81, we can subdivide eight eighth notes into two groups of three and one group of two: 3+3+2. Count out loud, "ONE-two-three, ONE-two-three, ONE-two," accenting each of the ONEs, and the result is an interesting syncopation, or shifting of the emphasis from strong beats to "weaker" beats. This rhythm is used in many styles around the world. Note that these groupings of three eighth notes are not triplets, so each group will add up to a total of a dotted quarter note (one and a half beats) not a quarter note.

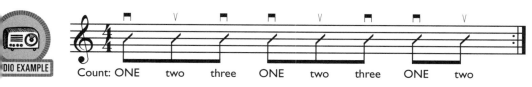

We can also play this rhythm without strumming every beat and create more cool syncopation, especially if a drummer or other instrument is playing quarter notes on the downbeats. When first learning the following rhythm, try counting all of the beats out loud, clapping only on the ONEs.

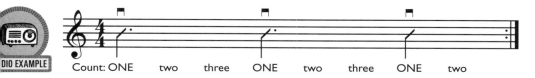

SPLIT STRUM

Uke players like Roy Smeck and George Formby traditionally used this rhythm in the split strum. Try the exercise, using downstrums and upstrums exactly as indicated. To do the split strum, the first downstrum is across all four strings, the first upstrum is mostly brushing strings 1 and 2, and the next downstrum is mostly brushing strings 3 and 4. Here it is, holding a C chord.

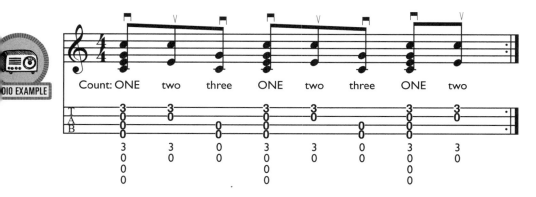

Now, we'll try adding a "tap" finger to the split strum, which brings out a ragtime type melody. To do this with a C chord, lift the left-hand 3rd finger off the fretboard to sound the open 1st string on the upstrums. This produces a tapping sensation and creates a three-note melody, the third note being on the 4th (high-G) string.

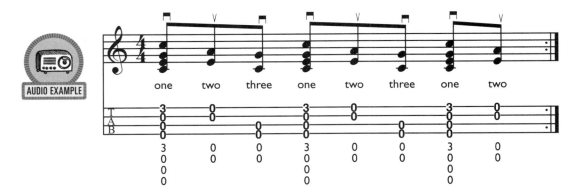

BO DIDDLEY BEAT, OR CLAVE

The 3+3+2 subdivision is also the foundation of the classic Bo Diddley beat, a powerful two-bar pattern. This is also known as the clave, and it is a common rhythm found in both Latin American and African music. In the first measure, we play just the ONEs instead of playing all the eighth notes. In the second measure, there's a rest on beat 1, and then we play quarter notes on beats 2 and 3, and another rest on beat 4. Practice until you can keep this going with a good groove.

Clave Strumming with Mute Notes

Now, we'll experiment with strumming continuous eighth notes, muting all the notes between the accented notes in the example below. Mute by slightly relieving pressure from your left hand while still holding the chord in place as you strum. This works best with *closed position chords*, which contain no open strings. This technique produces a cool, driving rhythm. Practice until you can keep this going with a good groove. Try it using a straight eight-note rhythm, and then try it using swing eighths.

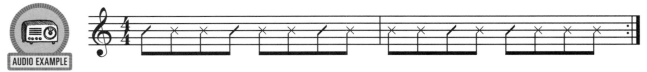

¾ AND 6/8 TIME SIGNATURES

In ¾ time, there are three beats per measure, with the quarter note receiving one beat. As with 4/4, the downbeats (1, 2, 3) will all be played with downstrums and the "&'s" will be played with upstrums. Following are some ¾ strum patterns. Each measure is a complete exercise to be repeated many times before going on to the next measure. There will be opportunities to use these strums in songs in a later sectoin. Also, you can incorporate these patterns into the ¾ songs you learned earlier in this book.

¾ *Strumming Patterns*

In 6/8 time, there are six beats per measure, with the eighth note receiving one beat. Typically, in 6/8 time, there are two accented beats, 1 and 4, so we would count: ONE-two-three, FOUR-five-six. In both ¾ and 6/8, there are a total of six possible eighth notes per measure; however, the accents in each time signature are completely different. Think of ¾ as being three quarter-note beats per measure, whereas 6/8 is two dotted quarter-note beats per measure.

There are a few different strumming approaches for 6/8. The first is to divide beats into quarter-eighth, quarter-eighth, or ONE-(rest)-three, FOUR-(rest)-six. Play the "ONE" and "FOUR" as downstrums and the "three" and "six" as upstrums. The next approach is to strum all six eighth notes, and we can do this either as down-up-down, down-up-down or down-up-down, up-down-up. Each option has a slightly different feel—the first is more driving, while the latter seems airier. Choose whichever strum sounds best for the song you are playing. Another strum you can use (which was covered earlier in the book) is down-down-up, down-down-up. Whichever pattern you choose, always make sure to accent the "ONE" and "FOUR."

Here are some 6/8 strums. Repeat each one many times before practicing the next measure.

6/8 *Strumming Patterns*

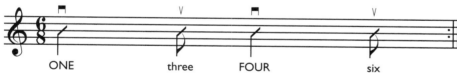

ONE   three   FOUR   six

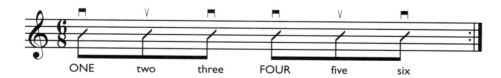

ONE   two   three   FOUR   five   six

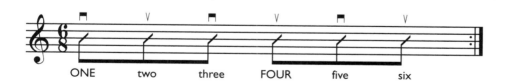

ONE   two   three   FOUR   five   six

KIND OF BLUE

When you go to a blues jam, the first song you'll often hear is a 12-bar blues. However, there are various other song forms used in blues. Being able to play these other blues forms will keep different songs from sounding too much the same. On page 131, we'll start learning some of these other forms, but first, let's review the 12-bar blues.

12-BAR BLUES REVIEW

As you recall from page 99, the 12-bar form is made up of three sung lines. The first line of lyrics repeats twice, and then it's "answered" with an ending line. Below is the chord progression for the 12-bar blues, shown with Roman numerals. Try it in different keys, using moveable chord forms from the previous section. Experiment using both major and dominant 7th chords, as they're often interchangeable in the blues.

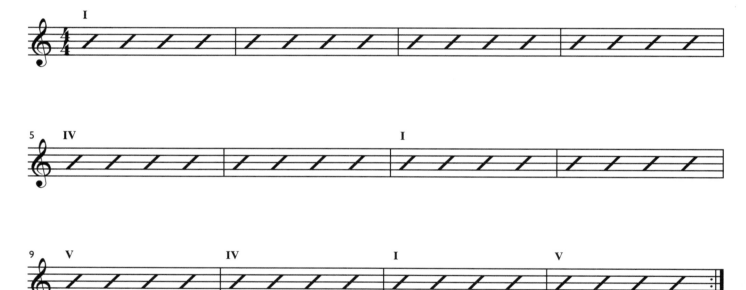

16-BAR BLUES

A common 16-bar blues form has four sung lines. The first lyric line repeats three times instead of two, and then there's the ending line. Below is a sample progression, based on 16-bar tunes such as "Lonesome Road Blues." There are also ragtime-style 16-bar blues forms that we'll be discussing soon. Again, try the example below in different keys, using moveable chord forms and various rhythms.

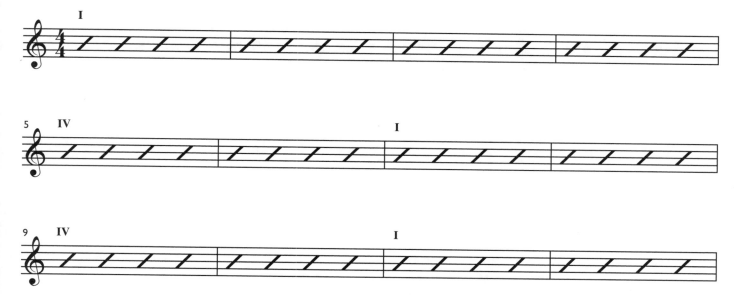

8-BAR BLUES

A common 8-bar form has two sung lines, the first lyric line doesn't repeat as it did in the other forms, and then there's an ending line. The example below is in the style of "Key to the Highway," a classic 8-bar blues in the key of A. It works well with the rhythm as notated, but also try using some of the rhythms we explored earlier.

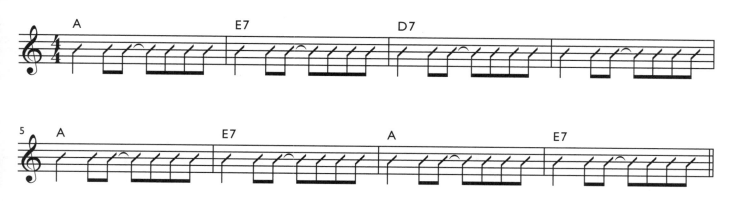

TURNAROUNDS

Often, near the end of a verse in a song, you'll hear what is called a turnaround. A turnaround occurs during the last two measures of each chorus (repetition of the song form) and is an excellent way to add variety. At bar 11 (of a 12-bar form), instead of playing the I chord for a full four beats, we'll play one beat of the I chord, followed by a melodic line that leads up or down to the V chord. Below are three turnarounds in the key of A.

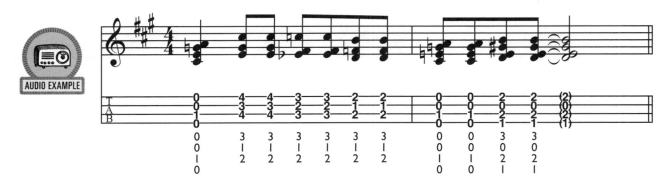

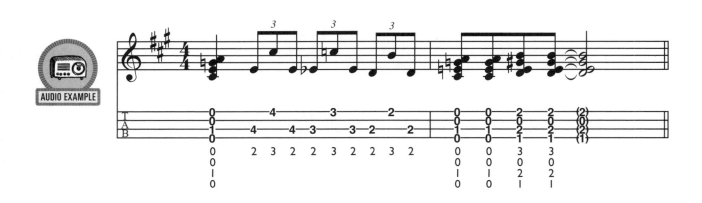

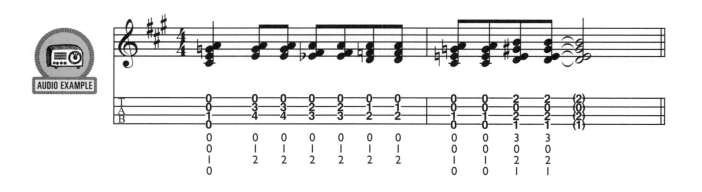

Following are some turnarounds in the key of C. Notice we're using the same shapes from the key of A but farther up the neck. You'll be able to transpose these ideas into other keys as needed.

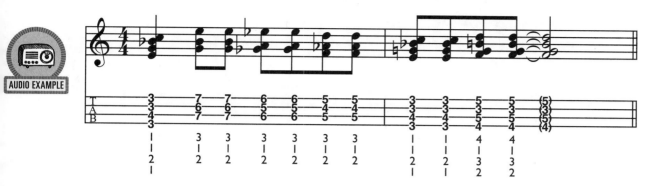

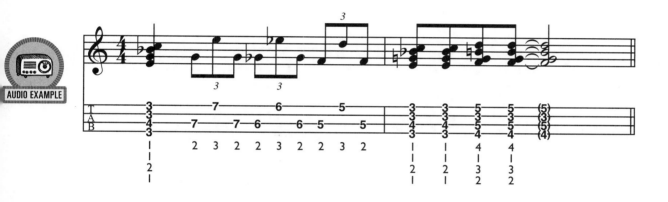

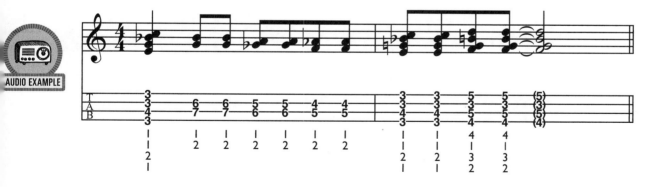

Here's a turnaround in the key of F.

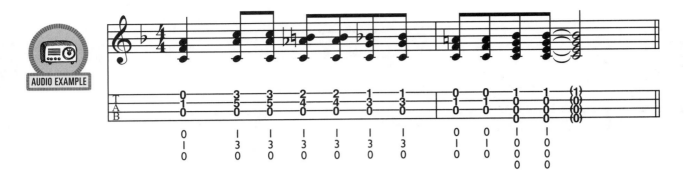

Below is that same turnaround but in the key of G. Again, notice we're using the same shapes but farther up the neck. You can try transposing these ideas into other keys. These same turnarounds will work for 12-, 8-, or 16-bar blues progressions.

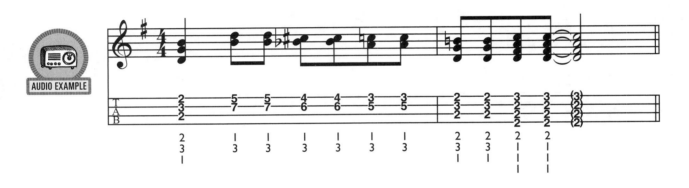

CIRCLE OF 5THS BLUES PROGRESSIONS

As you'll recall in on page 78, we discussed chord progressions that cycle counterclockwise through the circle of 5ths. For example, in the key of G, D7 is the V chord. The secondary dominant, or V of the V, is A7, which naturally leads back to the D7. The secondary dominant of A7 (in other words, the V of the V of the V), is E7, which naturally leads back to the A7.

Let's play "Salty Dog Blues," a classic 16-bar blues progression using this counterclockwise circle of 5ths progression. Although the song is in G, we don't encounter the tonic chord until measure 7, and again at 15. Notice that some chords have notes that change on the 1st string, which brings out the melody of the song.

Salty Dog Blues

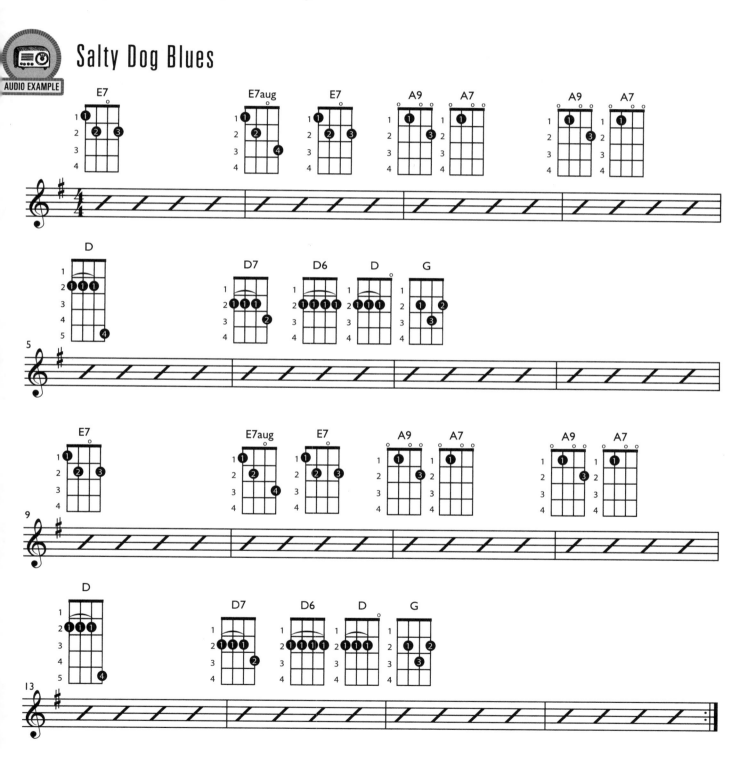

JAZZIN' THE BLUES

Now, we'll look at some ways to "jazz" up the blues. One common approach is to use secondary dominants as discussed in the previous lesson. We'll demonstrate using a standard 12-bar blues progression in the key of C. In C, the V chord is G7, the V of G7 is D7, and the V of D7 is A7.

Normally, measures 7–8 would be the I chord, leading to the V chord in measure 9. Instead, we'll cycle counterclockwise through the circle of 5ths, starting with A7 in measure 8. That leads us to D7 in measure 9, and, finally, the V chord, G7, in measure 10 (instead of its usual spot in measure 9).

Another variation is to play the IV chord in measure 2, and then go back to the I chord at measure 3, instead of staying on the I chord for the first four measures. We'll also play C7 at measure 4, which leads into the IV chord at measure 5. One more variation is to play a diminished chord on beats 3 and 4 of measure 2 and also at measure 6. In addition, you can use any of the turnarounds in the key of C for the last two measures.

As you'll notice when playing the following, it still sounds like the blues, but with more harmonically complex chord movement occurring in each measure.

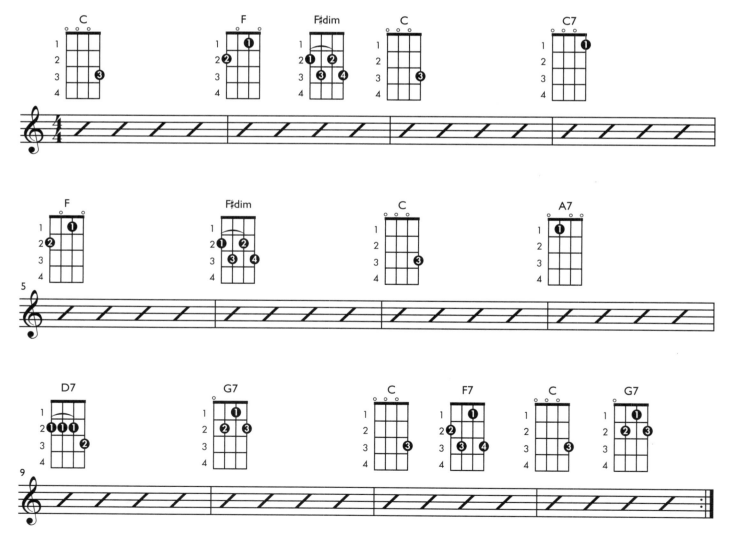

AUDIO EXAMPLE

Now, we'll vary this progression even more, using some of the moveable chord shapes from earlier sections of the book. We'll also play C7 instead of C for the I chord, which sounds bluesier; and at measure 4, we'll play another voicing of C7 higher up on the neck to lead us into the IV chord.

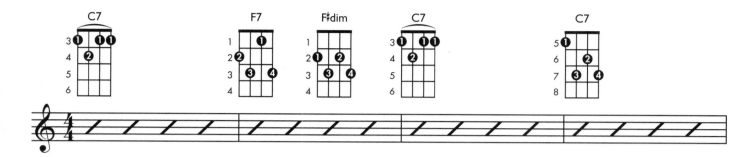

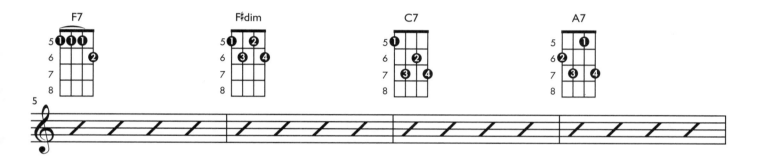

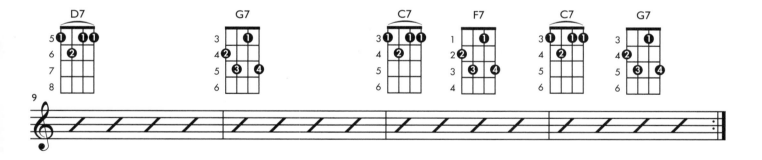

16-BAR RAGTIME BLUES

Now, were going to play "Alice's Red Hot Electric Rag," a 16-bar blues and ragtime progression that uses the counterclockwise circle of 5ths progression. A number of classic songs use this same chord progression, including Bessie Smith's " 'Lectric Chair Blues," Robert Johnson's "Red Hot," Sippie Wallace's "Women Be Wise," and Arlo Guthrie's "Alice's Restaurant."

In C, the V chord is G7, the V of G7 is D7, and the V of the D7 is A7. The A7 naturally leads back to the D7, and the D7 naturally leads back to the G7, our original V chord in C.

In the first four measures, we begin on C, and then jump to A7 to start working our way back through the cycle of 5ths to C. In the second four measures, we again begin on C, jumping to A7 to cycle back to G7, which then leads us to the third line. This third group of four measures is like a turnaround (I–I7–IV–IV°) and leads us to the final four measures, which are the same as the first.

Now, let's play "Alice's Red Hot Electric Rag."

Alice's Red Hot Electric Rag

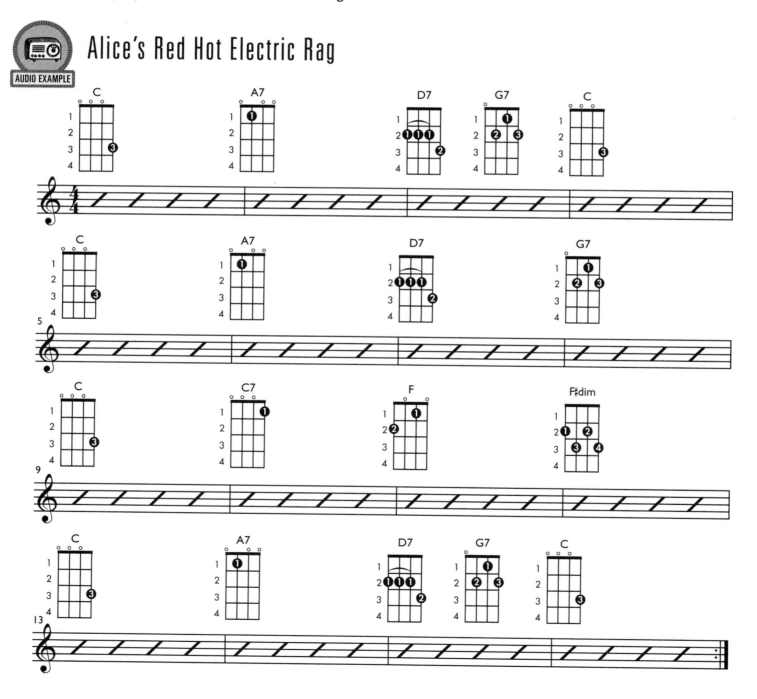

LET'S JAM: JAMMING ON THE BLUES!

When learning to play an arranged song, you know what the song is supposed to sound like before playing it, thus you can practice the same thing over and over, working toward a clear goal. Because an improvised solo never comes out the same way twice, learning to improvise can feel a bit more abstract and elusive.

In this section, you will be learning pentatonic scales in various positions. Pick one position and practice improvising with it for a while. Just practicing a scale over and over can get monotonous, so try using backing tracks to practice soloing over. In time, you'll get to know which finger movements will produce what kind of melodic movement within a position, eventually developing a sense for what something will sound like before you actually play it. Move on to the next adjacent position, and do the same. Notice the connecting notes in each position, then start to practice going between two positions during a solo.

A great solo tells a story and feels like it has a distinct beginning, middle, and end. We can achieve this goal by fully developing our melodic ideas, as opposed to just stringing together disparate riffs that don't relate to each other.

Great soloing is green, sustainable. Improvisers recycle and reuse ideas all the time. For example, play a short melodic phrase over the I chord, using just a few notes. When we get to the IV chord, play the same idea, slightly varying it rhythmically. When we get to the V chord, still use the basic shape of the original idea, but vary it even more to end the 12-bar phrase.

Call and response is a very effective technique. To use it, play the same original short idea, this time answering it with a different phrase that completes the sentence, so to speak. Now vary that idea as we discussed above, answering with the response, also varied, each time.

Finally, try singing your improvisational ideas, then see if you can find what you sang on your instrument. Often, what we sing comes out sounding better than the results we get from moving our fingers in familiar ways.

PHOTO • LARRY LYTLE

DID YOU KNOW?

Daniel Ho's simple philosophy of presenting music with sincerity and artistry encompasses six consecutive GRAMMY Awards, #1 albums on national airplay charts, and Top 10 albums on the Billboard charts. In 2010, his solo 'ukulele CD, Polani (Pure), was the first 'ukulele album in music history to receive a GRAMMY nomination. Daniel brings the same integrity to his instructional video 'Ukulele: A Beginning Method as well as his other instructional methods and song collections.

MORE ON PENTATONIC SCALES

Jamming with other people is among the most fun musical things to do. We'll explore the tools you need for improvising creative solos.

Pentatonic scales (see page 102) sound great and are extremely useful when improvising. The word "pente," from the Greek, means "five," and "tonic" means "tones," or "notes." Thus, pentatonic scales are scales containing five notes, instead of the seven notes found in major and minor scales. Pentatonic scales are ancient and are used in musical styles around the world.

MAJOR PENTATONIC SCALE

Let's look again at the major pentatonic scale. Leave out the 4th and 7th notes of the major scale, and the result is a major pentatonic scale. The formula to build a major pentatonic scale in any key is root–2nd–3rd–5th–6th. For example, a C Major scale is C–D–E–F–G–A–B–C. Leave out F (the 4th) and B (the 7th) and you get the C Major Pentatonic scale: C–D–E–G–A–C.

C Major Pentatonic Scale

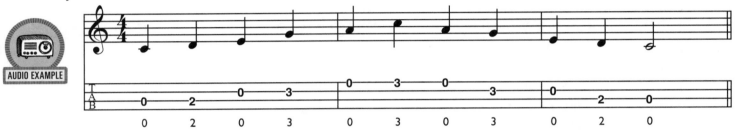

MINOR PENTATONIC SCALE

Using the exact same notes, but starting on A, the 6th degree of the scale, results in an A Minor Pentatonic scale: A–C–D–E–G–A. The A Minor scale is the relative minor of C Major. Notice the difference in sound, even though they use the same notes.

A Minor Pentatonic Scale

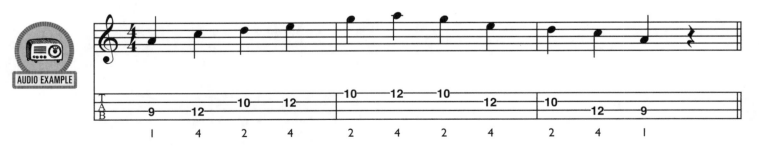

The formula to build a minor pentatonic scale in any key is: root–♭3rd–4th–5th–♭7th. We'll compare the two types of pentatonic scales from the same root, which will help you hear the differences. To construct a C Minor Pentatonic scale, start with a C Major scale. C is the root. Skip the 2nd degree of the scale, D. The 3rd is E—lower it by a half step, making it E♭. The 4th, F, and 5th, G, stay the same. Skip the 6th degree, A. The 7th note is B—lower it a half step, making it B♭. Here's the C Minor Pentatonic scale.

C Minor Pentatonic Scale

BLUES SCALE

There is also what is called the blues scale, which is a minor pentatonic scale plus one note, the ♭5th. In C, the 5th is G—lower it a half step and you get G♭.

C Blues Scale

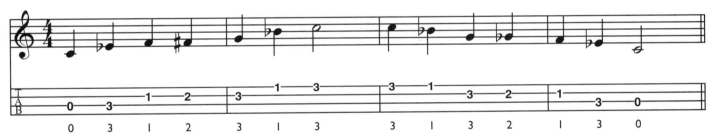

PENTATONIC SCALE POSITIONS

Below are moveable positions of the minor pentatonic scale that can be used to play up the neck and in any key. Each one connects with the next. Once you've learned all five positions, you can play the minor pentatonic scale spanning the entire fingerboard. (Note: To extend your improvisational range a 4th lower, consider trying the low-G tuning.)

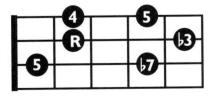
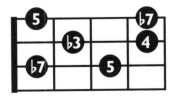
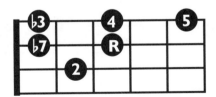

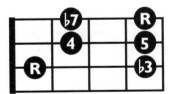
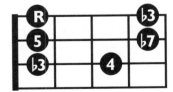

SOLOING USING THE MINOR PENTATONIC

Using our 12-bar blues progression in C from page 130, we'll play a sample solo based on the minor pentatonic scale. Also, remember the syncopated rhythms using triplets that we covered on page 126? We'll use one of them to create the melodic idea. When we get to the V chord, we vary the original melodic idea by moving it up a whole step. Finally, we end with one of the turnarounds in C that we covered on page 132. Recycle and reuse!

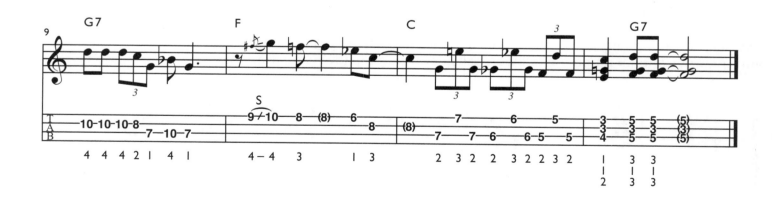

IMPROVISATION USING THE MAJOR PENTATONIC

The major pentatonic scale is a versatile scale for improvising and works in many styles from blues and bluegrass to country and rock. Recalling our discussion in the previous lesson on pentatonic scales, the major pentatonic scale contains the exact same notes as the minor pentatonic scale, just starting on a different root note. So the fingerings are easy to learn!

Let's improvise on the chord progression from "Rolling Down That Lonesome Road Blues," a 16-bar progression in G. Here's a sample solo using the G Major Pentatonic scale.

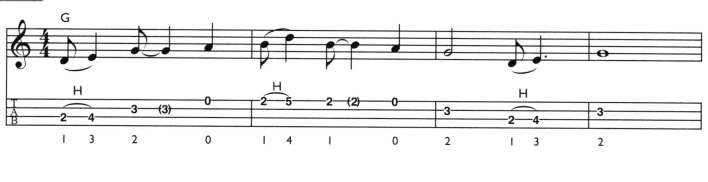

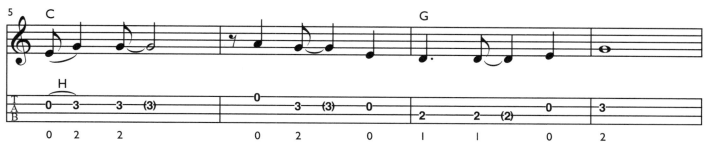

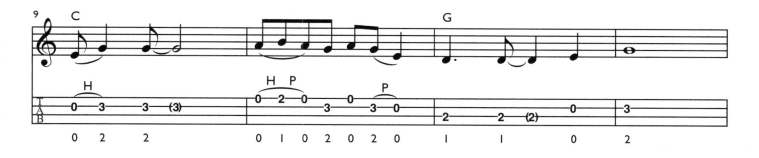

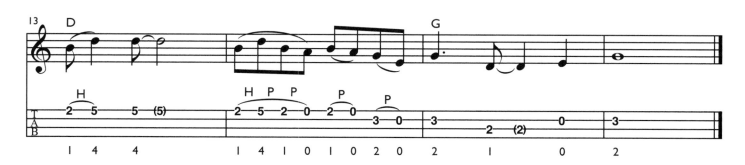

Now, let's explore changing major pentatonic scales over each chord. The G Major Pentatonic scale contains the following notes: G–A–B–D–E. The notes contained in a G chord are G–B–D, so the G Major Pentatonic scale contains all three chord tones. The notes in a C chord are C–E–G; the G Major Pentatonic scale contains the E and G, but not the C root. If we instead play the C Major Pentatonic scale, C–D–E–G–A, over the C chord, it contains all the chord tones.

The notes in a D chord are D–F♯–A. The G Major Pentatonic scale contains the D and A, but not the F♯, the 3rd of the chord. Similarly, if we play the D Major Pentatonic scale, D–E–F♯–A–B, over the D chord, it contains all the chord tones.

Perhaps the idea of changing scales over each chord sounds challenging, but it really isn't as difficult as it might seem. Looking again at the G Major pentatonic scale, it contains the following notes: G–A–B–D–E. The C Major Pentatonic scale contains C–D–E–G–A. Only one note changed, the B note moved up a half step to C. The D Major Pentatonic scale contains D–E–F♯–A–B. Comparing it to the G Major pentatonic, again, only one note changed, the G moved down a half step to F♯. Having these chord tones available for these chords really sounds great.

Below is another sample solo over the chord progression for "Rolling Down That Lonesome Road Blues," this time changing scales over each chord. Many of the melodic ideas from the previous version have been used so you can hear the difference between the two approaches.

COMBINING MAJOR PENTATONIC, MINOR PENTATONIC, AND BLUES SCALES IN A SOLO

There is no magic formula to which pentatonic scale should be used to solo over a song. Try different scales over the same progression and see which you prefer. Each scale will yield a very different sound and feel. Sometimes, you'll notice that both approaches sound good, and, in fact, we can combine different scales into our solos. Before trying to combine multiple scales in a solo, spend a lot of time practicing each scale individually.

We will now discuss how to combine scales in a solo. First, compare major pentatonic, minor pentatonic, and blues scales in the key of C.

C Major Pentatonic	C(R)–D(2)–E(3)–G(5)–A(6)
C Minor Pentatonic	C(R)–E♭(♭3)–F(4)–G(5)–B♭(♭7)
C Blues	C(R)–E♭(♭3)–F(4)–G♭(♭5)–G(5)–B♭(♭7)

Combine all the notes, and the composite scale contains: C(R)–D(2)–E♭(♭3)–E(3)–F(4)–G♭(♭5)–G(5)–A(6)–B♭(♭7). Here it is in open position.

The Composite Scale

The composite scale isn't really that useful to play exactly as it is over a progression; rather, it is a way to understand what notes are available to you within the overlapping scales. One approach you can use is to create a melodic idea from one pentatonic scale, and then answer it with an idea in another scale. Here's an example, using C and F Major Pentatonic for the "call" during the first two measures, and C Minor Pentatonic for the "response" in the next two measures.

The Composite Scale Over I to IV

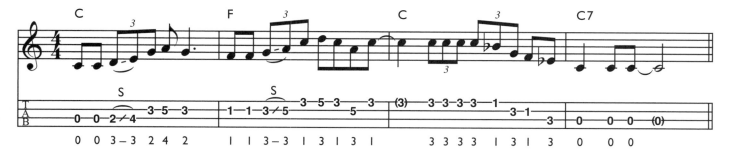

Below is a sample improvisation using our composite scale over the jazzy blues progression on page 136. A variation of the previous example is the basis for this solo. This solo is a variation of the previous example. We're Recycling!

The Composite Scale Over a Jazz Blues

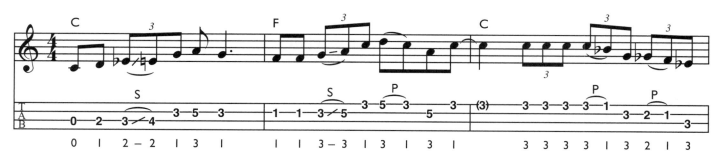

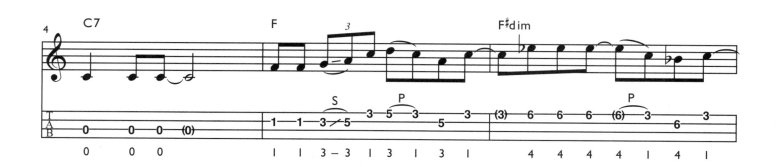

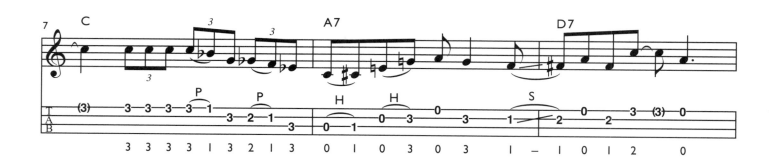

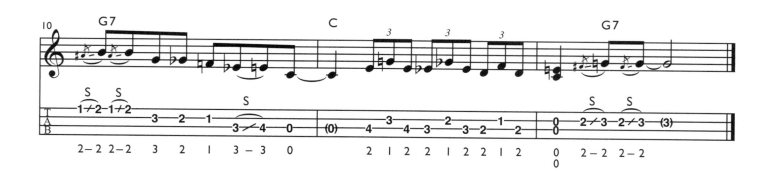

HOW TO DETERMINE THE KEY OF A SONG

Any song can be played in any key, but you'll find that it is easier for your voice if you choose the best key. Since everyone's voice is different, don't expect that your key will necessarily work for someone else.

Try this: Start strumming an F chord. Once you have the sound of it in your ear, begin singing "Oh Susanna!" If you're a male with an average voice or a female soprano, this key will probably be comfortable for you. You can then say "I sing 'Oh, Susanna!' in the key of F." If this key is too high or too low, try the next key on the list, the key of C. If neither key works, try the next key on the list. Find the key that doesn't strain your voice. (Since only a few songs are in a minor key, you may ignore the key of D minor for now.)

HOW TO PLAY AN ENTIRE SONG BY EAR

Once you've determined the key of the song, review the three magic chords you'll use. Let's say you're going to sing "Oh, Susanna!" in the key of F. The three magic chords are F, B♭ and C7.

Strum the I chord, F, and start singing until it seems a new chord is called for.

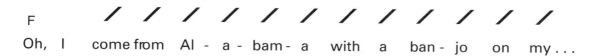

F

Oh, I   come from   Al - a - bam - a   with   a   ban - jo   on   my . . .

You can hear that on the word "knee" a new chord must be played. Try the IV chord in the key of F, the B♭ chord. Nope, that doesn't sound right. . . try the V7 chord. Yes, that does sound right:

C7

Knee,   and I'm . . .

On the word "goin'" we need another new chord. The IV, or B♭? No. How about going back to the I (the F)? Yes, that sounds right.

F   / / / / / / / / /   C7 /   F / / /

goin' to Lou'- si - an - na   for   my   true love (new chord) for to (new chord) see.

Now we get to use the IV chord or B♭.

B♭   / / / / / / /   F / / /   C7 / /

Oh,   Su - san - na   oh (newchord) don't you cry for (newchord) me.

See if you can work out the rest of it yourself.

Things to Remember

When working out a song by ear, keep these three major points in mind:

1. Most songs are in major keys. You know three possible major keys now: F, C and G. Try these first.

2. Folk songs and other simple songs almost always begin on the I chord. That is, a song in the key of F almost always begins on a F chord. A song in the key of C begins on a C chord, and so on.

3. Songs always end on the I chord.

HOW TO TRANSPOSE

Taking a song written in one key and playing it in another is called transposing. There are two important reasons why you might want to transpose a song.

1. It's written in a key that you don't know. If you buy collections of songs, you'll find that many of them will be in unfamiliar keys. To determine the key of a written song, look at the last chord in the song. If the last chord in the song is a G chord, the song is written in the key of G. That's fine, because you know the key of G. But what if the song is in B♭, or E♭ or A♭ or some other key that you don't know. What you do is transpose it to a key that you do know.

2. The song may be too high or too low for you to sing comfortably. Transposing the song into a more comfortable key will solve this problem.

The following chart will allow you to transpose from any key to any other key. Your main objective is to wind up in one of the three keys you know: F, C or G.

1	2	3	4	5	6
C	C♯/D♭	D	E♭	E	F
C♯/D♭	D	E♭	E	F	F♯/G♭
D	E♭	E	F	F♯/G♭	G
E♭	E	F	F♯/G♭	G	A♭
E	F	F♯/G♭	G	A♭	A
F	F♯/G♭	G	A♭	A	B♭
F♯/G♭	G	A♭	A	B♭	B
G	A♭	A	B♭	B	C
A♭	A	B♭	B	C	C♯/D♭
A	B♭	B	C	C♯/D♭	D
B♭	B	C	C♯/D♭	D	E♭
B	C	C♯/D♭	D	E♭	E

How to Use the Chart

1. Find the key the song is written in column 1. Let's say the song is in the unfamiliar key of D♭. Find D♭ in column 1.

2. Find the key you want to wind up in also in column 1. Let's say the key of G. You'll notice that G is six lines below D♭ in column 1.

3. Find the chords of the song in the D♭ row. Then replace them with the chords in the same column of the G row, exactly six lines below. For example, an G♭ chord would become a C chord. An A♭7 chord would become a D7 chord, and so on.

The chart can be used in this way to transpose from any key to any other key.

7	8	9	10	11	12
F♯/G♭	G	A♭	A	B♭	B
G	A♭	A	B♭	B	C
A♭	A	B♭	B	C	C♯/D♭
A	B♭	B	C	C♯/D♭	D
B♭	B	C	C♯/D♭	D	E♭
B	C	C♯/D♭	D	E♭	E
C	C♯D♭	D	E♭	E	F
C♯/D♭	D	E♭	E	F	F♯/G♭
D	E♭	E	F	F♯/G♭	G
E♭	E	F	F♯/G♭	G	A♭
E	F	F♯/G♭	G	A♭	A
F	F♯/G♭	G	A♭	A	B♭

HOW TO PLAY BY EAR
USING THREE MAGIC CHORDS

There are thousands of folk songs, country songs, early rock 'n' roll songs and blues songs that can be played using only three simple chords. Musicians call these the I (one), IV (four) and V7 (five-seven) chords. You already know all of these chords:

Key	I Chord	IV Chord	V7 Chord
F	F	B♭	C7
C	C	F	G7
G	G	C	D7
D minor	Dm	Gm	A7

As you can see, each key has a family of three chords which can be used to accompany many songs in that key.

You can review all of these chords in the Ukulele Chord Encyclopedia on pages 176–223.

PART 3: BEING A PROFESSIONAL UKULELIST PLAYER

Playing the ukulele in a band is fun and rewarding. Having acquired the skills and knowledge offered in this book so far, you are probably ready to play in a band. This section of the book provides tips on starting or joining a band, preparing for an audition, rehearsing and gigging. You'll also learn how to promote yourself, and even how to practice more effectively. Finally, you'll gain some insights into the music business, discover how to protect your interests and eventually get a recording contract. Let's get started.

FINDING, REHEARSING AND PROMOTING A BAND

HOW TO TELL IF YOU'RE READY TO PLAY IN A BAND

If you can play over a dozen songs from beginning to end without many mistakes and without losing the beat, then you are ready to play in a band. For a band to play live, they need to know at least a dozen songs.

HOW TO START A BAND

There are a number of ways to find other musicians to play with. One way is to ask an instructor if he or she has any students who might want to get together with you. Most instructors want to help their students find other people to play with, and they may already know who to suggest. This method can help you find other ukuleleists as well as bass players, drummers, keyboard players and any other kind of musician.

Another way to find musicians to play with is to put up an ad at your local music store. Make it brief and to the point, saying what type of players you are looking for. You can put the same ad in your local paper or classified Website. Many classified sections will charge nothing for this service.

HOW TO FIND AND GET INTO AN EXISTING BAND

It's a good idea to talk to people that you know in the music business and ask if they know of a band that is looking for a ukulelist. If they're not aware of any at the time, ask if they can keep you in mind and recommend you, or at least, let you know the next time they hear of an opening. You can make a personal webpage which tells about your experience, musical preferences, and equipment. Have business cards made which include your phone number, e-mail address and webpage address. Musicians tend to help each other, and hopefully someday you'll be in a position to return the favor.

Other ways of finding bands looking for a ukulelist are to look on bulletin boards in music stores and look in classified ads in newspapers and music magazines. You can also find bands that need ukulelists on the Internet. To access a number of musician referral services on the Internet, search: musician+referral service.

TIPS

HOW TO BE THE ONE EVERYONE WANTS IN THEIR BAND

1. **Show up at all rehearsals on time.** When it's time to start, have your ukulele already tuned, your amp set and be ready to go. This shows that you are enthusiastic about playing.

2. **Have your parts learned well.** Have the song arrangements memorized. Be ready to play the songs all the way through without making a lot of mistakes. Do as much preparation as possible outside of rehearsal.

3. **Have a good attitude.** Be enthusiastic about the group and about rehearsals. A positive attitude is contagious. If you're excited about playing, the other members will pick up on it and will become enthusiastic themselves.

4. **Be a team player.** Leave your ego outside the door. Keep in mind that everyone in the group is working towards a common goal. Have respect for the other members and their opinions.

5. **Help with the business of the band.** Do all you can to help with band promotion, getting gigs and keeping track of the finances. Remember that being in a band is being part of a business.

6. **When you're not playing a song, don't play.** Just turn your volume off. This rule applies to rehearsals, sound checks and performances. Don't play at all between songs. Playing between songs can be distracting and annoying to other members of the group and to the audience.

7. **Never tune your ukulele aloud**. Use a silent electronic tuner, one that cuts off the signal to your amp while you tune.

8. **Learn to sing**. Finding players who can sing is a big challenge for many bands. Knowing how to sing, even a little, can be the difference between you and the other guy getting the job.

YOUR PERSONAL PROMOTIONAL PACK

In order to join almost any established band, you will need to try to get an audition with that band. In order to get an audition, you may need to have your own *promo pack*.

WHAT YOUR PROMO PACK SHOULD INCLUDE

Your promo pack should contain:

- A photograph of yourself,

- A recording that has two or three minutes of your best playing,

- A biography that tells about your experience.

Make your promo pack as professional-looking as possible by having a good photographer take your picture, and have it enlarged into an 8x10 glossy. The recording should be one with songs that you have recorded in the studio and include parts of any songs that best demonstrate your abilities. If you can play in some different styles, be sure to include them on your recording. Versatility is always good.

If you haven't been in the studio, record yourself playing something at home that you can play well and shows your ability. Remember, most bands are looking for a player who can play solid rhythm ukulele as well as lead, so be sure to put something on your tape that shows you can play solid rhythm and not just solos. If there is a specific group for which you would like to audition, think of the kind of ukulelist that they may be looking for and make a tape especially for that group.

HOW TO PREPARE FOR AN AUDITION

Learning to audition well can be a huge asset to your musical career. A successful band will have several ukulelists competing for the position. Here are some tips that could make the difference between you getting the job and someone else getting it:

1. **Be well prepared.** When preparing for an audition, spend every spare minute learning the songs that you'll play at the audition. Play the songs over and over until you can play them in your sleep.

2. **Learn as much of the band's material as possible.** *Extra effort shows a good attitude and can be the reason that you are hired.* Show the band that if they were to hire you, you would be ready to start playing shows with only one or two rehearsals. In most cases, there will only be time for one or two rehearsals, so a successful band will need to work you in as quickly as possible.

3. **Your attitude can be as important as your playing.** The band will want to hire someone with a positive attitude, who is enthusiastic about the band and their music. When a band is looking for someone to hire, they know that they are going to be dealing with that person on a daily basis. Leave your ego at home when you are auditioning. If you are willing to relocate, be sure to tell them this. This can be a major factor in the decision of whether or not to hire you. The bottom line at an audition is that most of the time the person who gets the job is the person who wants it the most—the person with the "whatever it takes" attitude. Not all successful bands are looking for a jaded pro who has "been there, done that." A good attitude can compensate for lack of experience. Most bands are looking for members who are hungry for success. So, don't worry if you haven't played a thousand live shows or been on lots of albums. Despite your lack of experience, you could still be exactly the person they are looking for.

Good luck!

WHAT YOU MAY BE ASKED TO PLAY AT AN AUDITION

At most auditions, you will be asked to play some of the band's material. You may or may not be told ahead of time which songs you will play. You may be given a few minutes with a recording of a song to see how well you can learn it in a short period of time. It's likely that you'll be asked to play some of your own material as well, so have a few things prepared that you think will fit with the style of the band. The band may be interested in your songwriting style as well as your playing ability and attitude.

EQUIPMENT TO BRING TO AN AUDITION

Bring a spare ukulele to the audition. This way, if you should happen to break a string, everyone won't have to wait while you change it; you can just pick up your spare. Also bring a spare ukulele cable, an extension chord and a *ground lift* (an adapter that allows you to plug a three-prong plug into a two-prong outlet). By bringing the extension chord and ground lift, you know you'll be able to plug in your amp, which is a problem you don't want to have to deal with at the start of an audition. Change your strings the day before and make sure that all of your cables work. Before your audition, make sure that all of your equipment is in good working order. This is another way to show your professionalism.

REHEARSING AND IMPROVING THE BAND
REHEARSAL LOCATION

You can rehearse just about any place where you can play loudly without disturbing the neighbors. The ideal situation is one where you can leave your equipment set up and just walk in and start playing. If you can't rehearse at someone's house, check the phone book to find a rehearsal facility near you. Rehearsal facilities charge by the hour, by the day or by the month. A good way to save some money is to share the rehearsal space with another band and split the rent.

PHOTO • JOE BIELAWA

Jake Shimbukuro—This highly skilled ukulele player became famous in 2006 when a friend posted a video of his performance of "While My Guitar Gently Weeps" on YouTube. It quickly became one of the most-watched viral videos and kicked off his career as a performing artist and composer.

TIPS FOR MAKING REHEARSALS MORE PRODUCTIVE

1. **Have an agenda.** Decide on the songs to be rehearsed a few days before the rehearsal. Make sure that everyone has recordings of all relevant material.

2. **Don't be afraid to stop a song if there is a problem.** Go over the problem part a few times if necessary. Make sure everyone is clear on exactly how that part should go.

3. **Don't beat a song into the ground by playing it over and over.** After playing a song more than a few times, it becomes easy to lose your focus. It is more productive to move on, even if you haven't perfected the song yet. Then, come back to it after a while. This keeps rehearsals productive and also keeps the band from burning out on a song.

4. **Record your rehearsals.** Then listen to the recording and try to find which parts need more work. Do this as a group, if possible. This can be as productive as actual rehearsal because the band can discuss how to fix any weak spots. It can be easier to hear the weak spots while listening to a recording than to hear them when the band is playing. It's also much easier to stop the recording than it is to stop the band in the middle of a song to make a comment.

5. **Be sure that all song intros and endings are solid.** The audience may or may not hear a mistake made during the song, but a mistake in the very beginning or at the very end of the song will be the most noticeable.

6. **Band Members Only at Rehearsal.** The only people who should be at a rehearsal are the members of the band. Your rehearsals will be much more productive this way, because when there is even one other person in the room, the rehearsal becomes a performance. Constructive criticism between members becomes more difficult because no one wants to be corrected or criticized in front of an audience.

People outside the band will always want to watch you rehearse. Politely tell them that your band's rehearsals are "closed." Once you have the entire show together, an open rehearsal with some invited friends can be a good opportunity to try out a live show on an audience. An open rehearsal is more of a performance than a rehearsal and should only be done when the band feels like they are ready to perform.

7. **Controlling Dynamics.** Dynamics refers to varying the degrees of volume. One mark of a good ukulelist is the ability to know when to get louder or softer. Dynamics can be controlled in several ways. One is by the use of a volume pedal, and another is by how hard or soft one hits the strings. Also, the use of palm muting (laying the right side of your right palm gently across the strings near the bridge) is an effective way to control dynamics.

8. **A Good Way to Get Your Band Members Motivated** Book a gig. Having a show coming up will give everyone in the band something to anticipate and work toward. However, be sure that the band has enough time to prepare for it.

HOW LONG TO REHEARSE BEFORE YOU PLAY YOUR FIRST GIG

Before you play your first gig, you should have rehearsed the songs until you are just starting to get bored playing them. If you know a song well enough to be bored playing it, then you know it well enough to play it live. The band will probably be somewhat nervous during its first performance. The more automatic the songs are, the less chances there are of making mistakes due to nerves.

GETTING READY FOR THE GIG

The more prepared you are for a show, the more fun you'll have. You will be able to focus on enjoying yourself as well as focusing on what you are playing. You will always play your best when you don't have to think about what you're playing.

TIPS

HOW TO GET GIGS FOR YOUR BAND
THE BAND'S PROMO PACK

In order for your band to get gigs you will need to have a promo pack. The band's promo pack should contain:

1. **A CD or tape of the band.** If your band has a CD, include one in your promo pack. If it doesn't, record three of your best songs and include the recording in your promo pack. Club owners won't want to spend a lot of time listening to your demo so three songs will be plenty.

2. **A photo of the band.** You can either get creative here or have a simple photo of the band. If you choose to get creative, be sure that the photo reflects the style of music that you play.

3. **A brief history of the band, including:**

   A. A description of the style of music that the band plays

   B. The names of the band members and what instrument they play

   C. A list of songs that the band plays

   D. A list of places that the band has played before

   E. Anything interesting about the band

4. **Any newspaper articles, reviews or press about the band.**

   Good press or reviews about the band are a great addition to a promo pack. Photocopy any articles or pictures and include the name and date of the newspaper or magazine in which they appeared.

5. **The name and number of the businessperson for the band.** For example, "for booking and information, contact John Smith at (555) 555-5555." *Be sure that this number is given in several places in the promo pack*, especially on the recording package and on the photo. In case parts of the kit get separated, they will still be able to contact you. You will need to have an answering machine for your contact number so that the person who may want to book your band can leave a message. Remember that your promo pack reflects your band and its professionalism.

HOW TO USE A PROMO PACK

Give copies of your promo pack to the managers of clubs or other places that your band could play. It's also a good idea to give copies to booking agents because a good booking agent will be able to find you more gigs than you would be able to find on your own. The booking agent will charge a fee for each gig that he or she books. This may be a flat fee or a percentage of what the band is paid. You should also give copies of your promo pack to magazines and newspapers; they may want to do a review or a story on your band.

THE GIG

HOW TO GET READY BACKSTAGE

Here's a routine that will help you warm-up and get in the right frame of mind to perform. Start with stretching until you feel limber. Then start warming up on your ukulele. Play chords, licks and scales, starting slowly and gradually speeding up until your hands feel loose and ready to go. Don't go overboard, though. You could fatigue your hands before the show, which defeats the purpose of warming up. You may be nervous before a performance. Deep breathing and stretching exercises can be helpful for overcoming pre-performance jitters.

WORDS TO KEEP IN MIND TO HELP GIVE YOUR BEST PERFORMANCE

Instead of thinking, "let me *impress* the audience," think, "let me *entertain* the audience." Your main jobs when you're performing live are to have fun and entertain the audience. If you are having fun and are playing like there's no place you'd rather be than on stage, your audience will pick up on that attitude and enjoy watching you play.

WHAT TO DO IF YOU MAKE A MISTAKE

There are two kinds of mistakes: arrangement mistakes and playing mistakes. An arrangement mistake is when a player forgets how the song is supposed to go and, for example, plays the wrong section of the song at the wrong time. Arrangement mistakes are usually more noticeable and are a sign that the song still needs some work. If you know your songs well, you shouldn't be making these kinds of errors.

A playing mistake is when a player plays the wrong note or chord. These mistakes are a basic part of life—even the best players make them from time to time—and are usually easy to cover up. However, if you are making more than one playing mistake every few songs, you may want to practice your parts on your own, just to refresh them.

If you make a mistake when you're performing, just relax and jump back into the song. Try not to make a face or do anything that would let the audience know that you made a mistake. Chances are, unless the mistake is really obvious, no one will even notice. Don't dwell on the mistake, just continue in the song as if it never happened. Thinking about a mistake after you make it will only distract you and cause you to make even more mistakes.

HOW TO MAKE YOUR MISTAKES LESS NOTICEABLE

It's normal to make mistakes, but one thing you can do to make your mistakes less obvious is to play right through them. The way to practice this is to pretend you are performing. Play the song from start to finish and play right through any mistakes you might make. When you are playing by yourself, you may be tempted to stop when you make a mistake. Try to resist this temptation. The golden rule of performing is this: *No matter what happens, don't stop during the song.* When you are practicing a song from start to finish, follow this rule just as you would during a performance.

PRACTICE PLAYING THE SONGS WITHOUT LOOKING

The less you look at your ukulele, the more eye contact you can have with the audience. Playing the songs without looking shows that you have confidence in what you are doing. However, there are certain times when you should look at your ukulele. For example, when you are shifting from one part of the fretboard to another, it is better to watch where you are going than to make the jump without looking, which could cause you to land on the wrong fret. After you practice without looking for a while, you'll start to get a feel for where the notes are on the fretboard.

PHOTO • Ian Whitcomb

DID YOU KNOW?

Ian Whitcomb—As part of the British Invasion, Whitcomb's song "You Turn Me On" reach number 8 on the Billboard charts in 1965. Since then, he has helped stimulate the current revival of the ukulele through his songwriting and soundtrack work.

GET BETTER, SOONER

GETTING WARMED UP

One of the most important parts of a practice session is the warm-up. Playing vigorously without warming up can cause injury. Just as an athlete warms up before a strenuous workout, we must warm-up our fingers before strenuous playing.

To warm up properly, all of the muscle groups you use to play should be warmed-up slowly. Different muscle groups are used to play different things. For example, we use different muscles on the fretting hand for bending strings than for playing chords. Each of these different groups of muscles must be warmed up.

The key words for warming up are *slow* and *easy*. Let your hands gradually stretch out and get your circulation going. Start slowly and gradually increase the intensity of your playing. Starting slowly has two benefits. The first is that it allows your muscles to warm-up gradually. The second is that it will keep you relaxed. Tight muscles are enemies of speed and accuracy.

Your warm-up routine could start with scales or picking exercises, then move to string bending and licks and finish with strumming. Warming up usually takes between ten and fifteen minutes but can vary depending on how often you play. The longer the periods of time between practice sessions, the longer (and slower) your warm-ups should be.

TIPS

PRACTICING
SETTING-UP YOUR PRACTICE AREA

The best place to practice is someplace where you won't be disturbed. Your practice area should be a place where you can get away from the rest of the world and have "your time." If you are lucky, you'll have a place where you can leave all of your materials ready to use. Even a small corner of a room will do.

WHAT YOU'LL NEED IN YOUR PRACTICE AREA

When you're getting ready to play, have everything that you might need within reach. This way you won't have to interrupt your train of thought just to get up and get something you need. Here are some things to keep handy in your practice area:

1. Recording media (tapes, CDRs, whatever you use)
2. Recording device
3. Playback device (CD player, tape player, etc.)
4. Metronome or drum machine
5. Picks
6. Blank fretboard charts
7. Pencil with eraser
8. Any books or magazines that you want to work with
9. Tuner
10. Spare set of strings and a peg winder (in case you break a string)
11. Something to drink

WHAT AND HOW MUCH TO PRACTICE

When you are deciding what to practice, consider both long-term and short-term goals as a player. Your short-term goal may be to learn a song that you like or to master a new technique. Your long-term goals may range from playing for a few friends to becoming a successful recording artist. Whatever your goals are, and they may change often, try to select areas of study that will help you reach your goals. If one of your goals is to become a well-rounded player, it is important to vary your areas of study and not work on the same things during each practice session. Here is a short list of things to consider:

GIVE IT A TRY

Arpeggios	Note naming
Bending and vibrato	Phrasing
Chords	Playing songs from a songbook
Ear training	Practicing songs that you know Scales
Improvising	Songwriting
Lead ukulele	Technique exercises
Learning new songs	Timing and rhythm
New chords	

Before you start practicing, try choosing three or four different areas that you would like to work on that day. Once you have selected them, make a list. Put them in order, starting with the area that you feel you need to focus on the most. You could even date the list, so that you can keep track of the areas you have been working on.

Keeping areas of study listed in order of priority will keep you from always playing the same things when you pick up your ukulele. It will also keep you focused on your goals. As you start to get bored with your work in one area, you can refer to your list and know exactly which area to focus on next.

When you finish working on the last area, go back to the first. Continue this cycle until your practice session is over. If you don't get a chance to work on all of your selected areas one day, you may want to pick up where you left off during your next practice session. Make the last area you were working on the first during the next practice session.

MAKE PRACTICE A HABIT

In order to improve quickly, make practice a habit. If possible, practice at the same time each day. This is important for two reasons. The first is that things are easier to start if they are a habit. This is because you don't have to plan to do them. You just do them. For example, you don't have to plan to brush your teeth at night. You just do it. If you can make picking up your ukulele each day as automatic as brushing your teeth, you are bound to improve more quickly. The second reason is that if you play at the same time each day, you'll get into a groove where your schedule begins to form around this time. People will begin to know to leave you alone at that time of day.

HOW TO TELL IF YOU'RE IMPROVING

A good way to gauge your progress is to record yourself playing, write the date on the recording and then put it away for a few months. By making recordings every couple of months, you can listen back and objectively gauge your progress. Improvement comes slowly and it can be hard to tell when or how much you are improving. Ironically, the more you play, the harder it is to tell if you are improving. Just as it can be hard to notice when someone you see every day grows an inch over the course of a year, it can be difficult to notice improvement over less than a few months.

HOW MUCH YOU NEED TO PRACTICE TO BE A PRO

Most professional ukulelists go through a time when they practice several hours a day. If you would like to make a living playing ukulele, plan to practice around twenty hours a week, or more. Around three hours a day is a good goal. Some days you'll have more time to play than others. But, if you want to play professionally, you'll want to make playing and practicing a high priority.

HOW MUCH PRACTICE IS TOO MUCH

You are practicing too much when other parts of your life start to be neglected. No matter how badly you want to become a great ukulelist, you also need to have a life outside of the ukulele. Playing the ukulele can become an addiction. It can start to control your life instead of being a fun thing to do. Taking a day off every once in a while can actually be good for your playing.

In extreme cases, too much practice can even bring on repetitive stress injuries. If you are practicing several hours a day on a regular basis, then you need to be aware of repetitive stress injuries such as *tendonitis*. These injuries are often due to excess tension and strenuous playing without a proper warm-up.

HOW OFTEN YOU SHOULD PRACTICE

The more often you practice, the faster you'll improve. Try to pick up your ukulele at least once a day, five or six days a week, even if you only play for a few minutes. You'll find that the more you play, the more you want to play.

ELIMINATING FRUSTRATION

As soon as you begin to feel yourself becoming frustrated when practicing, try taking a few slow, deep breaths. This will help relieve frustration and help you concentrate.

Usually, that feeling of frustration comes from trying to learn too much at once. You have "bitten off more than you can chew." When you feel yourself getting frustrated, slow down a little and work on a smaller amount of material (take a smaller bite). Play that smaller piece until you can play it easily, then take another small piece and do the same thing. This will give you the sense of accomplishment that makes it fun to learn new things.

AVOID NEGATIVE THOUGHTS

Sometimes, when you are trying to learn something new and are having difficulty, there will be a negative thought going through the back of your mind saying, "This isn't that difficult, why can't you do this yet, what's the matter with you?" Everyone has this thought at one time or another.

Do your best to ignore this thought, and remember that listening to it will do nothing but add to your frustration. Negative thoughts will make you try to learn things too quickly and may even cause you to believe that you have something learned before you do. This may cause you to move on to something new before you're ready. It takes a conscious effort to ignore these negative thoughts and go ahead and learn at a comfortable, non-frustrating pace.

When you are working on something new, listen for this kind of thought and when you hear it, realize that it is your enemy. When you can do this successfully, learning and practicing will be less frustrating, more fun and more productive.

THE IMPORTANCE OF REVIEW

Reviewing what you have learned is an important part of learning to play. Each new thing that you learn builds on what you have learned in the past. Reviewing makes you more able to use the things you've learned by keeping them fresh in your mind. It speeds up the learning process. It will save you from spending time re-learning things. Every month, devote a day or two of practice to review what you've learned in the past few months.

PRACTICE STANDING UP

If you are a performer or you would like to be, it is a good idea to make your practice situation as close as possible to an actual performance. If you plan to perform standing up, then you should practice standing up. Playing the ukulele can feel a lot different when standing and if your seated position is less than perfect, your hands may be at a different angle than when sitting down.

WHY MANY SHORT PRACTICE SESSIONS ARE BETTER THAN A FEW LONG SESSIONS

You can learn more in a short, intense session than you can in a long, unfocused one. Your mind likes to learn things in small bits. When you're learning something new, it helps to learn in short sessions so that you can maintain a high concentration level.

Some days you will have more time to play than others. On days when time is limited, use the time to learn something new. Learn a new scale or chord, or a short, new part of a song. Then use the days when you have more time to polish the things you have learned. Repeat them until they become comfortable for you.

GETTING OUT OF A RUT

Every player, at one point or another, gets into a rut. We find ourselves playing the same old things each time we pick up the ukulele and our playing becomes stale.

The fastest way to get out of a rut is to play even more than usual. Also, try not to play any of your usual songs, licks or riffs for a week. If you tend to often play in one certain key, avoid this key completely for a week and instead play in other, less familiar keys. Each day, make it a point to learn a new song (or even part of one), or a scale or riff. Then record the new thing that you've learned and review what you've recorded the next day. Continue this until you're out of your rut.

MOTIVATION

The best way to get motivated to play is to plan a performance. The performance can be for a few friends or family members, or a larger group of people. The desire to perform well can be extremely inspiring and tends to bring a new focus and sense of urgency to your practicing. This focus can be great for your playing, especially if you feel like your playing is in a rut.

DID YOU KNOW?

Jimmy Buffet—Buffet is an American singer/ songwriter, author, actor, and businessman. His hit song "Margaritaville" is ranked number 234 on the Recording Industry Association of America's list of Songs of the Century. His beach-bum persona and island-themed songs evoke the relaxing sound of the ukulele.

PHOTO • Pamela Jones Photography, Shot at Tap Tap Haitian Restaurant in Miami Beach, FL

A FEW THINGS YOU NEED TO KNOW ABOUT THE MUSIC BIZ

GETTING WHAT'S COMING TO YOU
HOW TO COPYRIGHT A SONG YOU'VE WRITTEN

Once you have written a song and recorded it on tape, you automatically own the *copyright* to that song. This means that you alone have the right to make copies of the song and sell them. In order to protect that right, it is a good idea to have your song registered with the Copyright Office of the Library of Congress. Once your song is registered, you can prove in court that the song is yours (should anyone try to steal it).

To have your song registered, you'll need to visit this Website:

http://www.copyright.gov/

Navigate to "Forms" and download the forms, or go to "Electronic Copyright Office" (eCO), where you can register online.

The Copyright Office contact information, as of this writing, is as follows:

U.S. Copyright Office

101 Independence Ave. S.E.

Washington, D.C. 20559-6000

(202) 707-3000

There is a charge each time you register, but, you can register more than one song at a time. If you register more than one song at a time, the recording you send in will need to have a name, such as "Collection of Songs."

HOW YOU GET PAID WHEN YOUR SONG
GETS PLAYED ON THE RADIO

Technically, each time your song is played on the radio, on TV or anywhere else considered to be in public, you should be paid a fee. Because it would be impossible for you to keep track of each time your song is played and to collect the fee, there are agencies that do this for you. These agencies are called "performing rights collecting organizations." Their job is to monitor radio stations, TV stations and other places where songs are played for the public and pay you the fee for each time your song is played. The size of this fee depends on where your song is played. A hit song played all over the country can make the writer rich on performance royalties alone. The two main performing rights collecting organizations are ASCAP, which stands for the "American Society of Composers, Authors and Publishers" and BMI, which stands for "Broadcast Music Incorporated." To join either ASCAP or BMI, go to their Websites, or write them a letter requesting an application.

To contact ASCAP, write to: ASCAP, 1 Lincoln Plaza, New York, NY 10023 or see

www.ascap.com.

To contact BMI, write to: BMI, 320 West 57th Street New York, NY 10019 or see

www.bmi.com.

WHY YOU DON'T HAVE TO PAY WHEN YOUR BAND
PLAYS ANOTHER BAND'S MUSIC

Club owners and promoters pay a "blanket fee" to the performing rights collecting organizations. This fee covers all of the performance royalties for the music performed in their venue.

CAREER TIPS
WHERE YOU SHOULD LIVE

To become a pro, it will help to live in or near a major music city. Some cities that are known for their music scene are: New York, NY; Los Angeles, CA; Nashville, TN; and Austin, TX. There are many cases of bands making it out of small towns, but most successful bands are based in cities with thriving music scenes. There are several reasons for this. One is that major music cities have more places for bands to play. Another is that most music industry companies are in major cities.

NETWORKING AND HOW IT CAN HELP YOUR CAREER

Networking is the process of making contacts within the music industry. To a certain extent, the old saying, "it's not what you know but who you know" can be true. Who you know can play a large part in your success as a musician. Well-connected people have made a science out of networking. They know that the people who are on their way up are the people who make the best contacts.

Keep an eye out for energetic, ambitious people who are moving up in the industry. These are the people who will end up in high positions later on. You never know where someone will end up. A person interning at a record label could someday be the president of that label. The person who will be the most likely to help your career is a person that you have known for some time. The ideal contact is one who you knew when they were first starting out and have kept in touch with over time.

GETTING A RECORD CONTRACT

There are several different ways to get a record contract. To understand how to get a record contract, it will help to understand how a record company works.

A record company is basically a bank that lends artists money and is paid back through record sales. After the record company *recoups* (makes back all of the money that they spent on recording, promotion and tour support) the remaining money made from record sales is divided between the record company and the band.

The person at the record company that "signs" a band is called an "A&R" person (artists and relations). The A&R people take a big chance when they sign a band because they could end up losing their job if the band is not successful.

One way to get a record contract is to record an album yourself, sell as many copies as possible and build up a following by playing live and promoting your band. A record company is more likely to sign a band that has already proven itself by building up a fan base and selling albums on its own.

Another way to get a record deal is to make a demo of a few of your band's best songs and send it to an A&R person at a record company. If the A&R person hears the demo and thinks your band just may be the next big thing, he or she will want to see the band play live. The catch here is that the A&R person is unlikely to take the time to listen to your demo, unless they have already heard about your band from a trusted source.

The way to get them to listen to your demo is to be recommended by an inside source. For more information on the music business, check out the book *This Business of Music: The Definitive Guide to the Music Industry,* by M. William Krasilovsky, et al.

PERFORMANCE CONTRACT

Here is a sample contract for a private party or wedding gig. You can use this as a template to create your own contract, adding or subtracting points as necessary. Anywhere you see text underlines, just replace it with your own information.

(Your name, address, phone number, fax number and e-mail address here)

Dear John Doe,

This contract will confirm our engagement to provide music for your wedding reception to be held on June 17 in the year 2010 beginning at 7:00 p.m. We will play the equivalent of 3 sets of 50 minutes each between the hours of 7:00 p.m. and 10:00 p.m. with two short breaks of 10 minutes each, during which we will provide recorded music. Our attire will be suits and our repertoire will consist of see attached list. The band consists of Steven Jones, keyboards; Bill Smith, ukulele; John Brown, bass; Thomas Miller, percussion.

As agreed, I will provide the following equipment: all musical equipment, PA system, recorded music during breaks.

You will provide the following equipment: sheltered playing area, electrical power.

Food and drink of the same quality provided to your guests will also be provided for the band [note here whether the band is to be fed free of charge, are subject to a cash bar, etc.]. It is to be made clear to the caterer and/or staff at the venue that the band members are to be treated as your guests. [These items are pertinent mainly if you are playing a gig at which is food is to be served. Note that if your band consists of more than eight people, it may be difficult to get the client to agree to a "free food" arrangement.]

Our fee for this engagement will be $800.00, which includes all transportation costs. To activate this agreement I must receive a nonrefundable deposit of $80.00 by June 3, 2010. The balance is to be paid to me immediately following the engagement. If overtime is required, and if other obligations do not prevent us from continuing our performance, the rate is $150.00 per half hour, or any fragment thereof.

In case of injury or illness, at my sole discretion I reserve the right to replace any member of my group to ensure the quality of performance you have requested. Please make sure that we are advised of any special song requests well in advance. If you have more than one special request, additional rehearsal costs will apply. Also, please make sure to provide us with adequate directions to the engagement at least two (2) weeks in advance.

Please sign and immediately return both copies of this agreement to me along with the deposit. I will countersign and immediately send one copy to you for your files. If the deposit is in the form of a check, please make it payable to Steven Jones.

If you should have any further questions, feel free to contact me via the information above.

Sincerely,

Steven Jones

Accepted by (X) _____ dated February 1, 2010

Address_____

Telephone _____ Email_____

CHANGING STRINGS

Strings break for various reasons and sometimes they just become old, so when you need new strings you need to know how to replace them. Changing strings is easier than you think. Follow the steps below and you shouldn't have any trouble. If you are more comfortable having someone else change the strings, bring your ukulele to your local music store.

Before you start, make sure you have everything you need to change strings. You will need a new set of strings, a pair of scissors, and a flat surface to place your ukulele while you work on it.

REMOVING OLD STRINGS

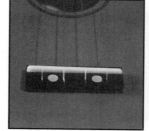

Standard Bridge   Tie-Bar Bridge

Step 1 Remove one of the old strings (start with the G string) by loosening the tuning peg until the string is loose enough for you to pull it gently off the headstock.

Step 2 Identify the type of bridge you have. The two most common bridges are the standard bridge and the tie-bar bridge.

Step 3 Standard Bridge: Pull the string gently towards the bottom of the ukulele and it should come free from the bridge. If the string is fitting tightly in the bridge, do not tug hard on the string to release it; be patient and continue to pull gently. The string will come loose and the bridge will not get damaged.

Tie-Bar Bridge: You will need to untie the string from the bridge by pushing the string towards the knot so it loosens. Once it is loose, pull the string through the bridge to remove it.

Before removing the other strings, replace the first string you removed by following the steps below.

ATTACHING NEW STRINGS

Step 1 Standard Bridge: Tie a knot at one end of the string, leaving about one inch of string from the knot to the end. Then tie a second not at the same place as the first knot so you now have a double knot. The knot will prevent the string from slipping out of the bridge when the ukulele is in tune. Place the knot under the bridge and pull the long end of the string towards the headstock. Pull with enough tension to make sure the knot will hold the string in place at the bridge.

Tie-Bar Bridge: Insert the string into the hole in the bridge so about two inches of string feed through towards the bottom of the ukulele. Loop the end of the string back over the bridge and around the string two or three times and finally pull the end of the string out the bottom so it tightens around the bridge (see photo above).

Wrap the strings from the inside of the headstock out.

Step 2 Attach the longer end of the string to the tuning pegs by passing the string completely through the hole with strings wrapping from the inside of the headstock out. Turn the tuners 3 (C) and 4 (G) so the strings are tightening counterclockwise, and strings 1 (A) and 2 (E) tighten clockwise (see photo to the right).

Step 3 Tune the string following the instructions on page 12. Since these are new strings, you will need to tune all the strings a few times before they stay in tune. Between tunings, stretch the strings gently away from the fretboard to help pull the strings into place and get them in tune faster.

Step 4 Once the ukulele is in tune, use scissors to trim off the excess string at the headstock and bridge.

Now go back to remove and attach the other three stings, one at a time.

PART 4: REFERENCE

CHORD THEORY: INTERVALS

Play any note on the ukulele, then play a note one fret above it. The distance between these two notes is a *half step*. Play another note followed by a note two frets above it. The distance between these two notes is a *whole step* (two half steps). The distance between any two notes is referred to as an *interval*.

A *scale* is a series notes in a specific arrangement of whole and half steps. In the example of the C major scale below, the letter names are shown above the notes and the *scale degrees* (numbers) of the notes are written below. Notice that C is the first degree of the scale, D is the second, etc.

The name of an interval is determined by counting the number of scale degrees from one note to the next. For example, an interval of a 3rd, starting on C, would be determined by counting up three scale degrees, or C–D–E (1–2–3). C to E is a 3rd. An interval of a 4th, starting on C, would be determined by counting up four scale degrees, or C–D–E–F (1–2–3–4). C to F is a 4th.

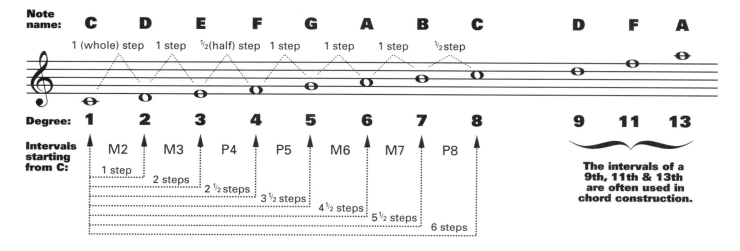

Intervals are not only labeled by the distance between scale degrees, but by the quality of the interval. An interval's quality is determined by counting the number of whole steps and half steps between the two notes of an interval. For example, C to E is a 3rd. C to E is also a major third because there are 2 whole steps between C and E. Likewise, C to E♭ is a 3rd. C to E♭ is also a minor third because there are 1½ steps between C and E♭. There are five qualities used to describe intervals: major, minor, perfect, diminished, and augmented.

M = Major   o = Diminished (dim)   m = Minor   + = Augmented (aug)   P = Perfect

Particular intervals are associated with certain qualities:

2nds, 9ths	=	Major, Minor & Augmented
3rds, 6ths, 13ths	=	Major, Minor, Augmented & Diminished
4ths, 5ths, 11ths	=	Perfect, Augmented & Diminished
7ths	=	Major, Minor & Diminished

When a *major* interval is made **smaller** by a half step it becomes a *minor* interval.

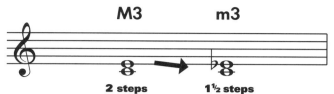

When a *minor* interval is made **larger** by a half step it becomes a *major* interval.

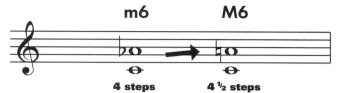

When a *minor* or *perfect* interval is made **smaller** by a half step it becomes a *diminished* interval.

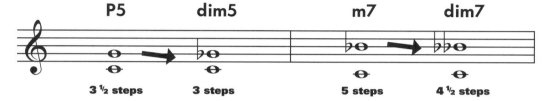

When a *major* or *perfect* interval is made **larger** by a half step it becomes an *augmented* interval.

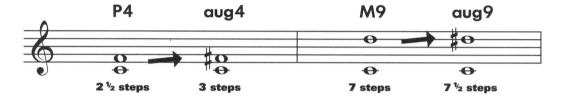

Below is a table of intervals starting on the note C. Notice that some intervals are labeled *enharmonic*, which means that they are written differently but sound the same (see **aug2** & **m3**).

TABLE OF INTERVALS

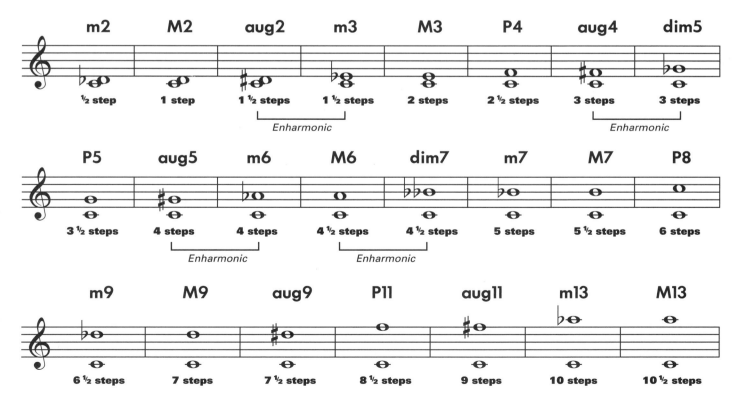

BASIC TRIADS

Two or more notes played together is called a *chord*. Most commonly, a chord will consist of three or more notes. A three-note chord is called a *triad*. The *root* of a triad (or any other chord) is the note from which a chord is constructed. The relationship of the intervals from the root to the other notes of a chord determines the chord *type*. Triads are most frequently identified as one of four chord types: *major, minor, diminished* and *augmented*.

All chord types can be identified by the intervals used to create the chord. For example, the C major triad is built beginning with C as the root, adding a major 3rd (E) and adding a perfect 5th (G). All major triads contain a root, M3 and P5.

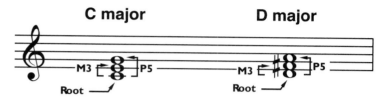

Minor triads contain a root, minor 3rd and perfect 5th. (An easier way to build a minor triad is to simply lower the 3rd of a major triad.) All minor triads contain a root, m3 and P5.

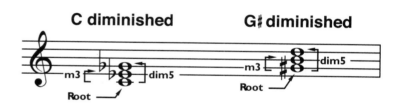

Diminished triads contain a root, minor 3rd and diminished 5th. If the perfect 5th of a minor triad is made smaller by a half step (to become a diminished 5th), the result is a diminished triad. All diminished triads contain a root, m3 and dim5.

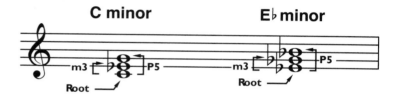

Augmented triads contain a root, major 3rd and augmented 5th. If the perfect 5th of a major triad is made larger by a half step (to become an augmented 5th), the result is an augmented triad. All augmented triads contain a root, M3 and aug5.

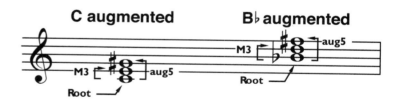

An important concept to remember about chords is that the bottom note of a chord will not always be the root. If the root of a triad, for instance, is moved above the 5th so that the 3rd is the bottom note of the chord, it is said to be in the *first inversion*. If the root and 3rd are moved above the 5th, the chord is in the *second inversion*. The number of inversions that a chord can have is related to the number of notes in the chord: a three-note chord can have two inversions, a four-note chord can have three inversions, etc.

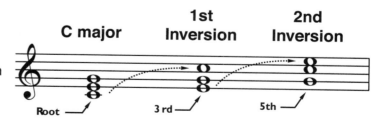

BUILDING CHORDS

By using the four chord types as basic building blocks, it is possible to create a variety of chords by adding 6ths, 7ths, 9ths, 11ths, etc. The following are examples of some of the many variations.

* The *suspended fourth* chord does not contain a third. An assumption is made that the 4th degree of the chord will harmonically be inclined to *resolve* to the 3rd degree. In other words, the 4th is *suspended* until it moves to the 3rd.

Up until now, the examples have shown intervals and chord construction based on C. Until you are familiar with all the chords, the C chord examples on the previous page can serve as a reference guide when building chords based on other notes: For instance, locate C7(♭9). To construct a G7(♭9) chord, first determine what intervals are contained in C7(♭9), then follow the steps outlined below.

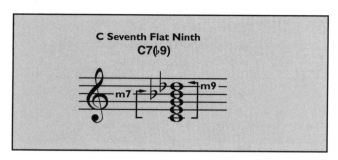

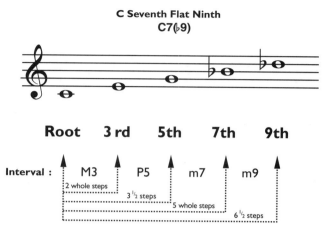

- Determine the *root* of the chord. A chord is always named for its root—in this case, G is the root of G7(♭9).

- Count *letter* names up from the *letter name of the root* (G), as we did when building intervals on page 168, to determine the intervals of the chord. Counting three letter names up from G to B (G–A–B, 1–2–3) is a 3rd, G to D (G–A–B–C–D) is a 5th, G to F is a 7th, and G to A is a 9th.

- Determine the *quality* of the intervals by counting whole steps and half steps up from the root; G to B (2 whole steps) is a major 3rd, G to D (3½ steps) is a perfect 5th, G to F (5 whole steps) is a minor 7th, and G to A♭ (6½ steps) is a minor 9th.

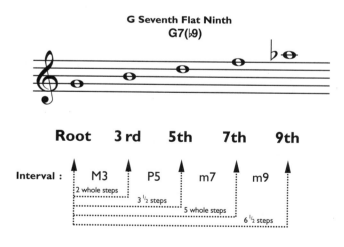

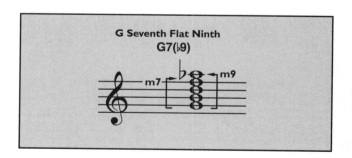

Follow this general guideline to figure out the notes of any chord. As interval and chord construction become more familiar, it will become possible to create your own original fingerings on the ukulele. Feel free to experiment!

INCOMPLETE VOICINGS

A *voicing* is an arrangement of the notes in a chord. Since your ukulele has only four strings, you can play only three- or four-note voicings, but it is not uncommon to omit the root from a voicing. In this book, a *rootless voicing* is indicated with a single asterisk (*) to the right of the chord diagram.

Sometimes, the 7th is omitted from an *extended chord*, which is a chord with tones that extend beyond the 7th, such as 9th, 11th, and 13th chords. In this book, extended chords with the 7th omitted are indicated with two asterisks (**) to the right of the chord diagram.

A NOTE ABOUT KEYS

The function of **Ukulele Chord Encyclopedia** (pages 176–223) is to provide access to fingerings of thousands of ukulele chords as well as introducing the fundamentals of chord construction. As the beginning ukulelist becomes accomplished in the recognition and construction of intervals and chords, the next natural step is to seek an understanding of the *function* of these chords within *keys* or *chord progressions*. Although it is not fundamental to playing chord changes, further study in harmony and chord progressions can only enrich the musical experience of the advancing ukulelist and is therefore highly recommended.

Ukulele Chord Encyclopedia is organized to provide the fingerings of chords in all keys. The *Circle of Fifths* below will help to clarify which chords are enharmonic equivalents (notes that sound alike but are spelled differently). The Circle of Fifths also serves as a quick reference guide to the relationship of the keys and how key signatures can be figured out in a logical manner. Clockwise movement (up a P5) provides all of the sharp keys by adding one sharp to the key signature progressively. Counter-clockwise (down a P5) provides the flat keys by adding one flat similarly.

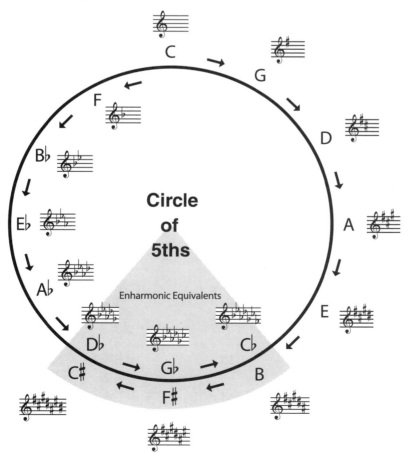

CHORD SYMBOL VARIATIONS

Chord symbols are a form of musical shorthand that give the ukulelist as much information about a chord as quickly as possible. Since chord symbols are not universally standardized, they are often written in many different ways—some are understandable, others are confusing. To illustrate this point, below is a listing of some of the ways copyists, composers and arrangers have created variations on the more common chord symbols.

C	Csus	C(♭5)	C(add9)	C5	Cm
C major	Csus4	C-5	C(9)	C(no3)	Cmin
Cmaj	C(addF)	C(5-)	C(add2)	C(omit3)	Cmi
CM	C4	C(♯4)	C(+9)		C-
			C(+D)		

C+	C°	C6	C6/9	Cm6/9	Cm6
C+5	Cdim	Cmaj6	C6(add9)	C-6/9	C-6
Caug	Cdim7	C(addA)	C6(addD)	Cm6(+9)	Cm(addA)
Caug5	C7dim	C(A)	C9(no7)	Cm6(add9)	Cm(+6)
C(♯5)			C9/6	Cm6(+D)	

C7	C7sus	Cm7	Cm7(♭5)	C7+	C7(♭5)
C(addB♭)	C7sus4	Cmi7	Cmi7-5	C7+5	C7-5
C7̵	Csus7	Cmin7	C-7(5-)	C7aug	C7(5-)
C(-7)	C7(+4)	C-7	C∅	C7aug5	C7̵-5
C(+7)		C7mi	C ½dim	C7(♯5)	C7(♯4)

Cmaj7	Cmaj7(♭5)	Cm(maj7)	C7(♭9)	C7(♯9)	C7+(♭9)
Cma7	Cmaj7(-5)	C-maj7	C7(-9)	C7(+9)	Caug7-9
C7̵	C7̵(-5)	C-7̵	C9♭	C9♯	C+7(♭9)
C△	C△(♭5)	Cmi7̵	C9-	C9+	C+9♭
C△7					C7+(-9)

Cm9	C9	C9+	C9(♭5)	Cmaj9	C9(♯11)
Cm7(9)	$C\frac{9}{7}$	C9(+5)	C9(-5)	C7̵(9)	C9(+11)
Cm7(+9)	C7add9	Caug9	$C7\frac{9}{-5}$	C7̵(+9)	C(♯11)
C-9	C7(addD)	C(♯9♯5)	C9(5♭)	C9(maj7)	C11+
Cmi7(9+)	C7(+9)	C+9		C9̵	C11♯

Cm9(maj7)	C11	Cm11	C13	C13(♭9)	C13($^{♭9}_{♭5}$)
C-9(♯7)	C9(11)	C-11	C9addA	C13(-9)	C13(-9-5)
C(-9)7̵	C9addF	Cm(♭11)	C9(6)	$C^{13}_{♭9}$	C(♭9♭5)addA
Cmi9(♯7)	C9+11	$Cmi7^{11}_{9}$	C7addA	C(♭9)addA	
	$C7\frac{9}{11}$	$C-7(^{9}_{11})$	C7+A		

CHORD FRAMES

Ukulele chord frames are diagrams that contain all the information necessary to play a particular chord. The fingerings, note names and position of the chord on the neck are all provided on the chord frame (see below). The photo at the right shows which finger number corresponds to which finger.

Choose chord positions that require the least motion from one chord to the next; select fingerings that are in approximately the same location on the ukulele neck. This will provide smoother and more comfortable transitions between chords in a progression.

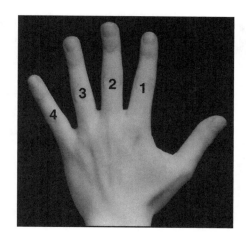

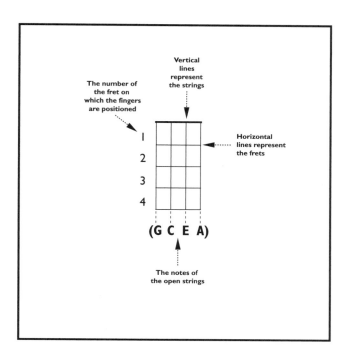

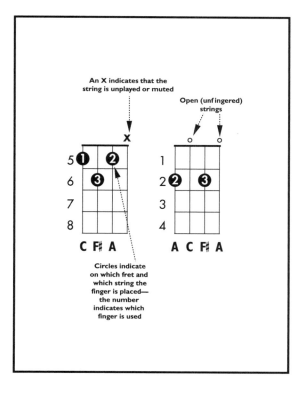

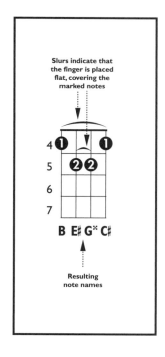

UKULELE CHORD ENCYCLOPEDIA

A♭

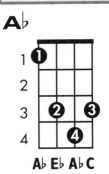

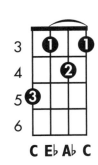

A♭ E♭ A♭ C

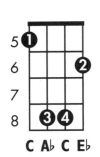

C E♭ A♭ C

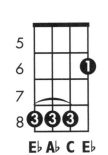

C A♭ C E♭

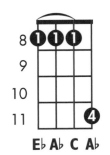

E♭ A♭ C E♭

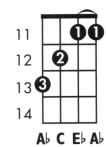

E♭ A♭ C A♭

A♭ C E♭ A♭

A♭m

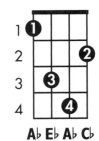

A♭ E♭ A♭ C♭

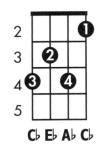

C♭ E♭ A♭ C♭

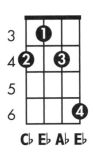

C♭ E♭ A♭ E♭

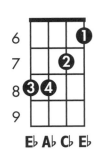

E♭ A♭ C♭ E♭

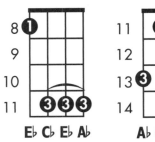

E♭ C♭ E♭ A♭

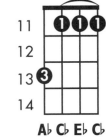

A♭ C♭ E♭ C♭

A♭°

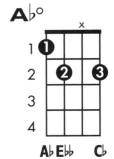

A♭ E♭♭ C♭

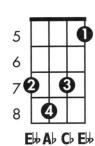

E♭♭ A♭ C♭ E♭♭

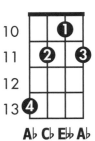

A♭ C♭ E♭♭ A♭

A♭+

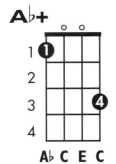

A♭ C E C

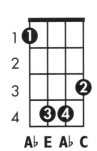

A♭ E A♭ C

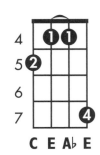

C E A♭ C

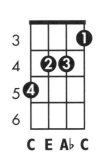

C E A♭ E

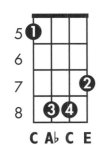

C A♭ C E

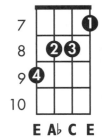

E A♭ C E

A♭5

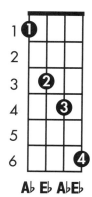

Ab Eb AbEb

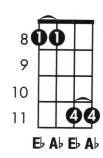

Eb Ab Eb Ab

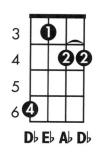

Ab Eb Eb Ab

A♭sus4

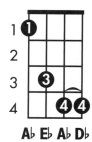

Ab Eb Ab Db

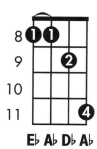

Db Eb Ab Db

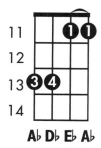

Eb Ab Db Ab

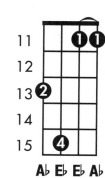

Ab Db Eb Ab

A♭6

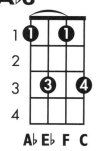

Ab Eb F C

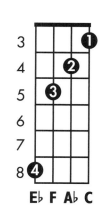

Eb F Ab C

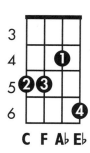

C F Ab Eb

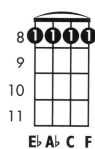

Eb Ab C F

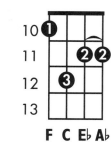

F C Eb Ab

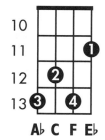

Ab C F Eb

A♭m6

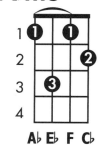

Ab Eb F Cb

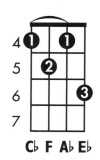

Cb F Ab Eb

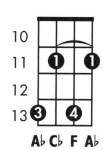

F Cb Eb Ab

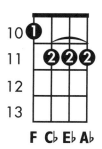

Ab Cb F Ab

A♭

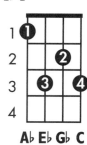

A♭7

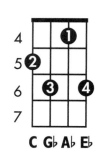

A♭ E♭ G♭ C   C G♭ A♭ E♭   E♭ A♭ C G♭   G♭ C E♭ A♭   A♭ C G♭ A♭

A♭maj7

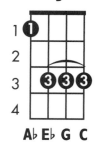

A♭ E♭ G C   C G A♭ E♭   E♭ A♭ C G   A♭ C E♭ G   G C E♭ A♭

A♭m7

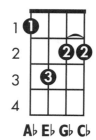

A♭ E♭ G♭ C♭   C♭ G♭ A♭ E♭   E♭ A♭ C♭ G♭   G♭ C♭ E♭ A♭   G♭ C♭ G♭ A♭

A♭m7(♭5)

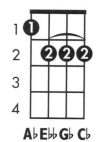

A♭ E♭♭ G♭ C♭   C♭ G♭ A♭ E♭♭   E♭♭ A♭ C♭ G♭   G♭ C♭ E♭♭ A♭

A♭°7

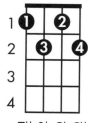

E♭♭ A♭ C♭ G♭♭

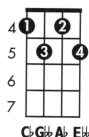

C♭ G♭♭ A♭ E♭

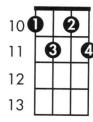

E♭♭ G♭♭ A♭ G♭♭

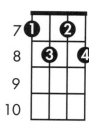

E♭♭ A♭ C♭ G♭♭

A♭(add9)

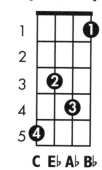

C E♭ A♭ B♭

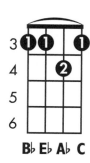

B♭ E♭ A♭ C

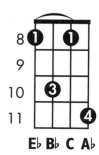

E♭ B♭ C A♭

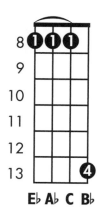

E♭ A♭ C B♭

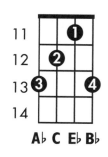

A♭ C E♭ B♭

A♭9

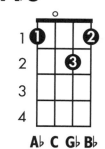

A♭ C G♭ B♭

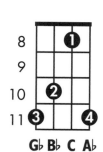

G♭ B♭ C A♭

A♭maj9

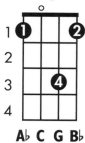

A♭ C G B♭

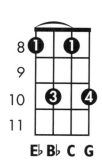

E♭ B♭ C G

A♭m9

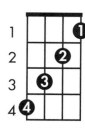

C♭ E♭ G♭ B♭

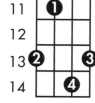

A♭ C♭ G♭ B♭

A♭7+

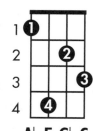

A♭ E G♭ C

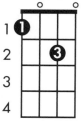

C G♭ A♭ E

A♭7(♭9)

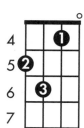

A♭ C G♭ B♭♭

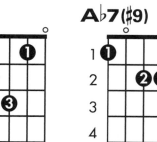

C G♭ A♭ B♭♭

A♭7(♯9)

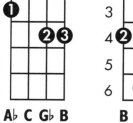

A♭ C G♭ B

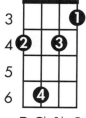

B G♭ A♭ C

A♭

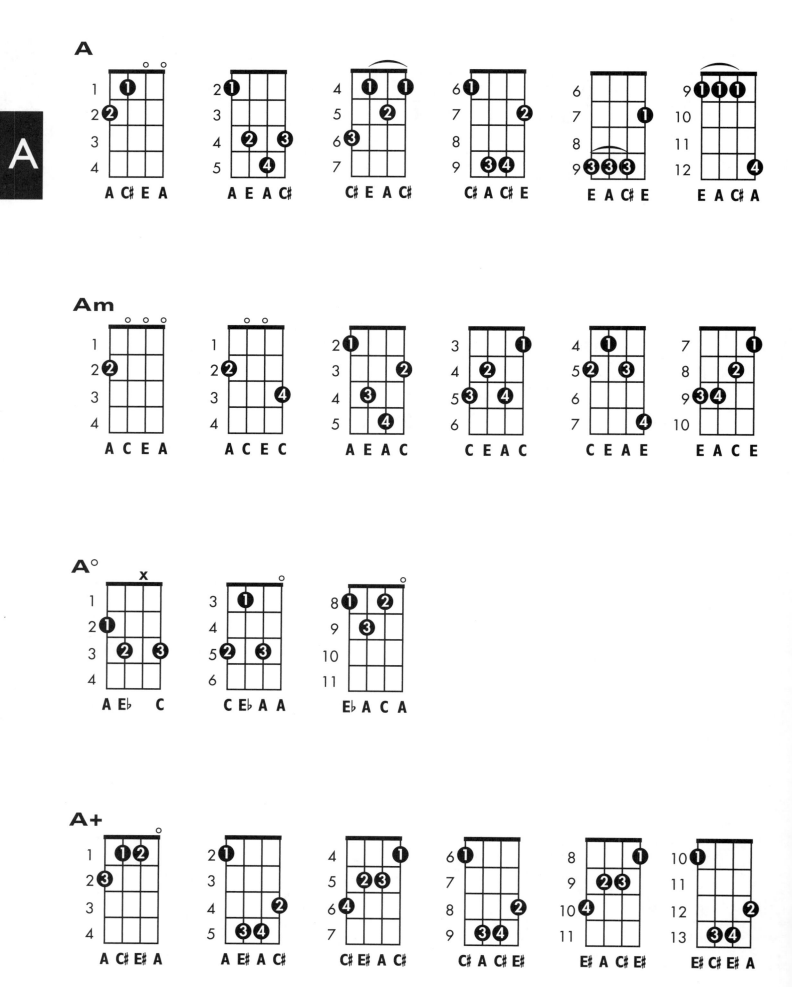

A5

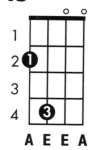

A E E A

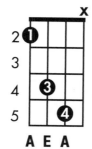

A E A

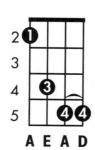

A E A E

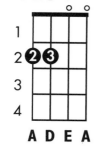

E A E A

A

Asus4

A D E A

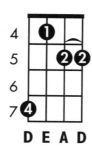

A E A D

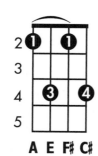

D E A D

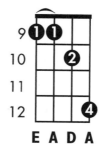

E A D A

A6

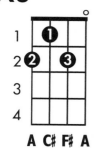

A C# F# A

A E F# C#

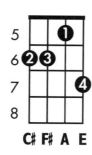

C# F# A E

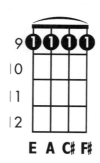

E A C# F#

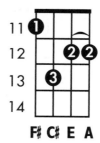

F# C# E A

Am6

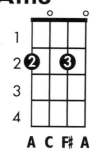

A C F# A

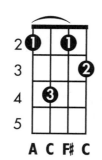

A C F# C

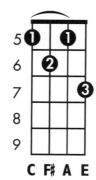

C F# A E

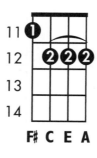

F# C E A

A7

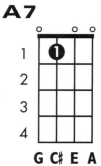
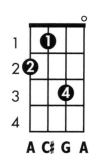
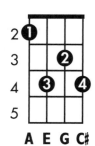
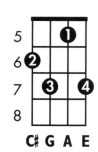

Amaj7

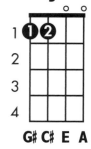
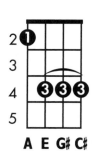
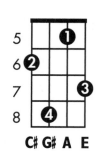
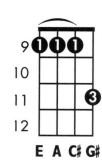
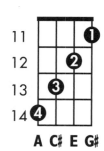

Am7

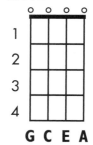
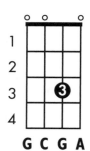
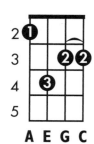
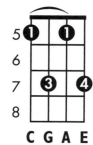
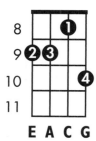

Am7(♭5)

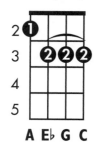
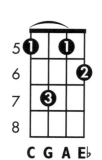
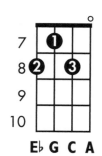
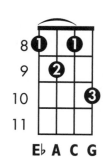
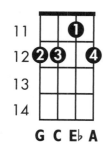

A

A°7

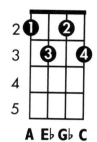

A E♭ G♭ C   C G♭ A E♭   E♭ A C G♭   G♭ C E♭ A

A(add9)

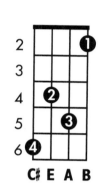

A C♯ E B   C♯ E A B   B E A C♯   E B C♯ A   E A C♯ B

A9

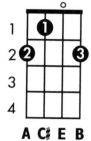

A C♯ G B   G B C♯ A

Amaj9

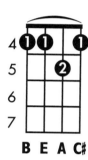

A C♯ G♯ B   C♯ G♯ B A

Am9

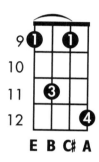

A C G B   C G B A

A7+

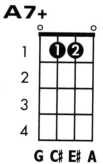

G C♯ E♯ A   A E♯ G C♯

A7(♭9)

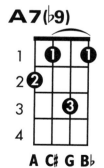

A C♯ G B♭   C♯ G B♭ A

A7(♯9)

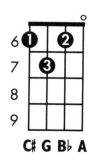
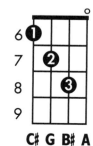

A C♯ G B♯   C♯ G B♯ A

B♭

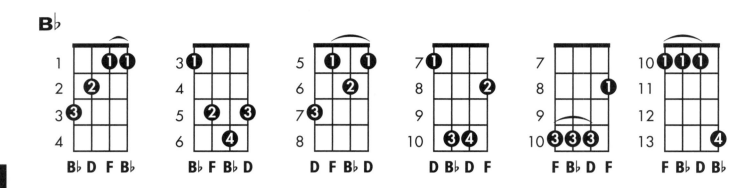

B♭m

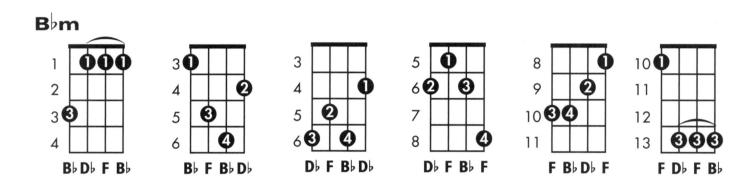

B♭°

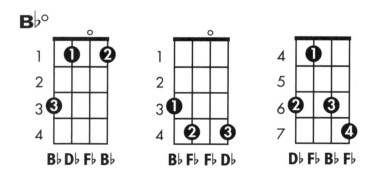

B♭+

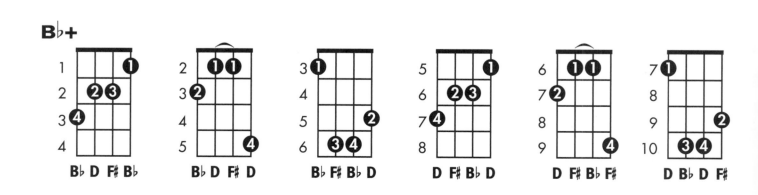

B♭5

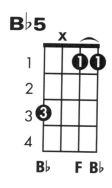
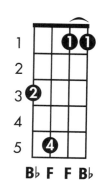

B♭ F B♭

B♭ F F B♭

B♭ F B♭

F B♭ F B♭

B♭

B♭sus4

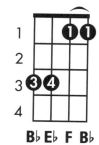
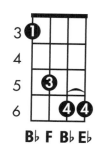
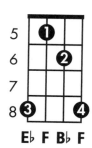
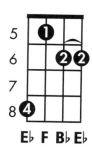
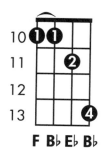

B♭ E♭ F B♭

B♭ F B♭ E♭

E♭ F B♭ F

E♭ F B♭ E♭

F B♭ E♭ B♭

B♭6

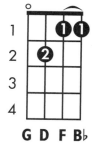
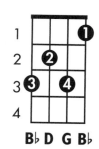
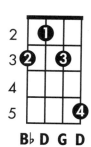
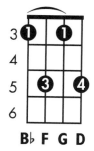
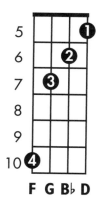
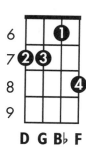

G D F B♭

B♭ D G B♭

B♭ D G D

B♭ F G D

F G B♭ D

D G B♭ F

B♭m6

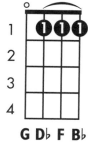
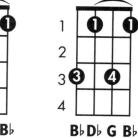
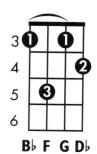
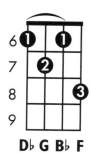

G D♭ F B♭

B♭ D♭ G B♭

B♭ F G D♭

D♭ G B♭ F

B♭7

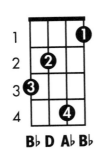
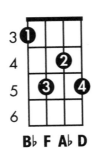

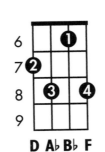
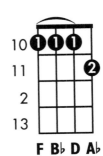

B♭maj7

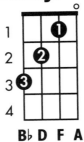
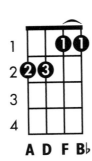
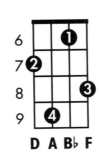
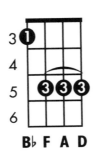
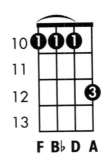

B♭m7

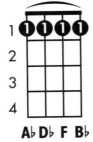
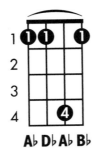
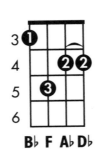
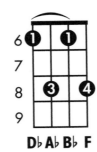
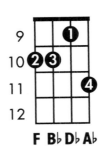

B♭m7(♭5)

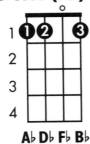
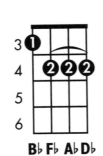
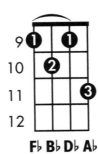

B♭°7

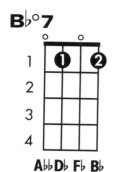
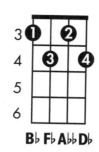
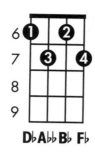
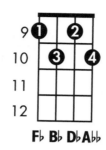

A♭♭ D♭ F♭ B♭   B♭ F♭ A♭♭ D♭   D♭ A♭♭ B♭ F♭   F♭ B♭ D♭ A♭♭

B♭

B♭(add9)

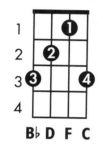
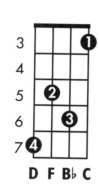
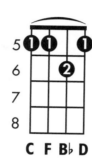
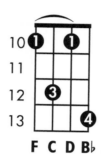

B♭ D F C   D F B♭ C   C F B♭ D   F C D B♭   F B♭ D C

B♭9

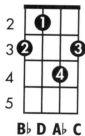

B♭ D A♭ C   C A♭ B♭ D

B♭maj9

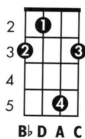

B♭ D A C   D B♭ C A

B♭m9

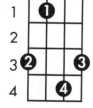

A♭ C F B♭   B♭ D♭ A♭ C

B♭7+

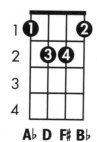

A♭ D F♯ B♭   B♭ F♯ A♭ D

B♭7(♭9)

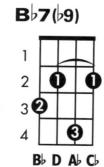
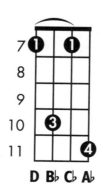

B♭ D A♭ C♭   D B♭ C♭ A♭

B♭7(♯9)

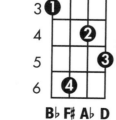
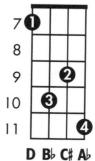

B♭ D A♭ C♯   D B♭ C♯ A♭

B

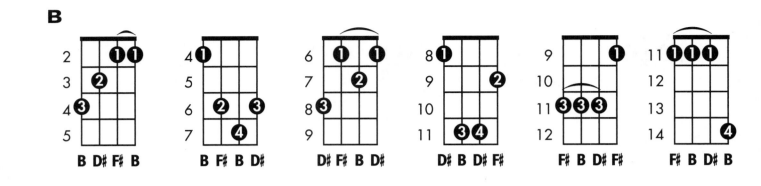

B D# F# B   B F# B D#   D# F# B D#   D# B D# F#   F# B D# F#   F# B D# B

Bm

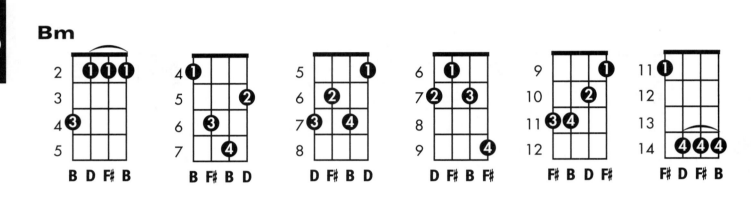

B D F# B   B F# B D   D F# B D   D F# B F#   F# B D F#   F# D F# B

B°

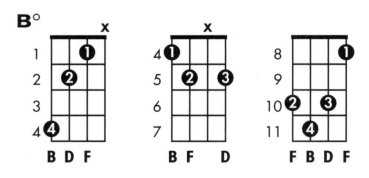

B D F   B F D   F B D F

B+

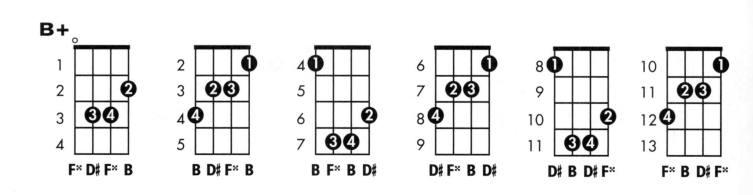

F✕ D# F✕ B   B D# F✕ B   B F✕ B D#   D# F✕ B D#   D# B D# F✕   F✕ B D# F✕

B 5

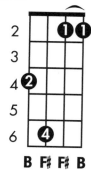

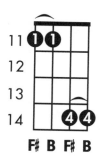

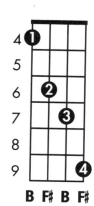

Bsus4

E F# B

B E F# B

B F# B E

E F# B E

F# B E B

B6

G# D# F# B

B D# G# B

B D# G# D#

B F# G# D#

D# G# B F#

F# B D# G#

Bm6

G# D F# B

B D G# B

B F# G# D

D G# B F#

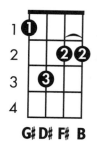
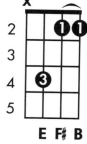

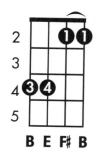
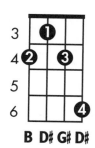
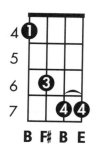
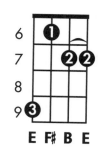
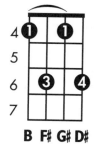
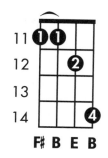
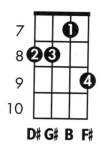
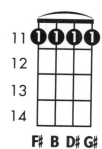
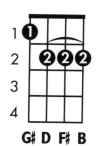
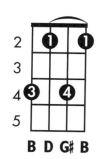
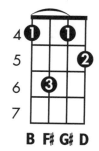
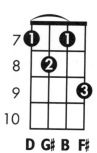

190

B7

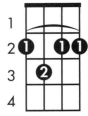
A D# F# B

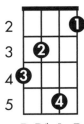
B D# A B

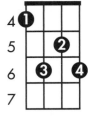
B F# A D#

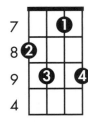
D# A B F#

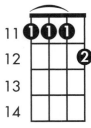
F# B D# A

Bmaj7

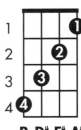
B D# F# A#

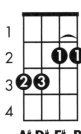
A# D# F# B

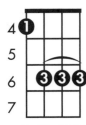
B F# A# D#

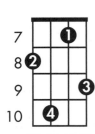
D# A# B F#

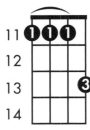
F# B D# A#

Bm7

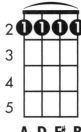
A D F# B

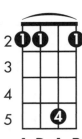
A D A B

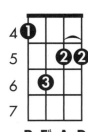
B F# A D

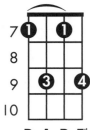
D A B F#

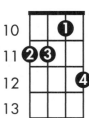
F# B D A

Bm7(♭5)

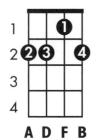
A D F B

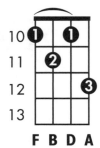
B F A D

F B D A

B°7

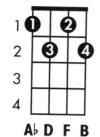
Ab D F B

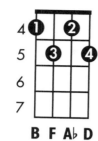
B F Ab D

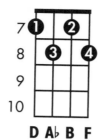
D Ab B F

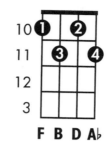
F B D Ab

B(add9)

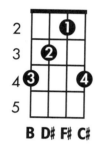
B D# F# C#

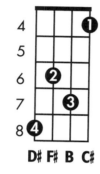
D# F# B C#

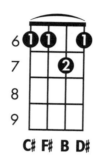
C# F# B D#

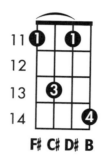
F# C# D# B

B9

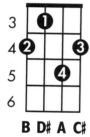
B D# A C#

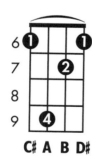
C# A B D#

Bmaj9

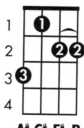
A# C# F# B

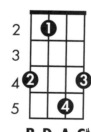
B D# A# C#

Bm9

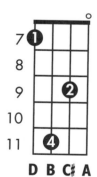
B D A C#

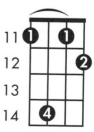
D B C# A

B7+

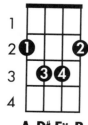
A D# F✕ B

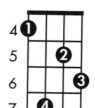
B F✕ A D#

B7(b9)

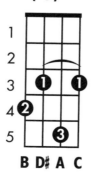
B D# A C

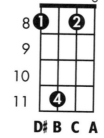
D# B C A

B7(#9)

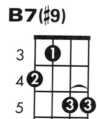
B D# A C✕

F# C✕ D# A

C

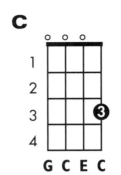

G C E C	G E E C	C E G C	G G C E	C G C E	E G C E

Cm

G Eb G C	C Eb G C	C Eb G Eb	G G C Eb	Eb G C Eb	G C Eb G

C°

C Eb Gb C	C Gb C Eb	Eb Gb C Eb

C+

G# C E C	G# E G# C	C E G# E	C G# C E	E G# C G#	G# C E G#

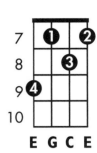
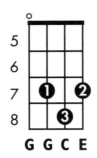
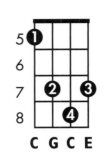
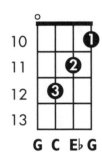
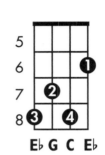
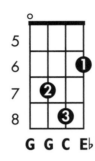
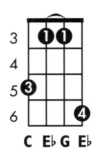
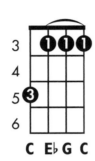
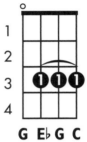
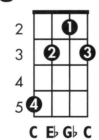
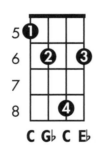
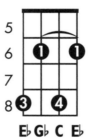
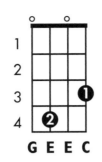
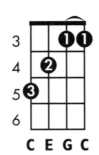
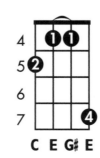
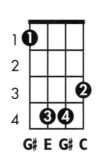
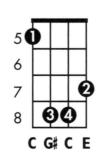
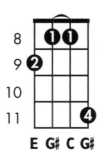
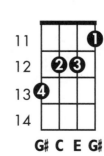

C5

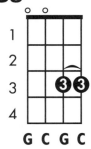 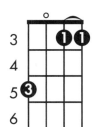 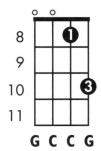 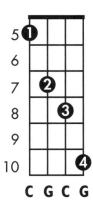

G C G C   C C G C   G C C G   C G C G

Csus4

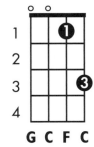 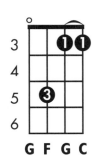 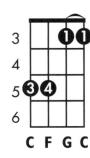 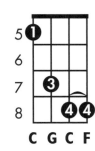 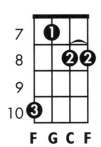

G C F C   G F G C   C F G C   C G C F   F G C F

C6

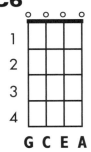 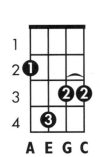 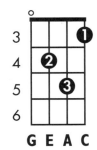 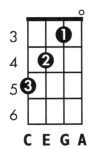 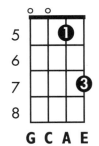 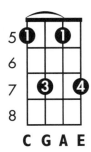

G C E A   A E G C   G E A C   C E G A   G C A E   C G A E

Cm6

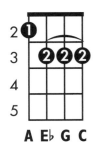 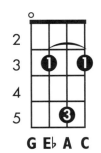 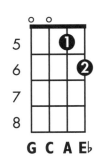 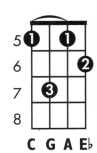 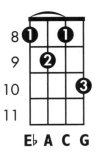

A E♭ G C   G E♭ A C   G C A E♭   C G A E♭   E♭ A C G

C7

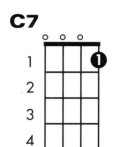
G C E B♭

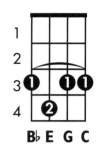
B♭ E G C

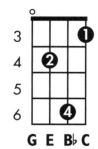
G E B♭ C

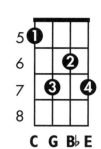
C G B♭ E

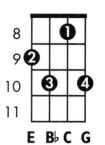
E B♭ C G

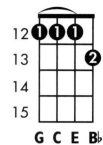
G C E B♭

Cmaj7

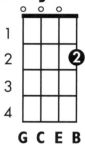
G C E B

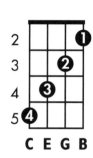
C E G B

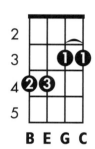
B E G C

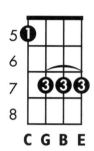
C G B E

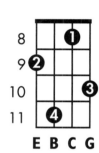
E B C G

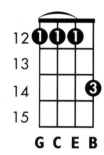
G C E B

Cm7

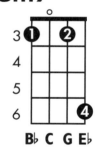
B♭ C G E♭

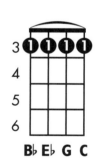
B♭ E♭ G C

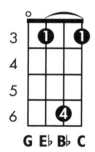
G E♭ B♭ C

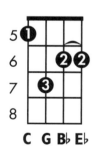
C G B♭ E♭

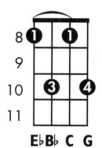
E♭ B♭ C G

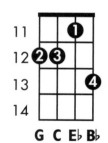
G C E♭ B♭

Cm7(♭5)

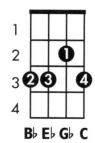
B♭ E♭ G♭ C

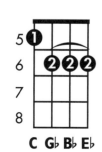
C G♭ B♭ E♭

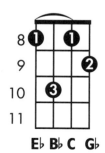
E♭ B♭ C G♭

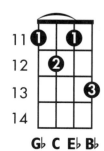
G♭ C E♭ B♭

C

C°7

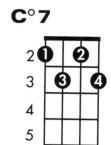
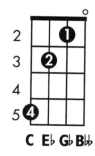
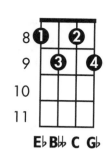
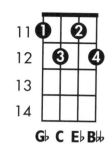

B𝄫 E♭ G♭ C   C E♭ G♭ B𝄫   C G♭ B𝄫 E♭   E♭ B𝄫 C G♭   G♭ C E♭ B𝄫

C(add9)

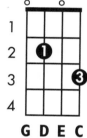
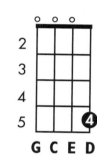
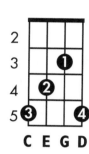
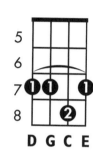
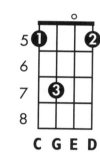
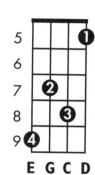

G D E C   G C E D   C E G D   D G C E   C G E D   E G C D

C9   Cmaj9   Cm9

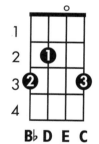
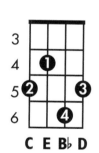
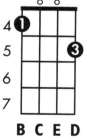
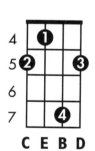
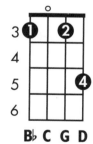
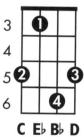

B♭ D E C   C E B♭ D   B C E D   C E B D   B♭ C G D   C E♭ B♭ D

C7+   C7(♭9)   C7(♯9)

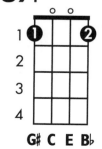
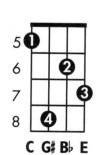
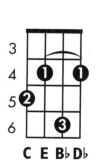
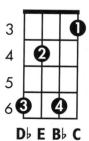
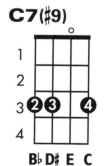
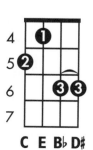

G♯ C E B♭   C G♯ B♭ E   D♭ E B♭ C   C E B♭ D♭   B♭ D♯ E C   C E B♭ D♯

C

C#

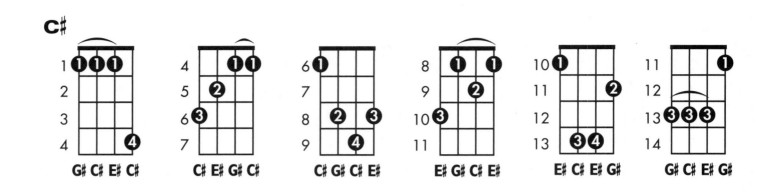

C#m

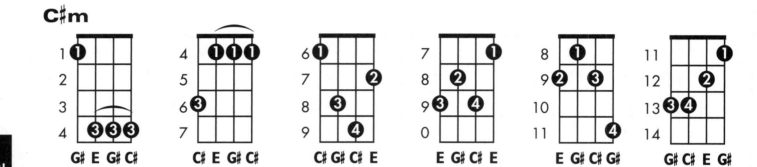

C#°

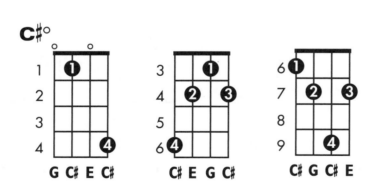

C#+

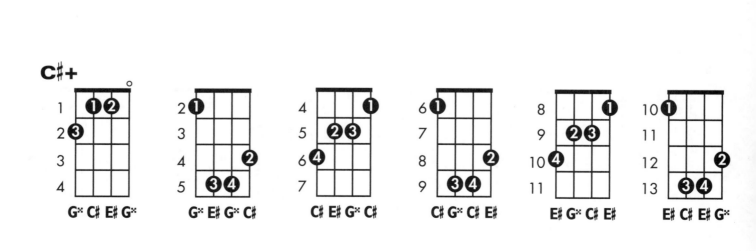

C#5

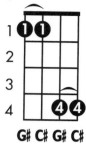

G# C# G# C#

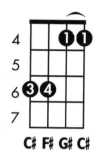

C# G# G# C#

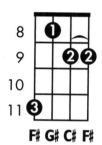

C# G# C# G#

C#sus4

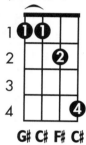

G# C# F# C#

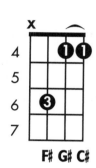

F# G# C#

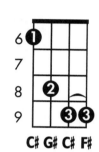

C# F# G# C#

C# G# C# F#

F# G# C# F#

C#6

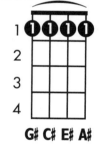

G# C# E# A#

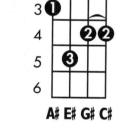

A# E# G# C#

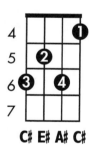

C# E# A# C#

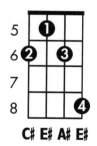

C# E# A# E#

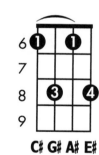

C# G# A# E#

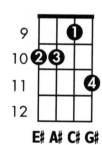

E# A# C# G#

C#m6

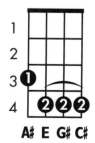

A# E G# C#

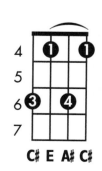

C# E A# C#

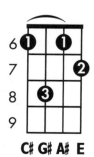

C# G# A# E

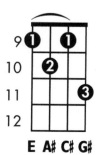

E A# C# G#

C#

C#7

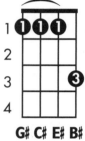

G# C# E# B

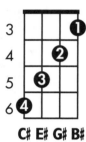

B E# G# C#

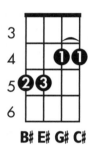

C# E# B C#

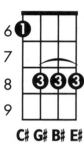

C# G# B E#

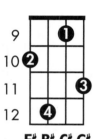

E# B C# G#

C#maj7

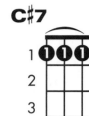

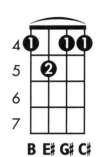
G# C# E# B#

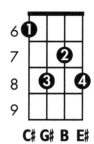
B# E# G# C#

C# E# G# B#

C# G# B# E#

E# B# C# G#

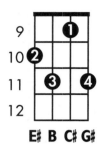
G# C# E# B#

C#m7

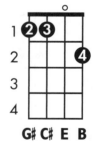

G# C# E B

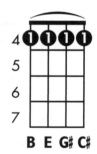

B E G# C#

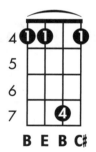

B E B C#

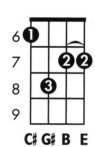

C# G# B E

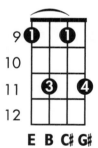

E B C# G#

C#m7(♭5)

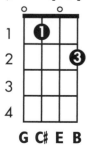

G C# E B

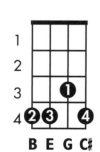

B E G C#

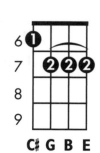

C# G B E

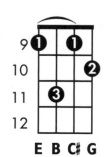

E B C# G

C#°7

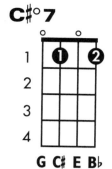

G C# E B♭   B♭ E G C#   C# G B♭ E   E B♭ C# G   G C# E B♭

C#(add9)

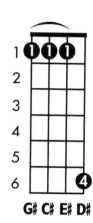

G# D# E# C#   G# C# E# D#   C# E# G# D#   E# G# C# D#   D# G# C# E#

C#9

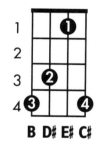

B D# E# C#   C# E# B D#

C#maj9

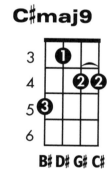

B# D# G# C#   C# E# B D#

C#m9

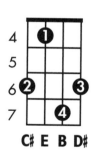

B D# E C#   C# E B D#

C#7+

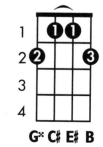

G* C# E# B   B E# G* C#

C#7(♭9)

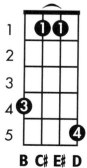

C# E# B D   B C# E# D

C#7(#9)

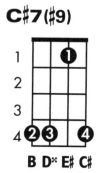

B D* E# C#   C# E# B D*

D

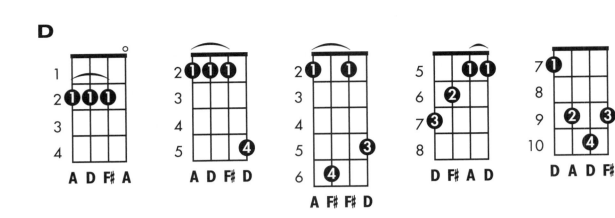

Dm

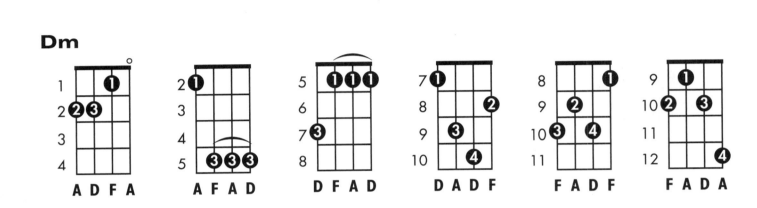

D

D°

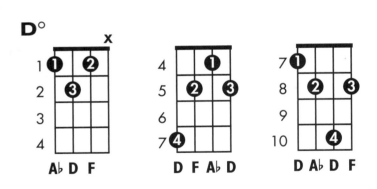

D+

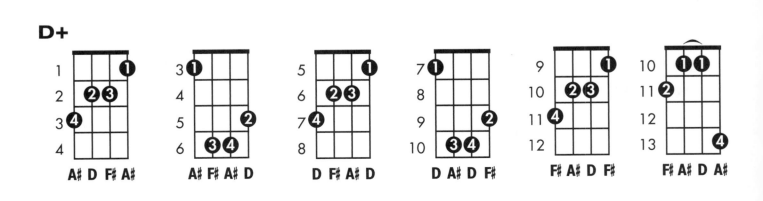

D5

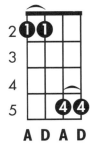
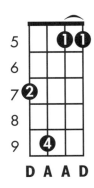
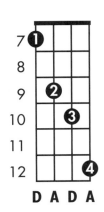

Dsus4

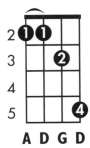
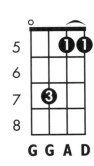
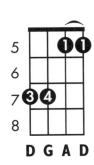
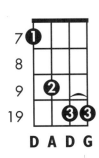
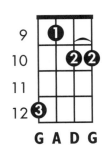

D6

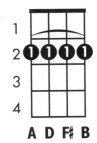
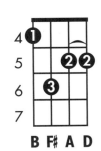
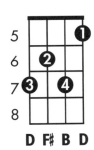
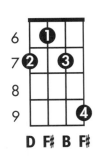
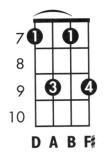
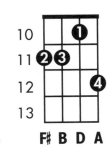

Dm6

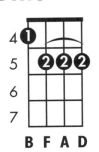
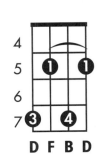
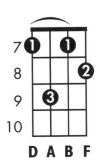
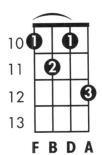

D7

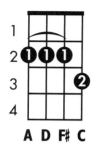 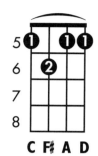 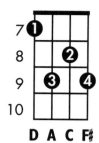 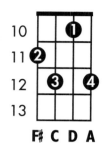 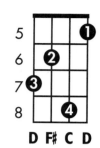

A D F# C   C F# A D   D F# C D   D A C F#   F# C D A

Dmaj7

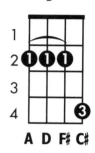 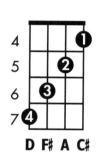 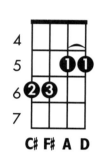 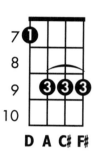 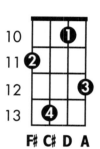 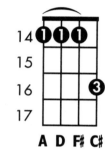

A D F# C#   D F# A C#   C# F# A D   D A C# F#   F# C# D A   A D F# C#

D

Dm7

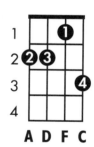 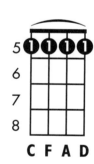 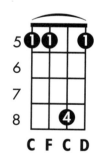 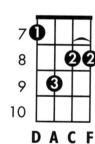 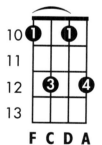

A D F C   C F A D   C F C D   D A C F   F C D A

Dm7(♭5)

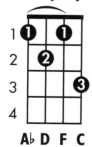 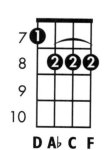 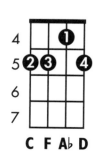 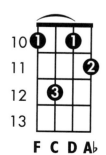

A♭ D F C   C F A♭ D   D A♭ C F   F C D A♭

D°7

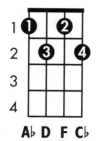 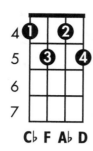 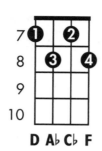 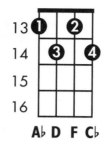

AbD F Cb   Cb F Ab D   D Ab Cb F   F Cb D Ab   Ab D F Cb

D(add9)

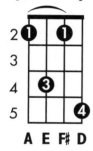 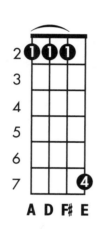 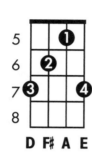 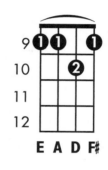

A E F# D   A D F# E   D F# A E   F# A D E   E A D F#

D9

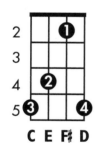 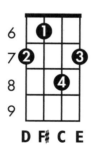

C E F# D   D F# C E

Dmaj9

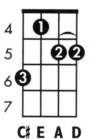 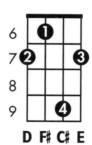

C# E A D   D F# C# E

Dm9

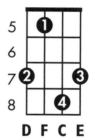 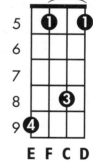

D F C E   E F C D

D7+

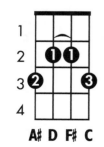 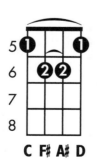

A# D F# C   C F# A# D

D7(b9)

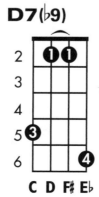 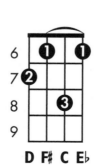

C D F# Eb   D F# C Eb

D7(#9)

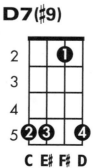 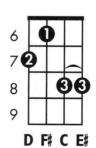

C E# F# D   D F# C E#

D

E♭

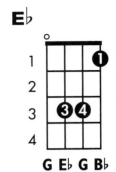

°		°			
1 ●	3 ●●●	6 ●●	6 ●●	8 ●	10 ●●
2	4	7 ●	7 ●	9	11 ●
3 ●●	5	8	8 ●	10 ● ●	12 ●
4	6 ●	9	9	11 ●	13
G E♭ G B♭	B♭ E♭ G E♭	G G B♭ E♭	E♭ G B♭ E♭	E♭ B♭ E♭ G	G B♭ E♭ G

E♭m

1 ●	3 ●	6 ●●●	6 ●●	8 ●	8
2 ●	4	7	7	9 ●	9 ●
3 ●●	5	8 ●	8 ●	10 ●	10 ●
4	6 ●●●	9	9 ●	11 ●	11 ● ●
B♭ E♭ G♭ B♭	B♭ G♭ B♭ E♭	E♭ G♭ B♭ E♭	E♭ G♭ B♭ G♭	E♭ B♭ E♭ G♭	G♭ B♭ E♭ G♭

E♭°

		°
1	5 ●	8 ●
2 ● ●	6 ● ●	9 ● ●
3 ●	7	10
4	8 ●	11 ●
B♭♭ E♭ G♭ B♭♭	E♭ G♭ B♭♭ E♭	E♭ B♭♭ E♭ G♭

E♭+

°					
1	2 ●	4 ●	6 ●	8 ●	11 ●●
2 ●	3 ●●	5	7 ●●	9	12 ●
3 ●●	4 ●	6 ●	8 ●	10 ●	13
4	5	7 ●●	9	11 ●●	14 ●
G E♭ G B	B E♭ G B	B G B E♭	E♭ G B E♭	E♭ B E♭ G	G B E♭ B

E♭5

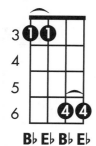
3 ① ①
4
5
6　④④
B♭ E♭ B♭ E♭

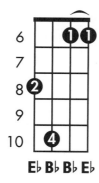
6　　① ①
7
8　②
9
10　　④
E♭ B♭ B♭ E♭

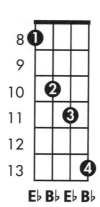
8 ①
9
10　②
11　　③
12
13　　　④
E♭ B♭ E♭ B♭

E♭sus4

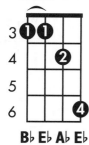
3 ① ①
4　　②
5
6　　　④
B♭ E♭ A♭ E♭

x
6　　① ①
7
8　②
9
A♭ B♭ E♭

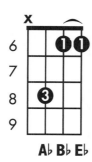
6　　① ①
7
8 ③ ④
9
E♭ A♭ B♭ E♭

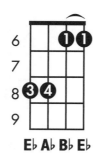
8 ①
9
10　②
11　　③ ③
E♭ B♭ E♭ A♭

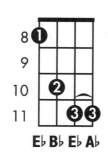
10　①
11　　② ②
12
13 ③
A♭ B♭ E♭ A♭

E♭6

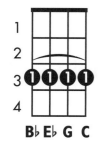
1
2
3 ① ① ① ①
4
B♭ E♭ G C

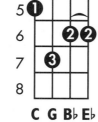
5 ①
6　　② ②
7　②
C G B♭ E♭

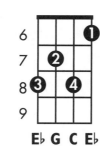
6　　　①
7　②
8 ③　④
E♭ G C E♭

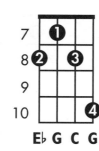
7　①
8 ②　③
9
10　　　④
E♭ G C G

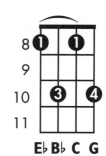
8 ①　①
9
10　　③　④
E♭ B♭ C G

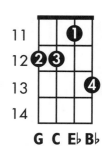
11　　①
12 ② ③
13　　　④
G C E♭ B♭

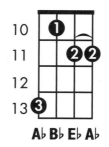
E♭

E♭m6

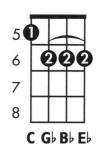
5 ①
6　② ② ②
7
8
C G♭ B♭ E♭

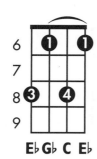
6　① ①
7
8 ③　④
9
E♭ G♭ C E♭

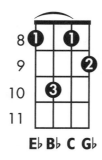
8 ① ①
9　　　②
10　③
11
E♭ B♭ C G♭

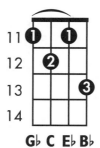
11 ① ①
12　②
13　　　③
14
G♭ C E♭ B♭

E♭7

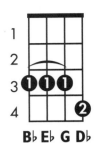
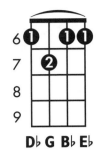
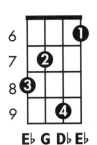
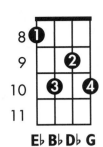
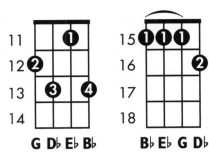

B♭ E♭ G D♭   D♭ G B♭ E♭   E♭ G D♭ E♭   E♭ B♭ D♭ G   G D♭ E♭ B♭   B♭ E♭ G D♭

E♭maj7

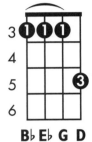
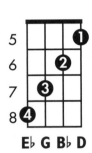
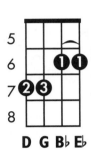
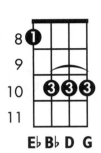
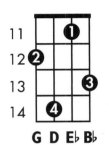
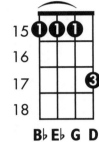

B♭ E♭ G D   E♭ G B♭ D   D G B♭ E♭   E♭ B♭ D G   G D E♭ B♭   B♭ E♭ G D

E♭m7

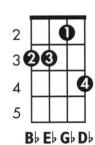
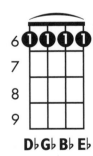
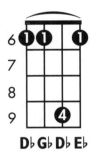
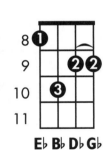
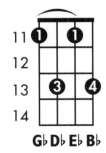

B♭ E♭ G♭ D♭   D♭ G♭ B♭ E♭   D♭ G♭ D♭ E♭   E♭ B♭ D♭ G♭   G♭ D♭ E♭ B♭

E♭m7(♭5)

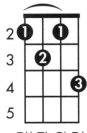
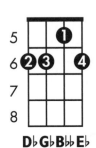
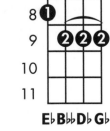
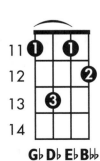

B♭♭ E♭ G♭ D♭   D♭ G♭ B♭♭ E♭   E♭ B♭♭ D♭ G♭   G♭ D♭ E♭ B♭♭

E♭

Eb°7

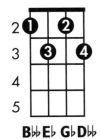 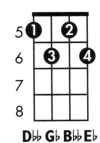 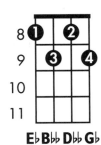 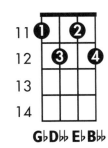 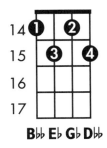

Bbb Eb Gb Dbb   Dbb Gb Bbb Eb   Eb Bbb Dbb Gb   Gb Dbb Eb Bbb   Bbb Eb Gb Dbb

Eb(add9)

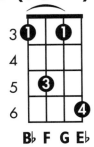 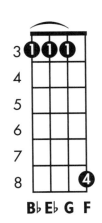 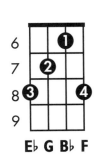 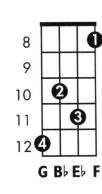 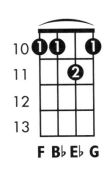

Bb F G Eb   Bb Eb G F   Eb G Bb F   G Bb Eb F   F Bb Eb G

Eb9

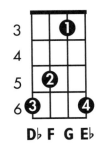 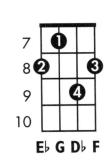

Db F G Eb   Eb G Db F

Ebmaj9

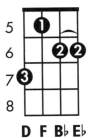 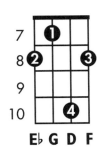

D F Bb Eb   Eb G D F

Ebm9

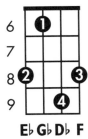 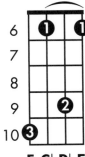

Eb Gb Db F   F Gb Db Eb

Eb7+

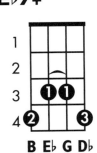

B Eb G Db   Db G B Eb

Eb7(b9)

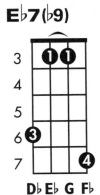 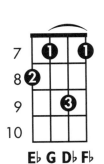

Db Eb G Fb   Eb G Db Fb

Eb7(#9)

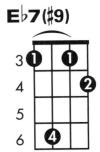 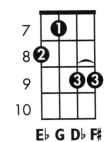

Bb F# G Db   Eb G Db F#

Eb

208

E

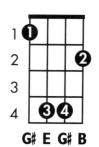

G# E G# B

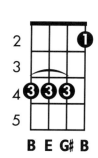

B E G# B

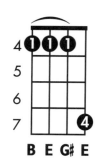

B E G# E

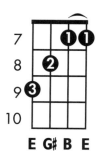

E G# B E

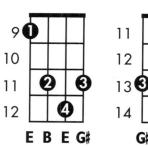

E B E G#

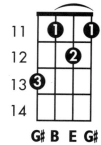

G# B E G#

Em

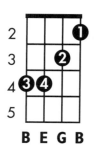

B E G B

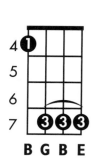

B G B E

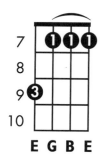

E G B E

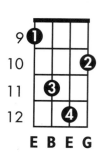

E B E G

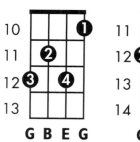

G B E G

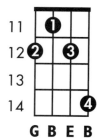

G B E B

E°

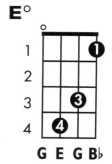

G E G Bb

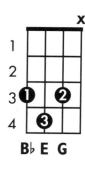

Bb E G

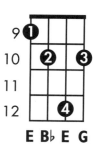

E Bb E G

E+

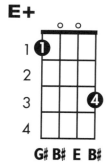

G# B# E B#

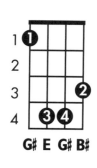

G# E G# B#

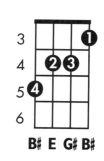

B# E G# B#

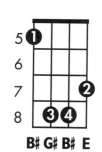

B# G# B# E

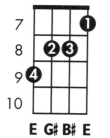

E G# B# E

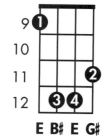

E B# E G#

E

E5

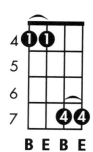 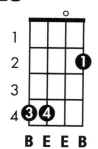 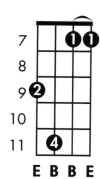 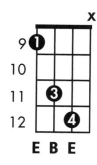

Esus4

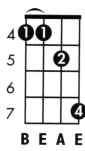 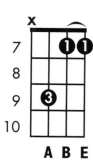 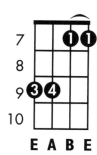 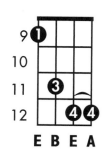 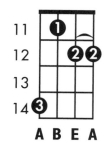

E6

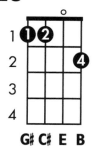 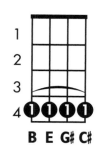 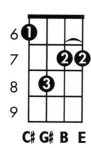 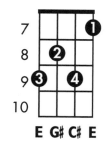 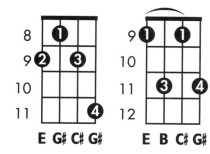

Em6

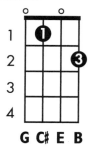 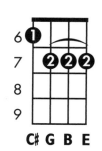 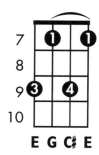 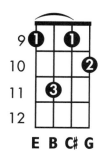

E

E7

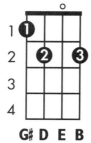
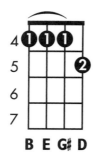
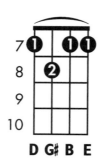
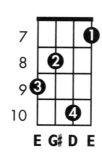
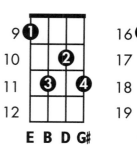
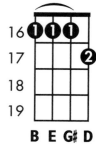

G# D E B   B E G# D   D G# B E   E G# D E   E B D G#   B E G# D

Emaj7

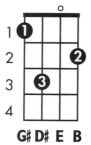
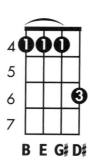
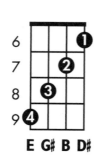
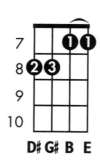
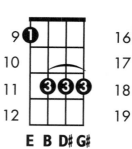
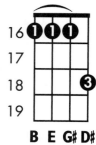

G# D# E B   B E G# D#   E G# B D#   D# G# B E   E B D# G#   B E G# D#

Em7

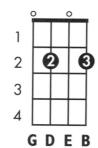
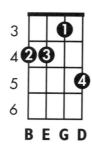
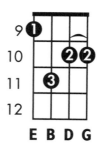
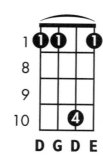
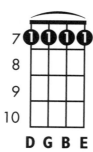

G D E B   B E G D   D G B E   D G D E   E B D G

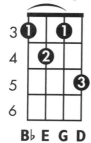

Em7(♭5)

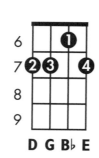
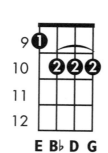
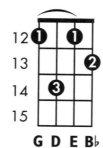

B♭ E G D   D G B♭ E   E B♭ D G   G D E B♭

E°7

| | | | |
|1|G D♭ E B♭|
|2|
|3|
|4|

B♭ E G D♭

D♭ G B♭ E

E B♭ D♭ G♭

B♭ E G D♭

E(add9)

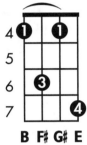 B F♯ G♯ E

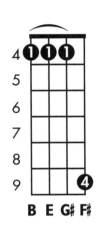 B E G♯ F♯

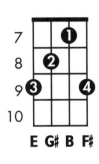 E G♯ B F♯

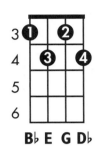 G♯ B E F♯

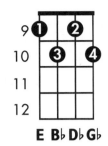 F♯ B E G♯

E9

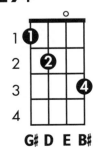 D F♯ G♯ E

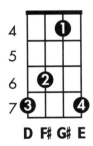 E G♯ D F♯

Emaj9

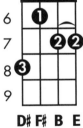 D♯ F♯ B E

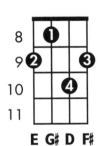 E G♯ D♯ F♯

Em9

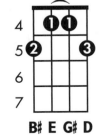 E G D F♯

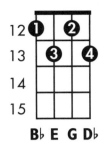 F♯ G D E

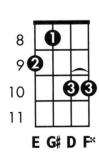

E

E7+

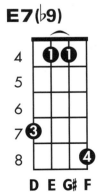 G♯ D E B♯

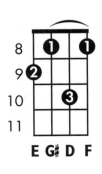 B♯ E G♯ D

E7(♭9)

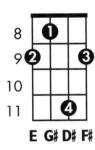 D E G♯ F

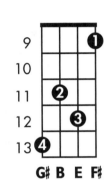 E G♯ D F

E7(♯9)

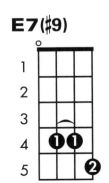 F✕ E G♯ D

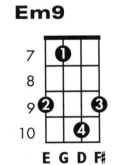 E G♯ D F✕

F

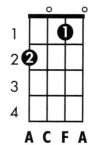
A C F A

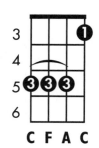
A F A C

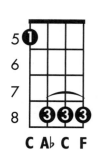
C F A C

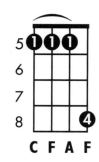
C F A F

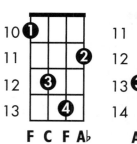
F A C F

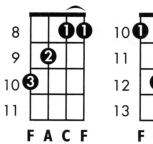
F C F A

Fm

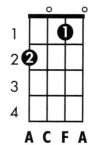
A♭ C F C

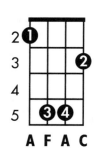
C F A♭ C

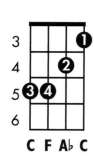
C A♭ C F

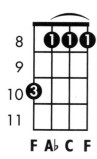
F A♭ C F

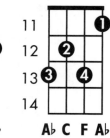
F C F A♭

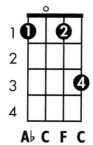
A♭ C F A♭

F°

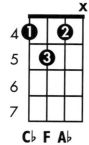
C♭ F A♭

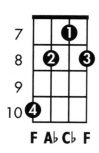
F A♭ C♭ F

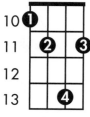
F C♭ F A♭

F+

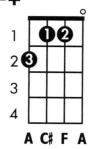
A C# F A

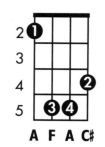
A F A C#

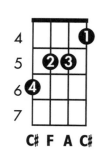
C# F A C#

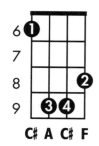
C# A C# F

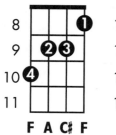
F A C# F

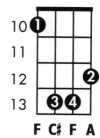
F C# F A

F5

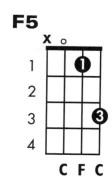

C F C   C F C F   F C C F   F C F   F C F C

Fsus4

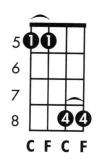 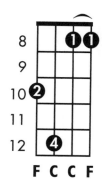 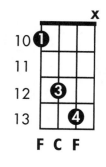 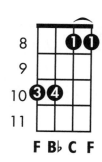 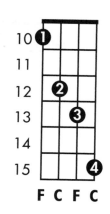

B♭ C F B♭   C F B♭ F   B♭ C F   F B♭ C F   F C F B♭

F6

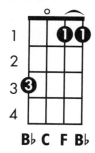 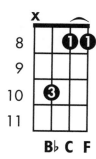 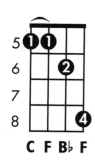 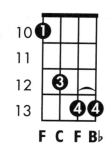

A D F C   C F A D   D A C F   F A D F   F A D A   F C D A

F

Fm6

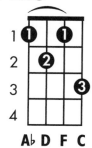 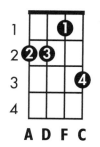 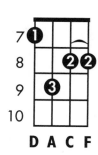 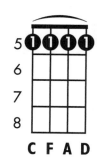 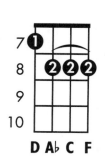 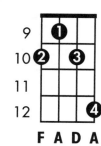 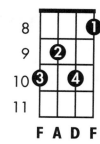 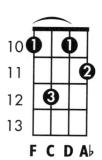 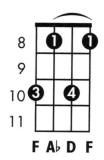 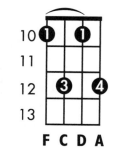

A♭ D F C   D A♭ C F   F A♭ D F   F C D A♭

F7

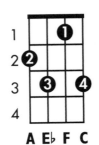 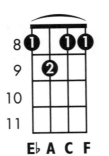 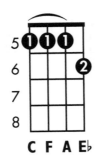 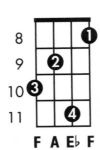 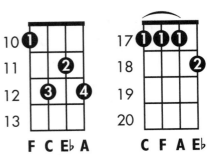

A Eb F C   C F A Eb   Eb A C F   F A Eb F   F C Eb A   C F A Eb

Fmaj7

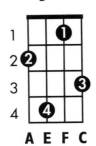 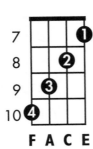 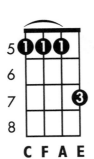 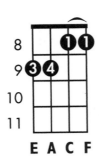 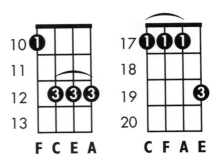

A E F C   C F A E   F A C E   E A C F   F C E A   C F A E

Fm7

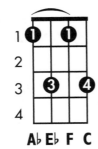 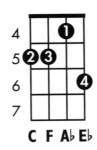 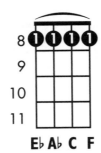 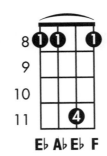 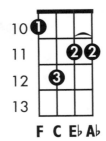

Ab Eb F C   C F Ab Eb   Eb Ab C F   Eb Ab Eb F   F C Eb Ab

F

Fm7(b5)

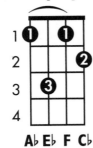 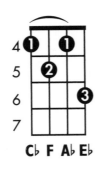 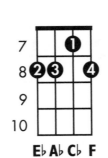 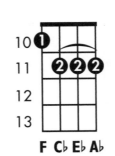 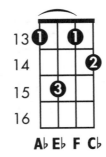

Ab Eb F Cb   Cb F Ab Eb   Eb Ab Cb F   F Cb Eb Ab   Ab Eb F Cb

F°7

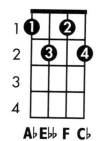 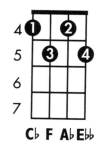

Ab Eb F Cb   Cb F Ab Ebb   Ebb Ab Cb F   F Cb Ebb Ab   Cb F Ab Ebb

F(add9)

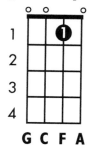 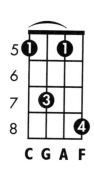 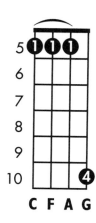 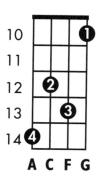 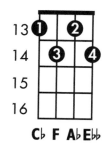

G C F A   C G A F   C F A G   F A C G   A C F G

F9   Fmaj9   Fm9

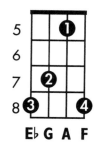 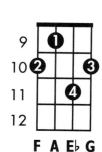 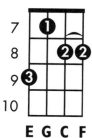 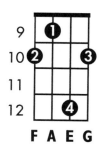 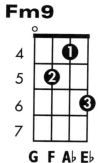 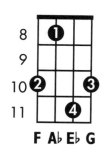

Eb G A F   F A Eb G   E G C F   F A E G   G F Ab Eb   F Ab Eb G

F

F7+   F7(b9)   F7(#9)

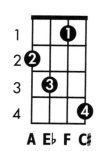 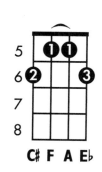 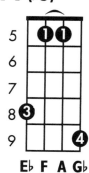 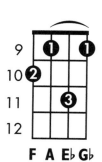 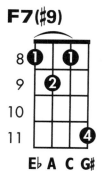 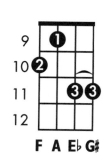

A Eb F C#   C# F A Eb   Eb F A Gb   F A Eb Gb   Eb A C G#   F A Eb G#

F#

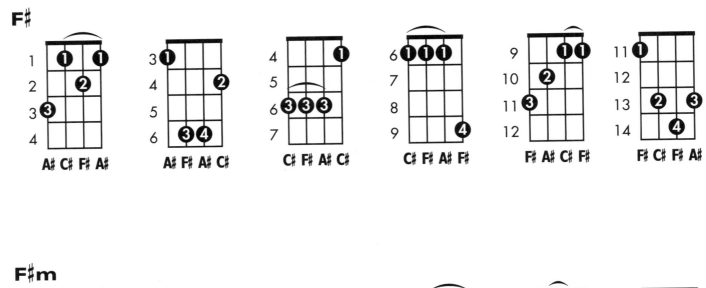

F#m

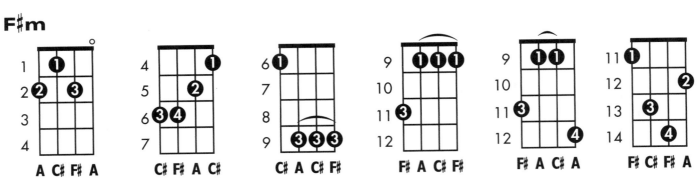

F#°

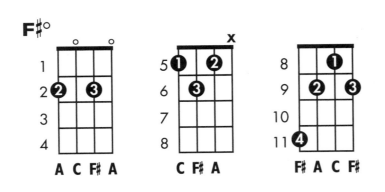

F#+

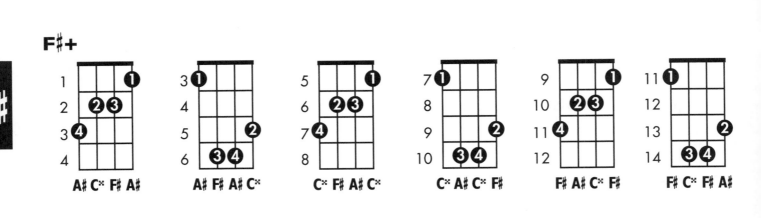

F#

F#5

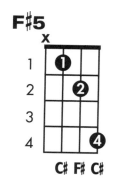
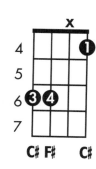
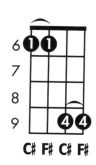
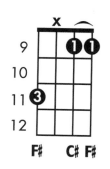
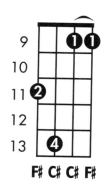

F#sus4

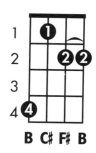
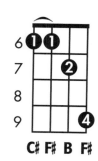
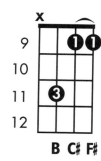
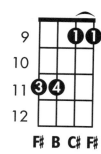
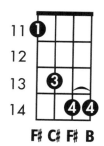

F#6

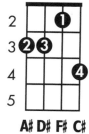
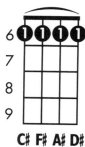
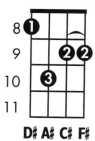
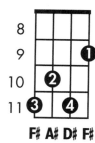
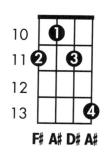
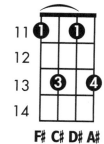

F#m6

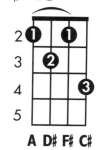
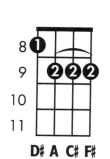
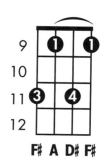
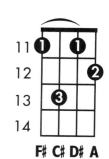

F#

F#7

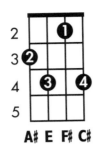
A# E F# C#

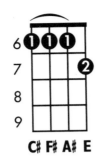
C# F# A# E

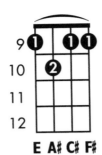
E A# C# F#

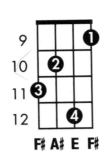
F# A# E F#

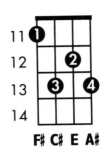
F# C# E A#

F#maj7

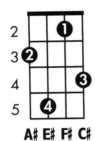
A# E# F# C#

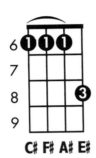
C# F# A# E#

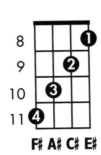
F# A# C# E#

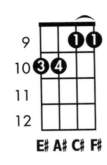
E# A# C# F#

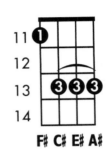
F# C# E# A#

F#m7

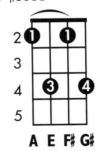
A E F# G#

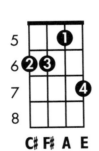
C# F# A E

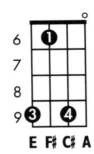
E F# C# A

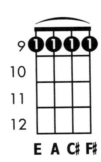
E A C# F#

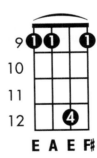
E A E F#

F#m7(♭5)

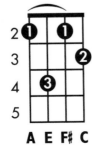
A E F# C

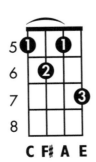
C F# A E

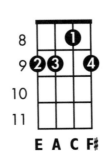
E A C F#

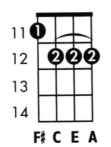
F# C E A

F#

F#°7

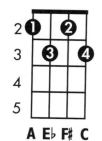

A Eb F# C

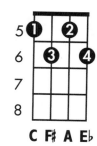

C F# A Eb

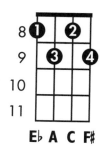

Eb A C F#

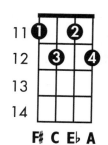

F# C Eb A

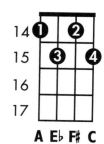

A Eb F# C

F#(add9)

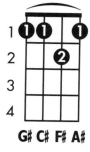

G# C# F# A#

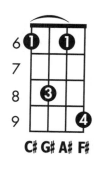

C# G# A# F#

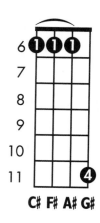

C# F# A# G#

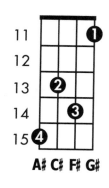

F# A# C# G#

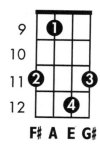

A# C# F# G#

F#9

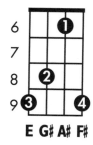

E G# A# F#

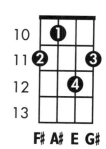

F# A# E G#

F#maj9

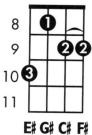

E# G# C# F#

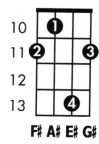

F# A# E# G#

F#m9

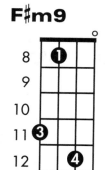

F# G# E A

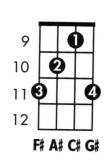

F# A E G#

F#7+

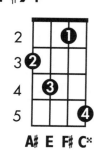

A# E F# Cⁱ

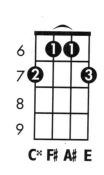

Cⁱ F# A# E

F#7(b9)

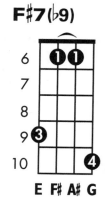

E F# A# G

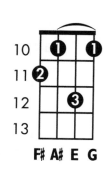

F# A# E G

F#7(#9)

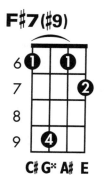

C#ⁱ G#ⁱ A# E

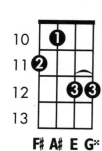

F# A# E G#ⁱ

F#

G

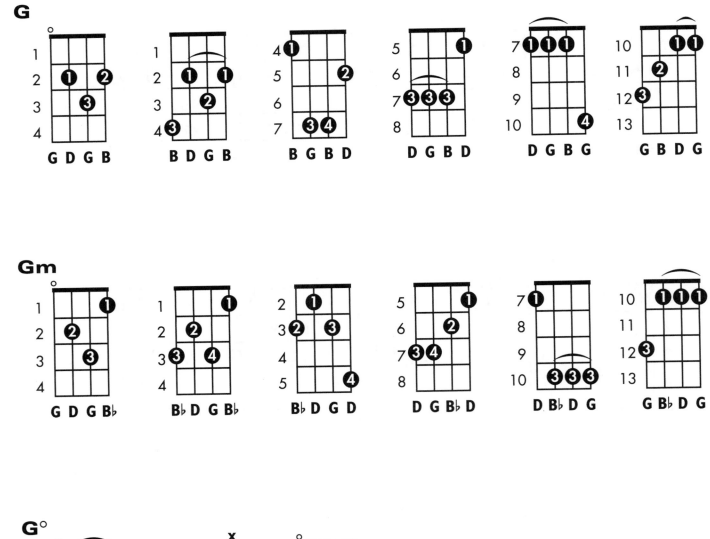

Gm

G°

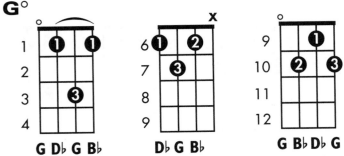

G+

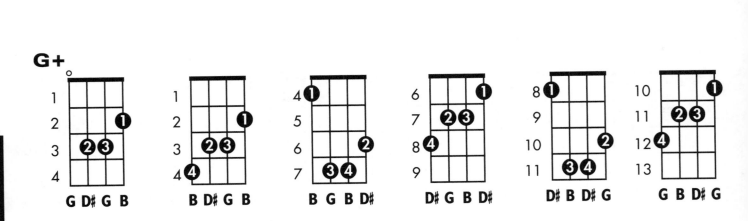

G

G5

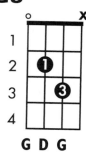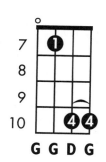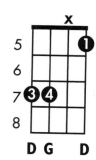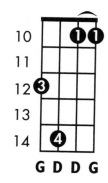

GDG   DGD   GGDG   DGDG

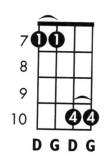

GDDG

Gsus4

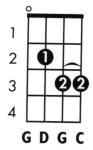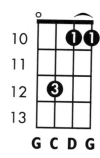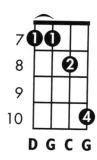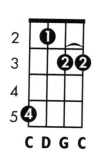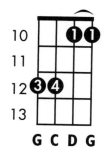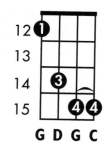

GDGC   CDGC   DGCG   GCDG   GCDG   GDGC

G6

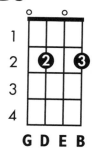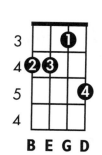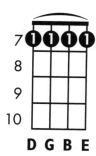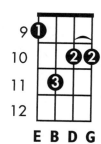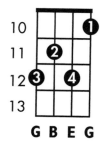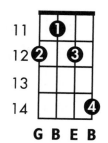

GDEB   BEGD   DGBE   EBDG   GBEG   GBEB

Gm6

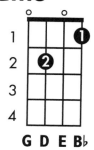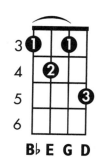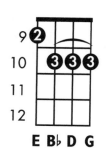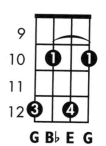

GDEB♭   B♭EGD   EB♭DG   GB♭EG

G

G7

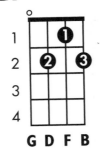 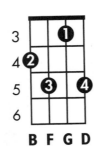 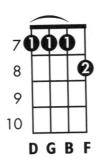 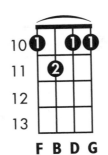 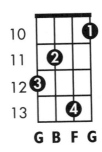

G D F B   B F G D   D G B F   F B D G   G B F G

Gmaj7

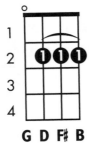 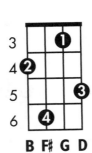 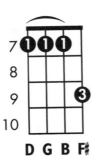 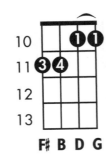 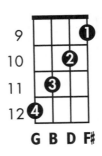

G D F# B   B F# G D   D G B F#   F# B D G   G B D F#

Gm7

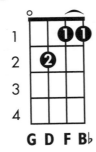 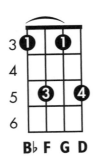 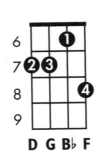 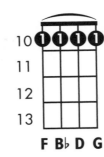 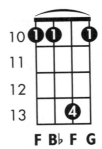

G D F B♭   B♭ F G D   D G B♭ F   F B♭ D G   F B♭ F G

Gm7(♭5)

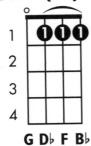 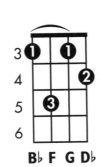 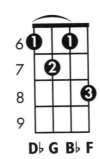 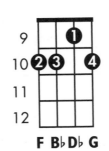

G D♭ F B♭   B♭ F G D♭   D♭ G B♭ F   F B♭ D♭ G

G

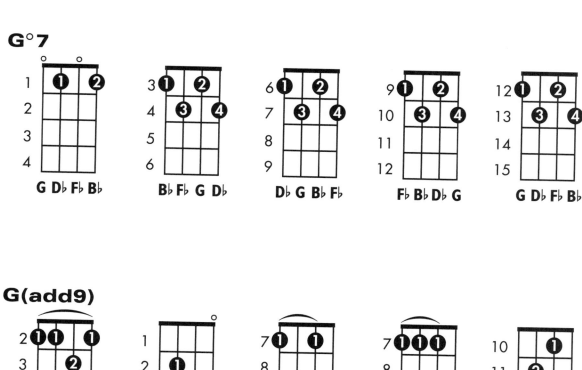

G°7

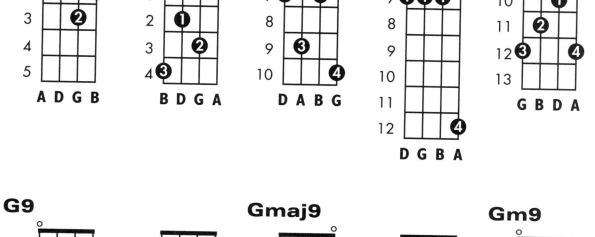

G(add9)

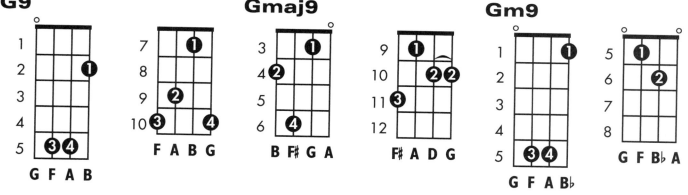

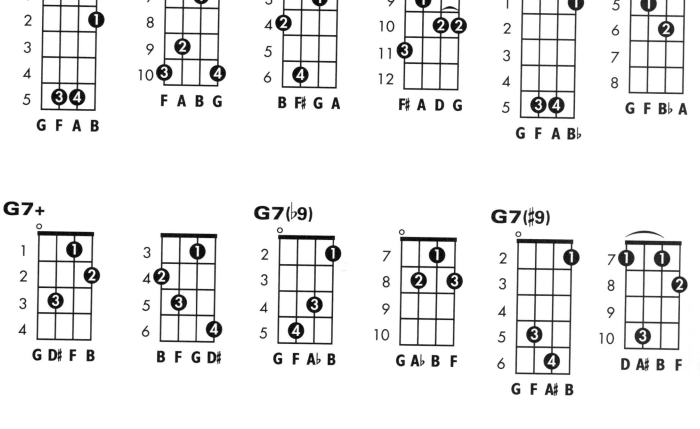

G

Ukulele Fingerboard Chart
Frets 1–12

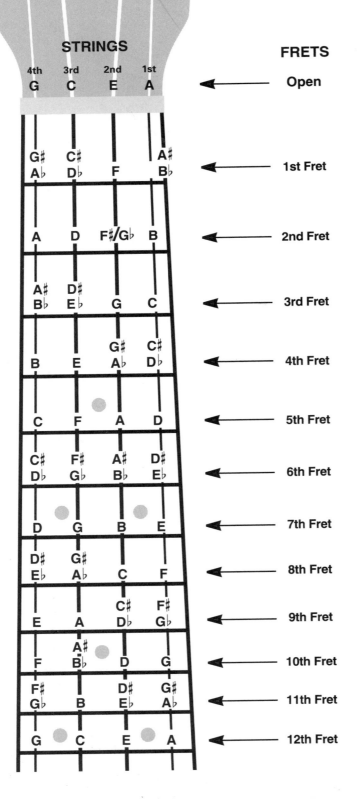

STRINGS

4th	3rd	2nd	1st
G	C	E	A

FRETS

Open

1st Fret

2nd Fret

3rd Fret

4th Fret

5th Fret

6th Fret

7th Fret

8th Fret

9th Fret

10th Fret

11th Fret

12th Fret